THE CRITICAL PULSE

COLUMBIA UNIVERSITY PRESS   NEW YORK

THE CRITICAL PULSE

THIRTY-SIX CREDOS BY CONTEMPORARY CRITICS

Mark Bauerlein | Lauren Berlant
Michael Bérubé | Marc Bousquet
Morris Dickstein | Rita Felski | Diana Fuss
Judith Jack Halberstam | Amitava Kumar
Lisa Lowe | Mark McGurl
Toril Moi | Cary Nelson | Andrew Ross
Ken Warren and twenty-one
other critics

EDITED BY **JEFFREY J. WILLIAMS**
& HEATHER STEFFEN

COLUMBIA UNIVERSITY PRESS

Publishers Since 1893

New York   Chichester, West Sussex

cup.columbia.edu

Copyright © 2012 Columbia University Press

Library of Congress Cataloging-in-Publication Data

The critical pulse : thirty-six credos by contemporary critics / edited by Jeffrey J.
Williams and Heather Steffen.

p. cm.

Includes bibliographical references.

ISBN 978-0-231-16114-5 (cloth : acid-free paper) — ISBN 978-0-231-16115-2
(pbk. : acid-free paper) — ISBN 978-0-231-53073-6 (e-book)

1. Criticism—Authorship.   2. Critics—United States.   3. Literature—History and
criticism—Theory, etc.   I. Williams, Jeffrey, 1958–   II. Steffen, Heather.

PN85.C686 2012

801'.95,dc23

2012020432

Columbia University Press books are printed on permanent and
durable acid-free paper.

This book is printed on paper with recycled content.
Printed in the United States of America

c 10 9 8 7 6 5 4 3 2 1
p 10 9 8 7 6 5 4 3 2 1

Cover Design: Shaina Andrews

CONTENTS

ACADEMIC LABOR

DECLARATIONS OF POLITICS

PEDAGOGICAL MOMENTS

THE DEFENSE OF LITERATURE

NEW TURNS

ACKNOWLEDGMENTS

Seventeen of these essays first appeared in a special issue of *the minnesota review* 71–72 (2009), marking the conclusion of Jeffrey Williams's editing the journal (he had edited it for eighteen years, and Heather Steffen served as managing editor for five years). Both editors would like to thank Bill Germano for advice along the way, Philip Leventhal for his seeing the value of the collection and overseeing its path into print, and the other staff at Columbia University Press who helped at various stages. In particular, Heather would like to thank Patrick Callahan, Salita Seibert, Eric Vázquez, and Jess Wilton, as well as her family, for their friendship and support. Jeff would especially like to thank Vincent Leitch for his constant support of the project and David Downing for a ready ear in the neighborhood.

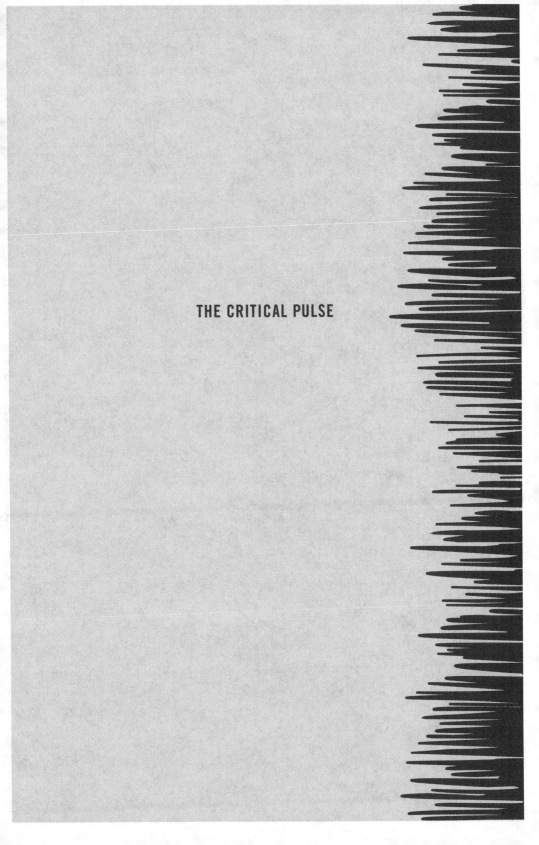

THE CRITICAL PULSE

INTRODUCTION

CRITICISM IN A DIFFICULT TIME

The *Critical Pulse* gathers thirty-six "credos," short essays in which contemporary critics tell what they think criticism should do and why they do it. The essays strip away academic edifice to give forthright accounts of critics' views. They propose a number of ways to do criticism now.

"Credo," from the Latin, translates literally as "I believe," and the genre of the credo typically suggests a statement of religious belief. Criticism leans in the opposite direction, suggesting skepticism or negation. Rather than beliefs, contemporary critics typically speak about theories, which tack to the scientific, focusing on the structures that embed literature and culture, such as the conception of society postulated in Marxism or feminism or the individual psyche in psychoanalysis. Theories inform the approaches that critics take: one might look through a Marxist or feminist or deconstructive or postcolonial "lens." But theories can be like masks that one might slip on and off, requiring no particular commitment from the critic. One can, for instance, easily produce a Marxist reading of a literary work but have little belief that class struggle is a preeminent category of analysis (and life), or feel that the collapse of the Soviet Union left Marxism in the dustbin of history.

A common metaphor for theory is that it provides tools. This figure works to dispel the sense of determinism that might attach to a theory, but it presents theory as a matter of opportunity. The use of such a tool can arise from a commitment or be arbitrary and stem from no necessary reason or be cynical. A theory does not get at what might motivate you or what calls your attention and why. That is the realm of the credo: credos boil things down to the premises that underlie one's theories and practices, to the individual motivations and stories that explain why we do what we do when we do criticism.

The following credos, we hope, will help clarify the role and possibilities of criticism in a difficult time, particularly as the humanities have been pared down to a skeleton crew, publishing has retreated to the higher-stakes bet of best-sellers, and the university, the home of criticism since the Great Depression, has become infatuated with the protocols of the market, aiding and abetting capitalism rather than keeping a distance from it. Criticism has a tenuous position in this new landscape.

The idea for this collection was prompted by a set of credos from a very different time. In 1950 and 1951, the *Kenyon Review* ran a series of essays under the heading "My Credo: A Symposium of Critics." *Kenyon* was a leading literary journal of the time, publishing a good deal of criticism as well as poetry and fiction. It is usually considered to have been the house journal of the New Critics, but it actually published a wide range of critics, such as the New York Intellectual Lionel Trilling (three of the chapters of his 1950 *Liberal Imagination* first appeared in *Kenyon*), the socialist Philip Rahv, and international figures like Jean-Paul Sartre. The symposium featured ten essays, from young myth critics Leslie Fiedler and Northrop Frye, the Harvard humanist Douglas Bush, the Americanist Richard Chase, the poet and occasional critic Stephen Spender, the biographer Arthur Mizener, and the appreciative critic Herbert Read, as well as those allied with the New Criticism (Cleanth Brooks, William Empson, and Austin Warren). The series was not a comprehensive survey—John Crowe Ransom, the editor, had originally intended that it would continue but was soon overtaken with other projects so abandoned it at an even ten essays—but it gave a sense of what professional critics of the era were about.[1]

The *Kenyon* credos came at a turning point. Criticism had been a minor pursuit and largely relegated to newspapers and sporadic comments by writers, but in 1950 it was becoming a major branch of literary study. It had also found its home, after the hardship of the thirties, in academe. There it vied for a place among scholarly practices dominant at the time—source studies and other staid forms of literary history, bibliographical compilations, etymological studies, and so on. Ransom had made an impassioned argument for the importance of criticism in his 1938 essay "Criticism, Inc.," and founded *Kenyon Review* a year later to provide a platform for it. Part of Ransom's argument, and the ensuing tendency of *Kenyon Review*, was to shore up literature as a discipline, with criticism as its central practice. Fittingly, a preoccupation of the *Kenyon* credos was specialization and whether criticism should be a science, with Frye voting yes, Fiedler voting no, and Read, observing from England, noting the American obsession with "scientific criticism." It was less science envy than a defensive reaction to the social sciences; those in literature were distinguishing the role of criticism from rising social sciences like psychology and sociology, as well as cousin disciplines like history. What they provided was different from those in the social sciences; it was unique to literature and offered special knowledge of it.

Ransom's arguments took hold after World War II with the ensuing build-up of higher education. Through the thirties, the American university struggled to tread water, but after the war it embarked on what historians call its Golden Age. The student population nearly tripled in twenty years, from about 1,101,000 in 1930 to 1,494,000 in 1940 to 2,659,000 in 1950, and faculty rose from about 82,000 to 147,000 to 247,000, as states provided subventions for a large share of tuition and the federal government chipped in with acts such as the GI Bill and, later, the 1958 National Defense Education Act, as well as underwriting a great deal of research.[2] Many flowers of criticism grew in the enriched soil of the postwar era, and it soon became known as the "Age of Criticism." The *Kenyon* credos reflected some of the hopeful confidence of the time, although they also reflected their time in other, less liberal ways— there were no contributions by women, people of color, or even those who espoused a strong political position, so their range was not quite as catholic as they presumed.

We are at another turning point, with criticism and critics facing depleted conditions. Since the 1970s higher education has shifted from being a flagship of the liberal welfare state, increasing opportunity for higher education as a public entitlement, to a flagship of the neoliberal state, reorienting attendance as a private consumer good and research as an arm of private for-profit businesses. (Jeff has characterized this as a shift from the welfare-state university to the post-welfare-state university.)[3] This has had far-reaching effects for students, who now carry a much larger percentage of the costs of education in the form of exploding tuitions and loans, and for faculty, who now are subject to a Hobbesian job system. Academic jobs have been reconfigured, with a majority of jobs given over to "casual" positions —part-time, adjunct, or other kinds of insecure. It is often said that this is a question of the market, but the demand for higher education has continued to grow through the past fifty years, with about 20,000,000 Americans now attending some form of it. In literary studies, according to Modern Language Association statistics, only 32 percent of the faculty have permanent berths, meaning that more than two-thirds do not. While the effects are obviously worse for those in precarious jobs, this also affects the increasingly rarefied minority who hold fully vested positions, leading to what one of our contributors calls "superservice" and other forms of speedup for those remaining, in a steep hierarchical system. Critics, like other human beings, are subject to their material conditions, and while critics in the postwar era faced expansive prospects, critics now face a shrinking room.

Moreover, criticism seems to lack definition. A generation ago, criticism largely meant theory, and one could readily map it into discernable camps. Now criticism seems more diffuse and harder to pin down. This might reflect the plateau between paradigms, when theory has become stale but no new paradigm has yet taken the field. Or it might represent an impasse in public legitimation, when it's uncertain what role criticism has and what constituency it speaks to (in the era of theory, criticism might not have been broadly public, but it spoke to an academic constituency concerned with specialized research). Criticism's purchase is hazy.

In the face of these conditions, there is a heightened need to clarify what we are doing in criticism and what we do it for. Though its current conditions might be cause for complaint or worry, the point of gathering this set of credos is to take stock, replenish supplies, and go back to it. *The Critical Pulse* aims toward renewal—toward reassessing criticism in the wake of the era of theory, discerning the social relevance of criticism now, and finding a way to reconfigure the university and work therein. We hope that the reflective pause and clarity of declaring one's belief might aid in renewal. To paraphrase Stuart Hall, it is a long road to renewal, but that is the road we need to take.

That contemporary criticism is housed in the university is often taken as its downfall. Sometimes criticism might fulfill the worst sense of "academic"—overly technical, expressing an incredibly narrow interest that no one else would ever entertain, almost solipsistic in its address to an audience, so heavily referenced as to be unreadable. But there's still much other criticism.

One of the purposes of this collection is to counter the usual aspersions of our academic position. We need make no apologies for working in universities. An academic purchase can grant us the training, time, credibility, and access to do criticism. Also, given that 70 percent of Americans attend some form of higher education, the university is not an ivory tower but a common experience. On the other hand, another purpose of this collection is to present, advocate, and model more straightforward critical writing. In a difficult time, we need to dispense with the needlessly obscure, the narcissistically narrow, the hopelessly roundabout. This isn't just a matter of style but of the topics we choose, and we have an obligation to choose topics that matter.

It is a mistake to see criticism as fallen from a purer state. Edmund Wilson, often taken as an exemplar of the public critic, reflected on the shift in criticism from the heyday of literary journalism to its roosting in the university in a piece called "Thoughts on Being Bibliographed." Though he worked as a literary journalist throughout his career, he had little nostalgia for the era of journalism. As he put it, one had to depend on the sometimes shallow dictates of editors and the demands of commercial magazines and learn how to slip "solid matter into notices of ephemeral happenings," against editors' "over-anxious intentness on the fashions of the month or the week [that] have conditioned them automatically to reject, as the machines that make motor parts automatically reject outsizes." Neither does Wilson take the usual tone of disdain toward the shift to the university. While he sees the pitfalls of both professions, journalistic and academic, he remarks that teaching is "a profession where they are at least in a position to keep in touch with the great work of the past."[4] Wilson had a practical sense about the conditions under which he and other critics worked, and he was something of a materialist, identifying the flourishing of journalism as a result of the financial flush of the 1920s and the shift from journalism to the university as a result of the economic scarcity of the Depression.

Sometimes it seems that criticism takes place in an airy realm of thought, detached from the conditions of its production. Though a good deal of contemporary criticism has looked at the historical circumstances embedding literature, little has looked at the circumstances embedding and producing criticism. Another purpose of this collection is to underscore that its material conditions shape criticism. Hence, a number of essays shine light on academic labor, graduate training, and the politics of higher education. They are part of the biography of criticism, but they are not merely biographical. They show the social and historical vectors that form criticism. As Antonio Gramsci observed, "The starting-point of critical elaboration is the consciousness of what one really is . . . a product of the historical process to date, which has deposited in you an infinity of traces."[5] These essays work to compile part of our collective inventory.

This direction and focus, on labor and politics, is perhaps the chief difference with the *Kenyon* credos. They were focused more on literature and the literary, whereas these deal more explicitly with cultural politics and see criticism as having a political responsibility. There are occasional jeremiads arguing that criticism's proper task is to focus solely on literature, but we believe that this relies on a wooden nominalism (because it is called "literary" criticism, it must focus on the literary). Rather, literary criticism, deriving from the branch of thinking called moral philosophy in the eighteenth century, has always encompassed a range of commentary, social and aesthetic, political and literary, historical and artistic. We believe that there are too many pressing problems confronting us, in the university as well as in the world around us, to indulge an interest narrowly in aesthetics or the literary. It is the power and hope of criticism that it reaches for something more.

This collection originated with a special issue of *the minnesota review*, a literary and critical journal that Jeff edited for eighteen years and Heather worked on as managing editor for five years. Jeff thought having people reflect on the purpose of criticism would be a good way to conclude his editorial run. From that issue we drew seventeen essays, and we have added nineteen more for this volume. While we tried to achieve some range and include varied perspectives, the contributions generally reflect the tendencies of the journal, sharing its focus on cultural politics, a belief in the public role of criticism, and a concern with academic labor. That is, this collection does not purport a comprehensive overview of criticism now; it does not, for instance, focus on accounts of particular literary fields or methods of reading. We feel that there is no lack of such accounts, and also we believe that the issue of academic labor, for instance, obligates our attention now. Still, one could easily imagine a platoon of additional contributors (and, as anyone who has embarked on such an undertaking can imagine, one is limited by what actually comes in). Making such a collection is part design and part accident.

The credo is less a statement of method than of stance, personal background, or motivation. It gets at *why* more than *what* we do when we do criticism. Thus we did not try to present an inventory of schools or theoretical positions nor a predictable list of major theorists. This volume no doubt includes some prominent critics, but we tried to bring in rising as well as established critics. We thus hope that the collection brings some surprise. One might be curious about what a well-known critic says, which might be different from what one expects, and one might read a contribution from a critic one did not know of. The purpose of the collection is to be not definitive but suggestive, to prompt you as a reader to reconsider the purpose of criticism, in answer to what you might read here, in agreement or disagreement.

We began by giving all of the contributors a simple assignment, asking them to tell us what they believed criticism should do and what they did in their own practice. We were stern taskmasters, specifying that the essays be relatively short (no longer than ten to twelve pages in typescript), with minimal apparatus and as straightforward as possible. The task was not as easy as it seemed, as many of our contributors attested and we discovered. It is hard to boil things down and recount one's basic motivations and principles. Moreover, there are few signposts. (The *Kenyon* credos, truth be told, are a bit dated.) But the contributors forged through, in a few different ways. Some of the credos are narrative, recounting a critic's experience; some are more impersonal, discussing critical views. Some advise a turn to a particular mode of criticism; a few are experimental. Many discuss the conditions of academic labor, but a good number look instead at traditional questions like the value of humanism. Most dwell on the relation between politics and criticism, and many aspire to a broader public than typical academic criticism.

To offer a rudimentary map, we have arranged the credos in six sections. The first, "A Critic's Progress," brings together credos that foreground the path a critic has taken and how he or she has changed the kind of criticism he or she does. Andrew Ross tells of leaving behind "armchair theory" to do "scholarly reporting," and Amitava Kumar recounts his departure from poststructural theory to find the most critical power in nonfiction writing. Lisa Lowe reflects on her father and how she has come to be a critic of globalization, and Vincent Leitch recalls forming his position, in part forged by difficult personal circumstances that represent neoliberalism in action. Craig Womack calls for more storytelling in criticism, and he reports how he has learned to be less combative and to listen to negative comments, while Jeff narrates his personal history and early literary aspirations, as well as the path he took from training in poststructural theory to his belief in the importance of socially responsible criticism.

The second section, "Academic Labor," features essays that foreground the work conditions we confront, from faculty to grad student. Sometimes this dimension seems external to literary study proper, but academic labor has become one of the more important veins of criticism and theory over the past decade. Marc Bousquet, as he has in many venues, underscores the conditions of our work lives and how important it is to reconceive academe as a place of labor and thus of organizing. Katie Hogan and Michelle Massé, coeditors of the recent volume *Over Ten Million Served*, point to a sometimes invisible aspect of our work lives, service, and how it has intensified over the past decade and has had its worst effects on women. John Conley recounts his experience of a graduate student strike at the University of Minnesota, from which he draws a strategy for resisting speedup, and Heather suggests ways for graduate students to organize without the benefit of a formal labor union, particularly in nonunionized academic shops.

Next, the section, "Declarations of Politics," gathers credos that focus especially on a critic's political experience and how it influenced his or her criticism. Paul Lauter recounts his work in the civil rights movement and other kinds of activism, and Barbara Foley tells about her roots in the radical movements of the late sixties, experiences that shaped their subsequent critical work. Cary Nelson explains how his scholarship interweaves with his politics, which he considers a way to internalize activism, and David Downing recounts how he became, from a child of the fifties, a critic of neoliberalism. Michael Bérubé offers a witty explanation of where he places himself amid the left, and Victor Cohen holds up the example of Studs Terkel as an engaged intellectual and argues for a renewal of a leftist cultural studies.

The fourth section, "Pedagogical Moments," assembles credos that ruminate on pedagogy in different ways, in the classroom as well as in writing or at professional events like conferences. Gerald Graff declares his goals as a teacher, bringing students into current intellectual debates without advocacy, while William Germano tells of his effort to make texts, especially historical texts, speak to contemporary students. Ann Pellegrini recounts how she challenges students to look at "inconvenient facts," particularly while teaching about gender and religion. Bruce Robbins likewise looks to the public importance of teaching, emphasizing that we might teach students to deal with "monsters" or others in the world, whereas Ken Warren recounts a key moment teaching a poem and how it opens onto histories of immigration and racism. Closing the section, Diana Fuss gives a nuanced account of the ways that pedagogy works without our control, rereading Paul de Man's idea of "the resistance to theory," and Lauren Berlant, teasing apart the significance of a misunderstanding at a conference, points out that pedagogy is an integral part of criticism.

Tapping into the tradition of the "Defense of Literature" (or poetry or criticism), the next section draws together essays concerned with the state of the humanities, the importance of literature, and the centrality of criticism. Toril Moi reaffirms some of the values of humanism—though not forgetting the insights of feminism—and the study of languages, and Morris Dickstein conceives of the role of the critic not in terms of the current academic conversation but the longer-sighted history of criticism. Rita Felski calls for a re-engagement with literature through a return to phenomenological criticism, and David Shumway defends the importance of criticism to literature. Mark Bauerlein issues a conservative challenge, calling us to teach basic literary understanding in the wake of a decline of reading, whereas Devoney Looser calls for both the conservative value of literary history and a renewed attention to women's literature, a task that we should not think is already done.

The final section, "New Turns," features essays from a rising generation of critics, beginning with Stephen Burt, a poet and critic who unapologetically sees criticism as a service to literature. Mark Greif takes a more capacious view and believes criticism should employ "all there is to use," unlike previous theories that demanded fidelity to one method, while Kathleen Fitzpatrick points to the shift augured by the Internet and how that will change the criticism we can do. Mark McGurl, speaking from his position as a member of a lost academic generation, after jobs dried up, suggests that critics return to a more existential sense, whereas Frances Negón-Muntaner, a filmmaker as well as critic, gives a personal account of the way that politics are not grand or global but small and incremental. Finally, Judith Jack Halberstam offers a lively account of what she calls "low theory," of how we should look at low as well as high texts, and also how many of the lessons we learn are in spite of rather than because of the formal strictures of education.

Probably the best way to use this volume is not to read it straight through, as one would a monograph, but to dip into it, reading one section or skipping around. It is not a definitive account of criticism and theory; rather, it presents a number of lenses, as in the facets of a prism, giving different angles and shifts of light on what we do when we do criticism. And though it generally does not foreground objective argument, it cuts through to a different level of truth, of what we actually believe, and of the different motivations we have for doing this work. One tacit lesson of the volume is to decipher one's own credo—perhaps taking from some of the credos here, perhaps countering them. We hope that these essays might prompt you to clarify what you aim for, as well as to help make our workplaces better places to do criticism.

NOTES

1. The contributions to "My Credo: A Symposium of Critics" appeared over three issues; in 12, no. 4 (Autumn 1950) were: 1. Leslie A. Fiedler, "Toward an Amateur Criticism"; 2. Herbert

Read, "The Critic as Man of Feeling"; 3. Richard Chase, "Art, Nature, Politics"; 4. William Empson, "The Verbal Analysis." In 13, no. 1 (Winter 1951): 5. Cleanth Brooks, "The Formalist Critics"; 6. Douglas Bush, "The Humanist Critics"; 7. Northrop Frye, "The Archetypes of Literature." In 13, no .2 (Spring 1951): 8. Stephen Spender, "On the Function of Criticism"; 9. Arthur Mizener, "Not in Cold Blood"; 10. Austin Warren, "The Teacher as Critic." Ransom had invited a number of others, such as I. A. Richards and Jean-Paul Sartre, who declined. Several had agreed to write but never delivered their essays, including F. R. Leavis, Philip Rahv, Allen Tate, and Trilling; see Marian Janssen, *The Kenyon Review, 1939–1970: A Critical History* (Baton Rouge: Louisiana State University Press, 1990), 175–79.

2. *Digest of Education Statistics* (Washington, D.C.: National Center for Education Statistics, 2006), http://nces.ed.gov/programs/digest/; Hugh Davis Graham and Nancy Diamond, *The Rise of American Research Universities: Elite and Challengers in the Postwar Era* (Baltimore, Md.: Johns Hopkins University Press, 1997).

3. Jeffrey J. Williams, "The Post-Welfare State University," *American Literary History* 18, no. 1 (2006): 190–216.

4. Edmund Wilson, "Thoughts on Being Bibliographed," in *Classics and Commercials: A Literary Chronicle of the 1940s* (New York: Farrar, Straus and Giroux, 1950), 112, 108.

5. Antonio Gramsci, quoted in Edward W. Said, *Orientalism* (New York: Pantheon, 1978), 25.

A CRITIC'S PROGRESS

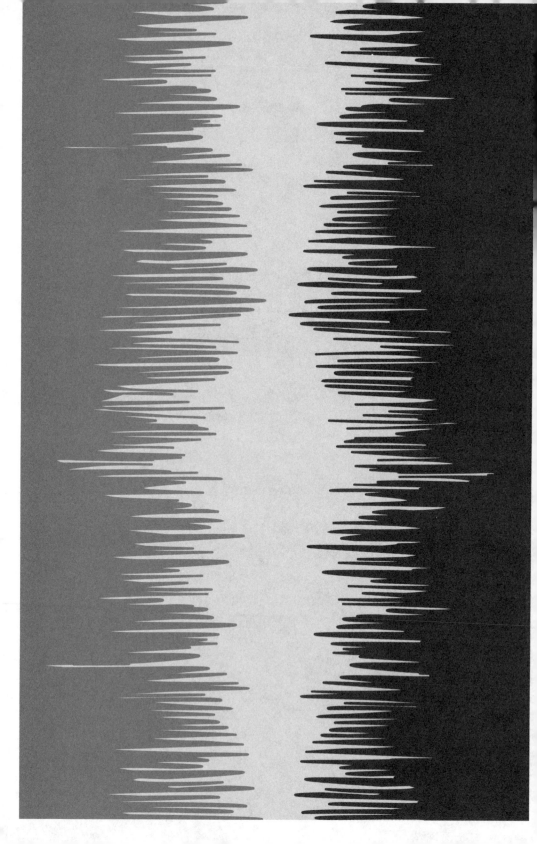

1 |
THE CASE FOR SCHOLARLY REPORTING

ANDREW ROSS

Not a few politically driven writers of my generation might say that they took their cue from the challenge set forth in the editorial of the *New Left Review*'s inaugural 1960 issue. It declared that "the task of socialism today is to meet people where they are, where they are touched, bitten, moved, frustrated, nauseated—to develop discontent and, at the same time, to give the socialist movement some direct sense of the time and ways in which we live." These words were not penned in the abstract. They were specifically intended as a gloss on the decision to take popular culture seriously by the editorial group of the new journal. Indeed, the words were probably written by Stuart Hall, who edited the *NLR* for the first two years, and whose subsequent patronage of the field of cultural studies is most associated with promoting critical analyses of popular expression. But the editorial declaration was also a firm rebuff of the mentality of the Old Left, which, far from meeting people where they are, had arguably more to do with telling people where they ought to be. In contrast to the announcement of this ostensibly clean break, the editors of, and contributors to, the *New Reasoner* and the *University and Left Review*—the two post-Suez journals which had merged to form the *NLR*—had included figures like E. P. Thompson, John Saville, Eric Hobsbawm, Christopher Hill, Dorothy Thompson, Alasdair Macintyre, and Raphael Samuel, all of whom had to wrestle with the legacy of Stalinism in the Communist Party of Great Britain in the course of rejecting it.

In time, under the successive editorships of Perry Anderson and Robin Blackburn, the prevailing tone of the *NLR* became decidedly more mandarin, and its content increasingly given over to macro-historical analysis or to sweeping surveys of the political scene. The *NLR*'s heady engagement with Western Marxism and Continental theory in the 1970s and 1980s, while perceived as a necessary educational route for the left, was even more of a detour away from the 1960 injunction to "meet people where they are." The spirit of the latter was more evident, if anywhere, in the fledgling precincts of cultural studies, where on-the-ground analyses of everyday life provided a documented, usable record of how youth, in particular, were synthesizing new and old experiences of coping with market capitalism. Of course, socialists were not the only ones for whom this kind of knowledge was valuable. While leftists surely needed it to help "develop discontent," market researchers and corporate trend makers set on profiting from discontent eventually caught on, and the soul of cultural studies, and its methods, became as contested as the experiences its practitioners set out to analyze.

My own story intersects with these traditions in somewhat unorthodox ways. My first training, as a critic, came from academics in Britain who had sat at the feet of F. R. Leavis, and it was succeeded, in short order, by others who had translated, if not indigenized, Althusser and other *marxisant* Continental thinkers into the United Kingdom. It was not until I came to the United States in the early 1980s to absorb the living poetry scene that the methods and more populist instincts of cultural studies called out to me, and they did so primarily because of my need to learn what cultural citizenship really amounted to in the streets, bedrooms, bars, theaters, offices, factories, and classrooms of North America.

Though I was recruited by Princeton's English Department in 1985 to teach poetry, no one, in that zone of gentility (we called the campus a "womb with a view") ever asked me to do so. As a result of that benign neglect, I took the opportunity to liberate myself, professionally, from the teaching of literature and self-apprenticed in the kinds of social and cultural analysis that American studies had established as a legitimate institutional niche on campus. As at Harvard, Yale, and Penn, the Princeton program had been around since the 1940s, and the NYU program, to which I subsequently moved, was only slightly younger. The longevity of American studies was a blessing to myself and many others who needed a haven where the gatekeepers of disciplinary turf had no authority. For sure, American studies had its own lineages and custom-bound tendencies, but the policing of the field was weak and almost nonexistent by the standards of the major four-walled disciplines. At Princeton, faculty recruitment meetings were occasionally punctuated by someone musing about what R. P. Blackmur would have thought about this or that candidate. It's impossible to imagine anyone in American studies raising a similar inquiry by invoking Henry Nash Smith.

American studies provided a home for the kind of criticism I wanted—which looks at society as a whole, deploys whatever methods are necessary to do so, and makes a real effort to meet people where they are. All the same, it took me a long time to work off the habits of my training and find my own voice as a practitioner of scholarly reporting—the genre in which I have come to feel most comfortable. There were particular obstacles in the path. I had been trained, first and foremost, as a "reader," alert, above all, to decoding the secret life of words. This meant that I was not a very good listener, especially to the spoken testimony of others. Indeed, the Derridean paradigm of literary reading taught its practitioners to distrust the authority accorded the spoken word—phonocentric was the somewhat derogatory label that accompanied this distrust. My second training was that of an armchair theorist, pledged to the synthesis of ideas. This sedentary art meant that I had no particular understanding of what a "field" of evidence had to offer. Indeed, theory's advocates often cast aspersions on the gathering of any kind of data; empiricism was the derogatory label which accompanied that form of distrust.

Overcoming these obstacles was by no means easy, and it took several years to acquire the confidence to pursue research against my instincts. Even the elementary task of scheduling and conducting a field interview took some doing at first. Nor had I any real preparation for the patience required to build a credible picture of a community, workplace, or labor market—to cite three of the field units I have researched, respectively, in *The Celebration Chronicles*, *No-Collar*, and *Fast Boat to China*. These books were researched in a mode that crossed ethnography with investigative journalism, and each was written to be published by a trade press. It might be appropriate here to reflect on the motives and circumstances that led to these publications.

American studies has always had time for ethnographic study—the defunct program at Penn was especially known for its espousal, and at NYU, ethnography has become one of our three sponsored methods—but it is fair to say that it has not been anywhere near the forefront of a discipline that is still hard-pressed to attract social scientists. Yet the lineage that runs from the Lynds's *Middletown* through Herbert Gans's *Levittowners* to Sudhir Venkatash's *American Project* and Aihwa Ong's *Flexible Citizenship* could hardly be more central to the concerns of American studies practitioners. So, too, the public orientation of the discipline encourages critical investigation of current affairs in ways that overlap with sustained journalistic inquiry. Classics like Anthony Lukas's *Common Ground*, Susan Faludi's *Backlash*, or Barbara Ehrenreich's *Nickel and Dimed* make this case quite clear. Not least, the cultural-investigation wing of American studies can claim Tom Wolfe as its most celebrated graduate, and, by extension, many practitioners of what Robert Boynton has termed the New New Journalism.

Modern ethnographers are all too aware of their professional rivals' claims on the knowledge extracted from their fieldwork, but, in my experience, they seldom acknowledge that they often compete directly with journalists. There are sometimes good reasons for this. For one thing, the core of their ethics are more or less at odds. Where journalists seek to authenticate their sources, ethnographers are supposed to protect or obscure their informants' identities. Where journalists will regard their methods as means to an end, the ethnographer will take pains to authenticate his or her methods of gathering data. Deadlines, even when they are generous, overdetermine the shape and depth of the journalist's study. Aside from considerations regarding tenure deadlines, a professional ethnographer is usually limited only by access to the field, which can most often be renewed without impunity. Finally, the journalist, who is almost always writing for a trade press, will already have internalized his or her publisher's desire for a take-home message that can be readily summarized for media and publicity purposes. Ethnographers tend to shy away from that kind of packaged delivery because they have internalized the credo that summary results do violence to their more holistic description of a field.

Though there are few instances when both kinds of professionals set themselves exactly the same investigative challenge, that was indeed the case with the first of my books in this vein, *The Celebration Chronicles*. A husband and wife team of journalists, one of them from the *New York Times*, spent more or less the same amount of time as I did living in Celebration—our books were published at the same time, were usually reviewed together, and split the market sales down the middle. It was partly under those circumstances, but also because journalists made regular pilgrimages to Celebration, that I developed the kind of scholarly reporting that characterized that book. Residents who felt dirtied by genre stories about "trouble in paradise," or who believed their community had been portrayed as one-dimensional in the mass media, were more willing to open up to a scholar who was not on a short deadline or looking for dirt and who they therefore concluded would be more accountable in the long run. But while most expected me to record their trials and efforts in a more responsible manner than the press had done, they also assumed that I was writing a narrative with a strong story line, one that not a few tried to influence. Meeting the Celebrationites where they were was quite a social challenge to me—after all, most were high-end suburbanites looking to leverage a merchandized Disney dream. But the political pay-off was worth it—I was documenting knowledge about the anxieties and aspirations of white middle-class families living on the fault-line of U.S. politics—Florida's I-4 corridor, which bisects Celebration, turned out to be the decisive swing vote in the 2000 election.

Consequently, there were aspects of that book I wrote in the "you are there" mode, but there were many others when immediate details are interpreted against an academically informed historical and sociological backdrop. Though the task of reconciling these impulses lay ultimately with my editor at Ballantine, a very commercial press that had given me a generous advance to fund my year in residence, I internalized it from the outset. Balancing the publisher's need to harvest returns on their advance (the Ballantine catalogue promoted my book on the page opposite *Chicken Soup and Other Folk Remedies*) with my own intellectual goals produced a genre of writing which mined the overlap between ethnography and journalism.

For *No-Collar*, my second book in this vein, I chose sites much closer to home—two new media companies in New York's Silicon Alley. Once again, coverage of dot-com start-ups had been a favored topic in the press at the height of the so-called New Economy. It occurred to me that the most important story about these companies—the nature of the workplaces—was being sidelined by the Internet gold rush. The press had shown some early interest in the maverick ethos of work organization and employee conditions, but follow-the-money stories about young entrepreneurs very quickly came to dominate all media attention. No one had done a close analysis of the workplaces from the point of view of employees themselves, and my hunch was that this angle would be lost to history in the event of an economic downturn. The window of opportunity to do my study proved to be even tighter than I expected. What emerged in the book was a profile of the adolescence of the self-directed work mentality that is the core ethos of the so-called creative class.

In my field work for these books, I worked out a hybrid formula for identifying informants. Those who spoke ex officio and who were used to speaking to the press were usually identified, as were those who wanted to be named and who waived the offer of anonymity. All other subjects were treated with full confidentiality, and many were given faux names. This formula satisfied the need for reportage to have a series of identifiable characters, around which to weave a storyline while it also offered ethical protection against exposure for other kinds of informant.

The same formula was applied in the third volume, *Fast Boat to China,* which looked at white-collar outsourcing from the perspective of Chinese employees who had taken over jobs transferred from high-wage countries. Media coverage of skilled outsourcing had reached a high pitch by 2004, but there were few accounts of the phenomenon from an offshore point of view, and most of them were Friedmanite paeans to the free-market opportunities afforded to young Indian IT employees. In addition, there were precious few ethnographies of workplaces in China's transitional economy that focused on the Yangtze Delta, and none at all on the high-tech sector that was emerging as the region's economic engine. Once again, the goal I set for my interviews was to take away some usable political knowledge—in this case, about the mentality of the embryonic Chinese middle class and the skeptical view that employees (and their managers) took of their global capitalist employers. Once again, I found that, as a scholar with an academic name card, I had more chance of access to companies and interviewees than if I had been a journalist, and the quality of response from employees and managers was likewise different.

I've taken the time to elaborate on the circumstances of these three volumes to describe what I have called the acquisition of a "voice." More than just a writing style, this involves an explicit orientation toward methods of research, expectations of audience response, fulfillment of contracts (formal and informal) with interviewees and publishers, and judgments about political utility. When we talk about this or that critic's credo, we most often assume that he or she chose a methodological approach that corresponds to some deeply held belief in the righteousness of principle. But it may be more honest to acknowledge that our practice is almost always shaped by circumstances—institutional conventions and rewards, public opportunities, the influence of peers and gatekeepers, the political and social climate, and the serendipity with which certain events enter our radar field of view.

Reading through the contributions of the (mostly) New Critics who filled the pages of the *Kenyon Review* in 1951, it's clear that all of these factors were considered extraneous and, for some, heretical to their observations on the function of criticism. It's not that they were unaware of them, but rather they believed their job was to try to be adequate to the truth about aesthetics *in spite, and not because,* of the circumstances in which they plied their trade. In addition, though most had little or no truck with what would become known as the Old Left (Leslie Fiedler, Stephen Spender, and Kenneth Burke are no-table exceptions), they shared the propensity of that era to tell people where they ought to be, regardless of their circumstance. Critics of my generation are loath to issue such decrees. We think of ourselves as more worldly—more attuned, at least, to the conditions under which criticism is made. But when it comes to the conditions under which other people make history, that is something that requires a little more legwork.

DECLARATIONS OF INDEPENDENCE

AMITAVA KUMAR

I'm in an overheated hotel room in Beijing, reading a *New Yorker* travel piece about China by Jonathan Franzen. The essay is describing the ecological devastation caused by rapid development, but what stops me is a remark that Franzen makes about his Chinese guide. David Xu has "the fashionably angular eyeglasses and ingratiating eagerness of an untenured literature professor." In that throwaway phrase, in its quick malice and wit, I come home. Whether this is revealing of the traveler's loneliness abroad or not, I find myself thinking that I belong not to India or to the United States but to the academy. I realize that I'm a sad provincial; for years, I've been living in a place called the English Department.

Which leads me to declare my first credo. The most significant turns in my scholarship, and in my writing, have been attempts to first fit into, and then violently move away from, the existing codes of naturalization for gaining citizenship in the English Department. Of late, this movement of mine has appeared very much like a person lurching away from an accident—for anyone who has just arrived at the scene it is impossible to judge exactly where the screams are coming from, but what is undeniable is the fact of the twisted wreckage and the smoke and the shock.

"Haven't you noticed how we all specialize in what we hate most?" This is the question posed by James Dixon, the protagonist of *Lucky Jim* by Kingsley Amis. If there is abjection and fine defeatist humor there, it gets even better toward the end of the novel when Dixon is getting ready for his public lecture and quickly getting incapacitated with drink. In the course of his climactic, doomed lecture, our antihero will have proven himself unfit for the teaching profession and, more happily, drawn the approval of a rich patron who will offer him suitable employment in faraway London. But before this happens, while in conversation with said patron, Dixon declares:

> I'm the boredom-detector. I'm a finely-tuned instrument. If only I could get hold of a millionaire I'd be worth a bag of money to him. He could send me on ahead into dinners and cocktail-parties and night-clubs, just for five minutes, and then by looking at me he'd be able to read off the boredom-coefficient of any gathering. Like a canary down a mine; same idea. Then he'd know whether it was worth going in himself or not. He could send me in among the Rotarians and the stage crowd and the golfers and the arty types talking about statements of profiles rather than volumes and the musical . . .

We know from Dixon's experience—and, sadly, our own—how this talent for discerning boredom is the result only of a long intimacy with it. An intimacy nurtured over countless departmental meetings, lectures, corridor conversations, numbing conferences, not to mention attendance at academic parties, where neurotics are nearly as numerous as blowhards.

You'd think there would be regular revolts against this culture of oppression. But we hardly witness any institutional uprisings. A few novels written about poisonous campus life, sure, but no prison breaks. In fact, going by what I have seen at the places where I have worked, it is more common to see the formerly oppressed slip easily into the role of the new, more brutal jailers. The behavior of some of my coercive colleagues in a department where I worked was regularly explained away as only the result of "past wounds" inflicted during the process of acquiring tenure.

But I digress. I was talking about boredom. One of the things that can be said about much of postcolonial criticism is that it is boring, although it'd be more accurate to say that it is often unintelligible *and* boring. However, when I arrived in this country in the late eighties and read postcolonial critics for the first time, I was intrigued. They seemed such a welcome change from my teachers in Delhi. As an undergraduate at Hindu College, I would take a bus to the university. I'd look out of the window, and when we were crossing the gates of Nigambodh Ghat, I'd sometimes see men carrying in their arms little bundles wrapped in white. Each bundle was a child whose corpse was being taken to the river by the father. A small mute procession would follow some men, but often a man would be alone with his enormous burden. I would watch for a few moments from the bus—and then I'd arrive in class.

My professors would be delivering lectures on Locke or Rousseau from notes held together with tape—the yellowing paper would flake off in little pieces when shaken in the air.

The pedagogical climate appeared dramatically different when I came to the United States. In this country, I suddenly felt that criticism was something that was both fresh and live. My teachers were the critics whose writings one read in academic journals. What I was being taught was original work. In some classes, such work also felt urgent. I had never read Edward Said before, or others whose names brought them somehow closer to me in my imagination, critics like Homi Bhabha and Gayatri Chakravorty Spivak. But I didn't share the belief, seemingly dear to the editors of special issues devoted to postcolonial theory, that the 3.2 million poor in Chiapas or the half-million beggars in Calcutta hungered to read debates between the elite of New York and New Delhi in the pages of scholarly journals. My indifferent education in Delhi meant that I hadn't received any real training in writing, academic or non-. But it became clear to me, as the years passed, that I wanted the words I wrote on the page to be worldly, sensual, even personal. I was trying to make postcolonial theory look more like what the larger world associated with postcolonials like Salman Rushdie. Couldn't our analyses become more exuberant, imaginative, and even playful? I wanted very badly to be a writer, and any writer needs readers, but it seemed impossible that postcolonial theorists would ever acquire a real audience.

May I posit a second credo here? A part of the search for readers is a search for venues that will publish you. I was fortunate to receive valuable support from this journal. As a beginning assistant professor, I published in these pages one or two critical pieces but also poems, photographs, and even a bit of doggerel verse written on the evening of Princess Di's death. And during those years, the journal's editors, Jeff Williams and also Mike Hill, collaborated with me in several discussions about academics and intellectuals who wrote for a wider public. While this was an often repetitive and even self-congratulatory exercise on our part, it also represented a demand for legitimation, and a search for a broader argument on behalf of a brand of writing that would earn us, if not hordes of readers, then at least tenure.

I'm talking of events that occurred more than a decade ago. The book that earned me tenure was *Passport Photos*, a multigenre report on what has been called immigritude. The book was published at a time when not only postcolonial theory but the entire enterprise of pure theory was beginning to lose its hegemony. I was very much aware that there were no *people* in postcolonial theory, and I tried to put in my book details of ordinary lives, including photographs and poetry about migrants. Tenure should have freed me to pursue more unconventional writing, but I have never again attempted the formal experimentation of *Passport Photos*. What tenure really allowed me to do was to quietly settle into the habit of writing what, till recently, I would have considered unexciting because it wasn't fragmentary or hybrid and relied on narrative, the style more associated with memoirs and long-form journalism.

In this turn toward more old-fashioned writing, I was helped by the emergence of a new, younger body of Indian writers who were just then making their mark in India as well as abroad. I'm talking now of the latter part of the nineties and names like Arundhati Roy, Pankaj Mishra, Amit Chaudhuri, Raj Kamal Jha, and Jhumpa Lahiri. I remember reading these writers and experiencing a great deal of excitement; I made an effort to get in touch with them, and some of these writers also became my friends. It couldn't have happened overnight, but in those days it seemed as if this single fact had allowed me to escape the small world of the English Department. For years, I had not read a single novel; now I began to read fiction written by both well-known and emerging Indian writers. This was also the time when the Internet arrived and, suddenly, the Indian newspapers I was reading were no longer two weeks old. This meant that the new fiction I was devouring no longer seemed to be reporting on an impossibly distant country. Cricket matches, riots, the deaths of politicians, murders as well as mergers, the release of Bollywood films, literary gossip, everything that was happening in India acquired an immediacy again. It became easy for me to write for the Indian newspapers and magazines that I was regularly reading on the Web. "Location, location, location" sounds very much like a postcolonial mantra, but it has amazed me—and this, too, amounts to a credo—how profoundly a writer's sense of the world, and also of fellowship, has been transformed by the emergence of the World Wide Web. You can be working at a disgustingly badly paid job in an acrimonious English Department at the University of Florida, but when you sit down at the computer and are able to file a story for a newspaper in India, a story that will appear in its published form on your screen only a few hours later, it becomes easy to imagine that you have escaped your immediate setting.

A few years before the period I've been just describing, I had read an article by Frank Lentricchia that had been published in the now-defunct journal *Lingua Franca*. Lentricchia's essay, which was entitled "Last Will and Testament of an Ex-Literary Critic," was an odd, slippery text. One moment it seemed to be arguing against overly political literary criticism, but just when you were expecting an elaboration of an alternative literary approach,

Lentricchia slipped into a more vociferous railing against the incompetence of all literary critics. In the end, you could forgive the essay's incoherence because the argument Lentricchia was putting forward was against any system or method of literary appreciation. All one could hope to do, and all that Lentricchia himself wanted to do, was become a worshipper of great literature.

But this was not my aim. Unlike Lentricchia, I had much still to learn. About theory and criticism and also about literature and the world. I didn't see myself reading the Indian writers I liked without exercising my judgment, and I certainly didn't want to write while pretending that I was in some kind of a trance. For good or bad, I was still very much a part of the academy.

The best allies I found in developing a language of reading not only texts but also people and places were academics from my field, or fields close to mine, who were writing long narrative pieces as well as books that mixed memoir and analysis.

One of my earliest models was Manthia Diawara's *In Search of Africa*. It was an inventive book and yet it performed the old task of storytelling. In the book, Diawara goes back to Guinea looking for his childhood friend. This search, spanning the course of the entire book, becomes a way of introducing the reader to everything from the legacy of the dictator Sekou Touré to the traditional arts of the griots and mask makers. Diawara also exercised an additional fascination over me. I had tried my hand at documentary photography for several years, and Diawara interested me because he was making documentaries about Africa. In a wonderful example of counter-anthropology, he had made a film called *Rouch in Reverse* about the classic French filmmaker Jean Rouch. Even *In Search of Africa* was actually the result of a documentary project of the same name. In elegant essays on photography, particularly in his studies of West African photographers like Seydou Keita and Malick Sidibe, Diawara would offer a language that I had wanted to use for so long. He wrote simply and yet with sensuous precision. Equally important, departing from the kind of sour, astringent critique that quickly becomes second nature to academic critics, Diawara celebrated the practice of art. He found joy in the work of street photographers, and his writing eloquently communicated that joy to the reader. After a decade of metacritical discourse about the constructedness of culture, it was refreshing to find in Diawara a sophisticated but honest search for authenticity and the good life. When I finished reading *In Search of Africa*, I couldn't wait to begin writing about Hindi poets struggling in obscurity or the Indian novelists that I admired and even the Bollywood filmmakers I had adored since childhood.

There were also other writers from inside academia who helped me give shape to a narrative voice. The names that readily come to mind are Amitav Ghosh (*In an Antique Land*), Michael Taussig (*Nervous System*), and Edward Said (*Out of Place*). But perhaps the example that meant the most, and which I also offered to my students as a model, was *Dreambirds* by Rob Nixon. As a graduate student, I had read Nixon in the pages of the *Village Voice* or the *Nation*, and later still I pored over his magisterial book on V. S. Naipaul. But in *Dreambirds*, which came out in 1999, Nixon successfully enacted the turn I had been practicing in the privacy of my room, the transformation of the critic into a memoirist and travel writer. Brilliantly using the ostrich and its migration across history and continents, Nixon had produced a book that was as much a rich cultural history of capitalism as it was a deeply affecting memoir about his own South African childhood.

Later, when offering a course for graduate students that I had entitled Top Ten Reasons for Doing Cultural Studies, I used Nixon's *Dreambirds* as a prime example. Apart from some of the books mentioned above, the other books on the course list that semester were Michael Bérubé's *Life as We Know It*, Barbara Ehrenreich's *Nickel and Dimed*, Susan Sontag's *Illness as Metaphor*, and Alain de Botton's *How Proust Can Change Your Life*. These weren't all books by academics, nor were these the only books used in that course, but these titles most clearly represented what I wanted my students to attempt in their writing. Not simply the range from the journalistic to the philosophical, or from the overtly political to the very playful, but also the right mix of the personal and the public. God knows, I was trying my best to do the same. I had long complained that ideological certainties arrived at in seminar rooms needed to be replaced by the real, often contradictory complexity of people's lives, and now I wrote narratives that relied a great deal on reportage. This turn toward journalism, in some instances resembling what Andrew Ross calls "scholarly reporting," seemed to be the right response to the dead end of postcolonial theorizing.

In the face of a dead critical vocabulary, what was needed were works of imagination. And I began to think that maybe even journalism wasn't the right answer, not conventional journalism anyway, with its pretense of objectivity and distance. We needed writing that examined entanglement, complicity, and compromise. In other words, writing that said clearly that there *is* no clean independence from anything. That too would be a sort of declaration of independence, I think.

That there is no escape into pure certainty or into some antiseptic haven of academic political correctness. That radical statements made at venues like the MLA Delegate Assembly falsely assume that bold posturing will change the profession and indeed the wider world. That, if we were more honest, there would be in what we say or do more self-questioning and doubt. And that our writing should express that condition. I'm putting this down, somewhat crudely and almost like bullet points, yet I realize that I should perhaps be doing a better job of it because for some years now I've adopted this position as a credo.

This position is far better described in a passage in V. S. Naipaul's *A Bend in the River*. The narrator is an African of Indian origin; he is named Salim and runs a shop in a turbulent republic that resembles Zaire. One night Salim is at a party at the home of a Western intellectual favored by the country's dictator. Two or three couples are dancing in the tastefully darkened room. There is music playing, Joan Baez is singing "Barbara Allen." And then other songs. Here's how Naipaul describes the scene:

> Not all songs were like "Barbara Allen." Some were modern, about war and injustice and oppression and nuclear destruction. But always in between were the older, sweeter melodies. These were the ones I waited for, but in the end the voice linked the two kinds of song, linked the maidens and lovers and sad deaths of bygone times with the people of today who were oppressed and about to die.
>
> It was make believe—I never doubted that. You couldn't listen to sweet songs about injustice unless you expected justice and received it much of the time. You couldn't sing songs about the end of the world unless—like the other people in that room, so beautiful with such things: African mats on the floor and African hangings on the wall and spears and masks—you felt that the world was going on and you were safe in it. How easy it was, in that room, to make those assumptions!

3 |
ON CRITIQUE AND INHERITANCE

LISA LOWE

For dialectical philosophy nothing is final, absolute, sacred.
It reveals the transitory character of everything and in everything; nothing can endure
before it except the uninterrupted process of becoming and of passing away,
of endless ascendancy from the lower to the higher.
—FRIEDRICH ENGELS, *The End of Classical German Philosophy*

For Juliet

There are many traditions of critique, but I have been involved in the ones that are dialectical and materialist: dialectical, in the sense that I understand the condition for critical thinking to be contradiction and I experience contradiction as the driving force behind difference, movement, and transformation; and materialist, in the sense that such thinking springs forth from within and prioritizes concern for the conditions under which production is organized. Within this situation of immanent self-contradiction, I have tried to practice critique as the persistent courage to inquire, to seek the possibility of just action. Much of my work has been concerned with the significance of Asian migrations in the nineteenth and twentieth centuries to the critique of the modern social formation of transnational capitalism.

My father passed away in July 2009, and since then, a significant part of my mourning has involved thinking deeply about the questions of critique and inheritance, reckoning and responsibility. During his lifetime, I found him occasionally enigmatic or awkward as a father but with retrospection I have come to appreciate his life and death differently, and his actions reverberate with an intimacy that I was able to grasp only in the last year of his life. I now comprehend his life and death as profoundly attentive, committed to this sense of critique, taking actions to resolve contradictions, even when those actions pronounced the realization of the impossibility of resolution.

He was born in China in 1928, and he had a wartime childhood that displaced him from Shanghai to Hong Kong, Burma, Yunnan, and Calcutta before arriving in the United States in 1945 at the age of sixteen. It was during the Second World War, two years after the Magnuson Act permitted a small quota of Chinese to enter, and it would be another two decades before the United States lifted prohibitions initiating general immigration from Asia. He and my mother were scarcely adults when they left wartime China and were among the very few Chinese at the University of Chicago in the early 1950s. I have often reflected that their unique shared history was likely the only reason they ever married, for they divorced by the end of the 1960s when I was still an adolescent.

My father was an intellectual historian and social theorist, who taught at several universities before settling into a career in the History Department at San Francisco State from 1968 to 1992, when he retired. Each of his three books was a serious meditation on the relevance of Marxism as an analysis of capitalist political economy, a philosophy of history, and a theory of subjectivity—the first with respect to modern China; the second, Europe; and the third, the United States. I know this because I have read his books rather than because he always shared his immediate concerns with me as he was writing them. Once I was an adult, our conversations became intellectual ones about ideas, history, and politics. I knew him as a man who understood his personal biography within the forces of history, who explicitly connected his intellectual preoccupations and penchants with this past of war and migration.

When I was a graduate student in the late 1970s and early 1980s, French poststructuralism had made its way into the U.S. academy. I read Althusser and Balibar with Hayden White, and Lévi-Strauss and Foucault with Jim Clifford. Gayatri Spivak, who had recently translated *Of Grammatology*, visited for a term. With Donna Haraway, our cohort of students—including Ruth Frankenberg, bell hooks, Chela Sandoval, Caren Kaplan, and others—read the feminists Kristeva, Cixous, Wittig, and Rose, alongside Lorde, Anzaldúa, Crenshaw, and Davis. In 1980, my father gave me his copy of Alexandre Kojève's 1934 *Introduction to the Reading of Hegel*. I had spent a year in France in the mid-1970s and studied European intellectual history as an undergraduate, but, initially, I assumed that his reference to Kojève was like an offhand remark, probably as distant in its relevance as I had found him emotionally remote as a father. Yet later, and several times over, I came to grasp the consequences if not the intention of his offering, for it directed me to an early moment in the French reception of Hegel that was elaborated not only in French philosophy but in French semiotics, psychoanalysis, and existentialist and poststructuralist Marxism, as well as deconstruction. It was a

FIGURE 3.1   San Francisco, 1985

lesson in the intellectual history of the dialectic and dialectical method. After the death of loved ones, we often subject to close scrutiny all of their many lost gestures, asides, and actions. In our mourning, we invest in making legible what has been lost, all the while knowing that there is something hidden within the recesses of the loss, something we will never know. As our gaze searches a photograph of the lost one, we are pierced by the understanding that what was will never be again, what Barthes called the *"punctum."*

In the late 1980s, I returned to Paris to do some work in the Bibliothèque Nationale on eighteenth-century travel narratives for my first book on French and British orientalisms. After finishing a day's work, I would rummage around secondhand bookstores in the Latin Quarter. One evening, I found in the corner of one store a shelf of old issues of *Tel Quel*, the avant-garde literary journal founded by Philippe Sollers in the 1960s that had come to symbolize French theory during the height of deconstruction. Intellectuals at *Tel Quel* had embraced Maoism as an anti-authoritarian theory and practice, and the Chinese Cultural Revolution was for them a utopian projection of "permanent revolution" after the disappointments of Mai '68. Among these old issues, there were several from 1971 and 1973, the journal's brief Maoist phase. Suddenly, I was startled, for in these issues, there appeared a translated chapter of my father's work, "Marx, Engels et la Chine."[1] In this, he observed that Western Marxism had misunderstood China when it cast the Asiatic mode of production as static and underdeveloped, while Lenin and Mao had rethought Marxism for Russia and China. I had inadvertently discovered him within this moment of *telqueliste* orientalism, in which French leftists searched for a political model outside of Western ideology.

I hold my father's copy of Kojève in my hands. Belatedly, but not too late, I take in that it may well have been the first expression that he had recognized in me an emerging intellectual. Read closely now, I see this gift of Kojève, rather than Hegel's *Phenomenology* itself, as an instance of the mediation of history in the productive generation of the unfolding dialectic of critique. That is, Kojève's exegesis of the Hegelian dialectic of universal History displaced that "original" in an *Aufhebung* or sublation that transformed it and raised it to another level in the unfolding of history. It is a wonderful object lesson in how a dialectical tradition can be "carefully disinterred" (in Stuart Hall's words), reread, and refracted through the contexts of another history. Kojève, a Russian émigré of the interwar years, had explicated Hegel in terms of Marx and Heidegger, and the insights of his rereading would inform Foucault, Lacan, and others, perhaps even more than Hegel himself. My father, a wartime Chinese émigré, was attuned to precisely these kinds of displacements, considering Marx's dialectical method transformed by the historically different conditions of China and Russia, in Maoist and Leninist thought.

In his later works, my dad used historical method to interpret the processes of modern perception and embodiment, and phenomenology to understand the emergence of modernity.[2] A modern emphasis on intentionality and structures of consciousness also marked the decisions he made in his life as he approached everything from the perspective of a critical being in relation to the possibilities for transformation. He regarded what appeared to be true, what may be seized as given in time, as phenomena ever to be questioned, as a mediation of processes that block their immediate availability. I watched him analyze the forces of fragmentation and reification that impede understanding. I believe that, for him, the sense that every thought and action is but one stage in an unfolding whose end cannot be known in the beginning was not merely a formal commonplace. For if this sense remained only formal, it would neither discern the true nature of contradiction, nor reckon adequately or materially with it. Until the end, he sought not only to confront contradiction but to act in ways that might fundamentally change the conditioning contradictions of his life: wealth and poverty, China and the West, duty and love. In his example, I saw a life dedicated to grappling with the great divides of accumulation and need, thoughtless comfort and unbearable vulnerability. And from his paternal regard, I learned some fundamentals that I practice in my own pedagogy: respect for the difference of the other, teaching method rather than imparting facts or opinions, engagement as a commitment to lifelong responsibility.

Inheritance is a complex and subtle process. The definitions of inheritance as determined by biology are as impoverished as the ones concerned with the passing on of names, property, station, or debts. It is, rather, as Engels describes dialectical history, an "uninterrupted process of becoming and of passing away," a metaphor for the endless process in which the next generation is bequeathed the conditions left by the former. My father's actions, made with full commitment in the face of an as yet unfathomed solution, deferred the contradictions he faced to be addressed at another level or in another manifested history. I receive in his dying my responsibilities.

For some years before his death, I had been writing a book that examines the abolition of slavery and the introduction of Chinese indentured labor as the historical conditions for the emergence of the dialectic at the center of liberal ideas of freedom. In recent years, I put this work aside when a series of unexpected events intervened. However, as I continue to collect details about the post-1840 "coolie" trade that dispersed millions of Chinese to the British West Indies, Spanish Cuba and Peru, French and Dutch colonies in the Indian Ocean, Australia, Hawaii, and the United States, it appears to me that these Chinese migrations had linked and heralded the world system in an unprecedented manner. The figure of the Chinese migrant mediated competing distinctions between "free" and "unfree," disrupted the dialectic and teleology of lord and bondsman, and marked the onset of a new division of labor within an international economy based on manufacturing and trade, the apotheosis of which we find in contemporary globalization. Asia figured as the supplement for *both* the Western imperial imagination *and* the black anticolonial one. My work interprets the European dialectical reckoning with Asia and ultimately pursues the possibility that the displacement of that dialectic into anticolonial and antislavery philosophies gave rise to notions of decolonization, emancipation, and independence that may account for Asia and, in doing so, not reproduce the same violence of an earlier dialectic.

With my father's passing, I have taken up this work again with a furious energy. It is my response to my father's final action, his last critique. As I excavate lost histories and decipher intimacies deferred, I learn to accept my inheritance.

NOTES

1. Donald M. Lowe, "Marx, Engels et la Chine," *Tel Quel* 56 (Winter 1973): 60–64. This was the first chapter of *The Function of "China" in Marx, Lenin, and Mao* (Berkeley: University of California Press, 1966).

2. Donald M. Lowe, *The History of Bourgeois Perception* (Chicago: University of Chicago Press, 1982); Lowe, *The Body in Late-Capitalist USA* (Durham, N.C.: Duke University Press, 1995). In later years, he was associate editor of the Asian studies journal *positions: east asia culture(s) critique*, edited by his second wife, Tani Barlow.

4 |
WHAT I BELIEVE AND WHY

VINCENT B. LEITCH

Although I completed my Ph.D. in literary studies during the early 1970s, I didn't assert an explicit point of view, an identifiable critical position, until the late 1980s. In an article I wrote in 1987, "Taboo and Critique: Literary Criticism and Ethics," I outlined my own project of cultural critique, fusing poststructuralism with post-Marxist cultural studies. First, I criticized the taboo on extrinsic criticism promulgated by the American New Critics and tacitly conveyed to me by most of my professors. Second, I sketched my own program by working through faults with the 1980s critical projects of Wayne Booth (liberal pluralism), Robert Scholes (structuralism), and J. Hillis Miller (conservative deconstruction), all major critical voices of the time. Where the New Critics focused on the literary text as an autonomous aesthetic object and explicitly forbade critics from linking it with society, history, psychology, economics, politics, or ethics, cultural critics of all stripes, myself included, accepted and affirmed such links. This is no easy road to travel. When Booth, Scholes, and Miller all insisted that close reading precede ethical critique, they foolishly retained a mandatory formalistic phase for all critical inquiry, keeping the literary text as a privileged aesthetic object on the way to broadened social concerns. They got things backward.

This became the opening pages of my book, an unabashed credo, *Cultural Criticism, Literary Theory, Poststructuralism* (Columbia University Press, 1992), arguing a handful of positions on perennial literary topics consistent with a cultural studies informed by poststructuralism. For anyone who might have been paying attention, it appeared evident from my 1987 article that I had bought into cultural studies, having been earlier identified with poststructuralism, particularly Yale deconstruction. However, my first book, *Deconstructive Criticism* (Columbia University Press, 1983), followed an arc from French structuralism and poststructuralism through Yale deconstruction to the *boundary 2* group (cast as an alternative deconstructive project) to the wide-ranging anarchist projects of Michel Foucault and of Gilles Deleuze and Félix Guattari. In the end, it parodied Yale deconstruction. Things became even clearer with my next book, *American Literary Criticism from the 1930s to the 1980s* (Columbia University Press, 1988), written between 1982 and 1986. It covered thirteen schools and movements, starting with Marxism and New Criticism, adding as a first for histories of American criticism a chapter on the early engagé social criticism of the New York Intellectuals, and ending with feminism, black aesthetics (another first), and cultural studies. The work traced over the course of 500 sober pages both formalist projects that dehistoricize, depoliticize, and aestheticize literary studies and antiformalist movements that deepen and extend cultural criticism. My trajectory was clear.

In 1987 I got divorced after seventeen years of marriage. Also I moved from working at a small private Southern liberal arts college for thirteen years to a large Midwestern state university. When the dust settled, I ended up a single parent with two young teenagers. Over the next ten years I shepherded them through high school and college. These were rough economic times. I learned about the economics and politics of postmodern families up close and personal.

On the verge of bankruptcy, having doled out $30,000 for expenses surrounding the divorce, I managed after eighteen months of hand-to-mouth apartment dwelling to buy a house. It was done through creative financing by a realtor along with his banker and appraiser colleagues. I rented the house for six months. That became the 5 percent down payment. I obtained a subprime adjustable-rate mortgage from a local bank, plus a small personal loan on the side from the realtor. It all seemed a miracle, going from near bankrupt to homeowner in eighteen months. Lucky for me, the interest rate did not shoot up, nor did the price of houses drop. Eventually, I was able to refinance with a new fixed-rate mortgage, which, however, cost $2,000 in closing fees added to the principal of the loan. Debt proliferates.

As you might imagine, during this period I felt chronically insecure. I was fearfully checking interest rates on a regular basis. I witnessed to my astonishment the flexibility (moral relativism) of the real estate, appraisal, and banking industries. By the late 1990s President Clinton solidified the changes going on, radically deregulating banking and investment and tearing down key firewalls erected during the Great Depression by President Roosevelt. Branch banks started to pop up all over the place. Credit was increasingly easy to get. Home ownership rates were rising. And single-headed households were more and more common. Cultural critics today realize, primarily in the wake of feminism, that the personal is linked with the social, political, and economic. My personal story felt more and more like a lesson in politics and economics.

The day the Clinton White House announced a freeing-up of student loans in the early 1990s, I was overjoyed and relieved as, it turned out, were bankers, politicians, and university administrators. My oldest child was just starting college on her way to BA and MA degrees—and ultimately $46,000 in loans, despite her scholarships, summer jobs, and teaching assistantship. My youngest child soon racked up $10,000 in loans on his BA degree. I don't recall anyone in my sixties generation carrying much debt for their college education, whereas my children, like the majority in the United States, face a decade or two or three of debt repayments. (When I was a visiting Fulbright professor in Northern Europe in the 1970s, I witnessed free university education where students received additional support from state stipends.) So I was misguided to be overjoyed at President Clinton's apparent munificence, not realizing from the outset it was a way to shift financing from institutions to individuals, enabling the state to withdraw from paying for education. I did not recognize nor condemn this move to privatization, but I did register it immediately in growing anxiety about interest rates, credit scores, debt loads, and the financial future of my children. There is a politics of feelings and everyday family intimacies that tells us what's really going on in the culture.

Around the time my children moved in with me, the nationwide retirement system for college teachers began to change after many decades of stability. When during the 1970s I first entered TIAA-CREF (Teachers Insurance Annuity Association–College Retirement Equities Fund), there were two accounts where I could allocate my money (a sum equal to 10 percent of my annual salary contributed by my college): (1) TIAA Traditional [Bonds and Mortgages] (founded 1918), and (2) CREF Stock (established 1952). Most new faculty members at that time split their funds 50/50 or 60/40, with other permutations possible. Arriving at a new university position in 1987, I continued the split I had had at the previous job (this time the school contributed a figure equal to 15 percent of my salary). But starting in 1988 things at TIAA-CREF changed more and more tellingly over the next two decades. In 1988 a new choice was added to the earlier two—the CREF Money Market Account. In 1990 two additional investment accounts appeared, CREF Bond Market and CREF Social Choice. Over the course of the nineties five far more risky CREF options became available: Global Equities (1992), Equity Index and Growth (both 1994), Real Estate (1995), and Inflation-Linked Bond (1997). Then in 2002 TIAA-CREF opened eighteen separate mutual fund accounts to retirement contributions. And 2004 witnessed seven brand new Lifecycle Funds, complemented by three more such accounts in 2007. In 2006 nine other TIAA-CREF retirement-class mutual funds emerged. If you're counting, this means that instead of the two previous choices, I and several million other participants now faced four dozen choices within the TIAA-CREF family of funds. During this period, many of us, me included, got befuddled.

Along the way I wondered, do I and my colleagues know enough about stocks, bonds, real estate, indexes, rating agencies, and so on to make good investment choices? By the mid-nineties, like it or not, we were all being turned into investors. That for me was a worrisome new burden. Previously I did not read investment-account prospectuses and quarterly reports, nor did I monitor investment news. When my home computer got linked to the Internet in the late nineties, I began to monitor finances, as well as to work, on a 24/7 basis. If it were not for their rules limiting the number of trades each quarter, TIAA-CREF might have turned me into a day trader over the course of the 1990s. This is my personal experience with mainstream casino capitalism, the triumphalist neoliberalism and free-market dogma spreading from the 1970s onward. It has become harder and harder for me not to talk about the recent reconfiguration of money, mortgages, debt, work, education, retirement, and their impact on the family as well as day-to-day life. The way I see it, this is the kind of cultural critique we need. It is different from the impersonal speculative way many do postmodern critique. Nearer home, the industry calls it "financial literacy."

The social as well as economic transformations of our times have affected me in dramatic ways. It first started to register on me and my family in the late 1980s and early 1990s. Before my generation, there were two divorces in my huge Irish Italian American Catholic family, a social network rooted in Islip and Babylon Townships on the south shore of Long Island. In my generation there have been several dozen divorces, plus lots of mobility given a nationwide job market. Personally, I feel I have been living in exile as migrant labor since I got my first job in the South, followed by positions in the

Midwest and the Southwest—several decades away from home and count-ing. The single-headed household, often uprooted from the extended family, caught up in mortgage and student debt, increasingly worried about health care expenses plus retirement, and befuddled by financial choices describes not only my reality but that of so many others in the shrinking middle class. I hasten to add that my two siblings, an older sister and a younger brother, have long shuttled in and out of the working poor, a new and growing class of the nickeled and dimed, without retirement accounts, college loans, or mortgages. So much for the world of family values.

The psychological syndrome that fits postmodern social insecurity is, I believe, panic attacks. I've had them. This is different from the paranoia typi-cal of the Cold War period of my youth. Panic attacks involve more or less continuous stress, anxiety, and distraction, compounded by overwork, caf-feine, sugar, excessive options at every turn, speed, multitasking, a 24/7 reality, too much news and media, an absence of quiet time and relaxation, not to mention leisure. Some people seem to thrive on this regimen. The rising gen-eration appears more adapted to it, texting like bandits while popping anxiety pills in record numbers.

The mode of criticism that is best suited to these times, it has seemed ob-vious to me, is a renewed cultural critique with political economy, particularly finance, at center stage. It should pay attention to the feelings, emotions, and intimacies that financial tides set in motion. Increasingly since the 1980s, I have felt that my job as a university professor entails teaching not only cul-tural literacy but intimate critique. Sadly, this world has bad effects on many, too many, of my students and their families.

Unplanned happenings, unexpected events, and accidents have played a decisive role in my personal life and career. Early on my economics teacher at the state Merchant Marine academy in New York told me to consult Heilbronner's *The Worldly Philosophers* for my course project on nineteenth-century economic theory. When I asked a librarian about worldly philosophy and Heil-something, he sent me to Heidegger. A fateful event. I was eighteen years old and just opening to the world of literature, philosophy, and econom-ics, but with neither direction nor mentor. Two years later, following a do-it-yourself immersion in existentialism, Beat literature, and left Keynesian economics, I walked out of the academy liberated (no more uniforms) and became a literature major.

The month after I started on my new road, my younger brother, a high school senior, died in a drunk-driving car accident. That had the effect of so-lidifying my anger at God into agnosticism and bouts of atheism. My eleven years of rigorous Cold War American Catholic education, all in uniform, predating the liberalizations of the Vatican II Council and teaching dreadful medieval dogmas, prepared me poorly for the world. Not surprisingly, I am a longtime secularist who believes in freedom from religion as well as freedom of religion. I have little good to say about fundamentalisms, which have visited members of my family as well as my country. I am nonplussed, if bemused, by New Age spirituality. I retain respect for liberation theologies. But, in general, I keep a wary eye on religion.

I had to play catch-up on literary studies, being two years behind my cohort. So I undertook a three-semester MA to compensate and satisfy my curiosities. The week I graduated a military draft notice arrived. It was a few days before Christmas, and I was applying for Ph.D. programs. Quickly I took a six-month spring semester teaching job in a local high school to earn money and to forestall the draft. It was 1968, and I decided unequivocally I would go into exile to Canada if I were drafted into the army. Vietnam changed forever my feelings about American imperialism and nationalism, teaching me the necessity of critical patriotism. The Vietnam War was stupid, immoral, and criminal as was the post-9/11 war in Iraq.

Let me jump ahead. By chance I was asked to referee a proposal in autumn 1994 for a "Norton Anthology of Literary Theory and Criticism." The publisher turned to me, I supposed, because of my prior books. I ended up endorsing the idea of a Norton anthology on theory but not the specific proposal, recommending against the proposer, sketching what shape a proper anthology should take, and listing who should be considered for the job (not me). A few months later the editor showed up in my office and asked me if I would be interested. I hesitated but ultimately accepted with two understandings: that I could recruit a team of editors and that revised editions, if deemed desirable, would happen on roughly eight-year rotations. I didn't want the anthology to become a way of life and a full-time job. And I believed a collective approach to the task, never tried before with large theory anthologies, made the best sense. This was summer 1995. Luckily, it was an opportune moment for me because I had just finished the manuscript of my book *Postmodernism—Local Effects, Global Flows* (SUNY Press, 1996). Happily, as it turned out, my next book was the *Norton Anthology of Theory and Criticism* (2001), with me as general editor along with a team of five hand-picked editors. The opening page of the preface, drafted by me and approved by the team, defined "theory" this way for new generations of students and faculty:

Today the term encompasses significant works not only of poetics, theory of criticism, and aesthetics as of old, but also of rhetoric, media and discourse theory, semiotics, race and ethnicity theory, gender theory, and visual and popular culture theory. But theory in its newer sense means still more than this broadly expanded body of topics and texts. It entails a mode of questioning and analysis that goes beyond the earlier New Critical research into the "literariness" of literature. Because of the effects of poststructuralism, cultural studies, and the new social movements, especially the women's and civil rights movements, theory now entails skepticism toward systems, institutions, norms; a readiness to take critical stands and engage in resistance; an interest in blind spots, contradictions, distortions (often discovered to be ineradicable); and a habit of linking local and personal practices to the larger economic, political, historical, and ethical forces of culture.

(xxxiii)

This is what I believe. And I came by it the hard way.

My motivation for undertaking the Norton anthology project was largely missionary. After I completed my Ph.D. on the history of poetry and poetics, I converted to criticism and theory as a specialty. There were no such specialty programs when I was coming up. Over the next decade I reengineered myself through self-directed study, research, and teaching, interrupted with short periods of formal education: NEH Summer Seminar (1976), School of Criticism and Theory (1978), Fulbright-Hays Theory Lectureship (1979), International Institute for Semiotic and Structural Studies (1981), Alliance Française in Paris (1982). I also completed a bachelor's program in French while I was working as a beginning professor during the seventies. In its post-formalist renaissance, theory in America was vital, exciting, life-enhancing, not the narrow and deadening dogma of the previous era. I was a convert.

For me the *Norton Anthology of Theory and Criticism* (2nd ed., 2010) was and is designed to accomplish several missions: to dignify and monumentalize theory; to consolidate the many gains of contemporary theory; to defend theory during the culture wars, which were started by the right wing in the mid-1980s and persist today; last, but not least, to introduce students and faculty, in the United States and abroad (where half of its sales happen), to a wide-ranging, provocative, and accessible textbook that is both scholarly and up-to-date, being constructed from the standpoint of twenty-first-century cultural critique. (Forgive the promo.) I see myself as both an insider and a populizer. I make no apologies to my hierophantic colleagues. The mission lives on.

Here is a piece of illuminating background. I was flabbergasted and bitterly angry when I heard ex-CIA agent Philip Agee on a 1970s late-night television interview explain how in the 1950s and 1960s the CIA recruited candidates at Catholic colleges. Why Catholic colleges? It turns out the CIA preferred to recruit there because Catholics understand hierarchy, discipline, and duty. "Son of a bitch," I spluttered. From kindergarten to tenth grade (ages five to sixteen years), I was enrolled in Catholic schools. I wore a uniform every day and marched to class, went to confession on Saturdays, attended 9:00 a.m. mass in uniform each Sunday. They taught me acquiescence to authority, selflessness, and endless rules (preconditions for fascism). As a theorist, I teach skepticism toward authority, self-assertive cultural criticism, and intimate critique.

My *Postmodernism—Local Effects, Global Flows* was followed by *Theory Matters* (Routledge, 2003) and *Living with Theory* (Blackwell, 2008). All three books are essay collections of cultural criticism and defenses of theory. What holds this later work together is an ongoing project of mapping as well as evaluating postmodern culture. I construe postmodernity as neither a philosophy nor style but a new period that started in the 1970s and 1980s. Not uncritically, I am working in the wake of Fredric Jameson, David Harvey, and especially the British New Times project, all dating from the late 1980s and continuing into the new century. My experience and observations confirm that we are living through a distinct post-welfare-state period, more or less helpfully labeled postindustrial, post-Fordist, consumer society, late capitalism, or globalization.

What most characterizes postmodern culture for me is disorganization. Think of the TIAA-CREF case. On the one hand, financial consumers are offered an excessive array of choices of investment products pitched to their tolerances for risk, time frames, and preferences. On the other hand, who has the time and expertise to make intelligent choices? I'm confused, stressed, perplexed. I seek a guide for idiots or dummies, the latest edition since the pace of change is rapid. This is a symptomatic genre for our times. As a wine drinker (my Italian heritage), I am befuddled by the number of decent Chardonnay and Syrah/Shiraz wines under twenty dollars a bottle. This largesse dates from the wine revolution that started in the 1970s and 1980s. *Wine Spectator* magazine (established 1976) nowadays evaluates 18,000 wines annually. I have a similar experience in a bookstore (for example, the self-help section), a supermarket (the cereal aisle), a footwear store (walls of sneakers). The speeded-up proliferation of commodities and choices, plus the disaggregation of niches and spheres, render the big picture inaccessible and, strictly speaking, unknowable. Hence, the need for mapping.

One last unexpected turn of events helps explain what I believe and why. I couldn't find a position the year I received my Ph.D., the job market having crashed several years earlier (1970, to be exact, and continuing today). So I ended up teaching on a one-year interim appointment in the Department of Humanities at the University of Florida. There I met Gregory Ulmer, a new Ph.D. in comparative literature who had just secured a full-time tenure-track job. Two decisive things occurred during that year. First, Ulmer introduced me to French structuralism and poststructuralism. That shook me up and helped me get past my New Critical frame of mind. Second, the job required me to teach multiple sections of Humanities 211, 221, and 231 during the fall, winter, and spring quarters. The course content was set by the department, with only a few open spots. One step ahead of the students, I learned and taught Ancient and Medieval, Renaissance and Enlightenment, and Modern Western Humanities. The curriculum programmatically juxtaposed art history, literature, philosophy, religion, and music (with the latter handled by a musicologist in large lectures). A typical module would be the Parthenon, Plato's *Republic*, Sophocles' *Antigone*, and Aristotle's *Poetics*, or Abstract Expressionism, Existentialism, Beat Literature, and Bebop Jazz. Although it covered old-fashioned intellectual rather than social history, the program put me in touch with big pictures. It struck a resonant chord within me. Early and late, my work aims for wide-ranging comparative history.

The program also introduced me to art history (specifically architecture, sculpture, and painting). Out of this latter came a lifelong interest in contemporary painting, plus modern museums, galleries, art journals and books, and local art scenes. When I came to address postmodernism, I naturally turned to painting as well as literature, philosophy, and popular arts (I am a child of the sixties). One of the genuine benefits of construing postmodernism as a period, not just a school of philosophy or a style, is the necessity to investigate political economy and society as well as the arts high and low. Postmodern fusion, pastiche, multiculturalism, and backlash manifest themselves, I find, in the period's food, wine, fashion, film, music, art, philosophy, religion, and literature. Through accidents and blindly, it appears, I was being prepared and preparing myself early on for a job of cultural criticism and critique. Our times demand it.

5 |
HEARING LOSSES AND GAINS

CRAIG WOMACK

Any damn fool can get complicated. It takes genius to attain simplicity.
—PETE SEEGER on Woody Guthrie

L ike any critic I locate my work inside stories, places, and dates. This is my most recent, and telling, story: On Monday, July 12, 2010, I drove over to my paternal great-uncle's place, east of downtown Eufaula, Oklahoma, and just off a little cove of the lake there. The visit was long over-due, and I had put it off for several years. Why? The music, for one thing. He always wants me and Dad and Dad's twin brother to play guitar, and he sings 1950s country songs like a bawling calf separated from its mother at branding time. I like Lefty Frizzell, and Hank (all three—Williams, Snow, Thompson), Kitty Wells, Little Jimmy Dickens, Johnny Horton, Ernest Tubb, Roy Acuff, and the rest of the crew as well as anyone and better than most my age, but I tend to jazz up the chords and take solos that lean away from the melody. My uncle, whenever I play anything other than simple changes, hollers, "Whoa, wait a minute!" and stops and holds on to both sides of his head. This means he, my dad, and my Uncle Foy do most of the playing since I tend to throw everybody off.

And that's the least complicated part. I never felt overt homophobia from any of them out that way, but that's because the subject is buried so deep in rural Oklahoma that people are even homophobic of homophobia. "Gay" pretty much tops the list of things you don't need to say that you don't need to say. So, I had always gone there without my partner. The question "never been married?" made its rounds for a few years until people realized I might feel inclined to answer. Guitar picking is the one thing that allows me to be there—if not on my own terms, at least on familiar ground.

My parents, who've lived in California for a long time and are often fuzzy on the details regarding people back home, told me my uncle had been sick, but they didn't say how come. On the drive out, I pulled into town before crossing the railroad tracks east of Main. I wanted to get a long-sleeve shirt at Sharpe's, the only department store, and cover the ceremonial scratches I'd just gotten during *buskita*, the second week of Green Corn at Tallahassee Wakokiye, the Creek grounds I belong to. While my uncle has some Cherokee ancestry, he is Baptist, and I didn't feel up to explaining why we do these things. Easier to hide them, and I've always been a sucker for snapping pearl buttons anyway.

I arrived at their rock-hewn modern ranch house in the early afternoon, and when my aunt let me in she told me my uncle was in the back room in bed. My uncle, one of the most active people I know for his age, is an old plow boy who never made it into the twentieth or twenty-first century. He is something of a horse whisperer. The last time I had seen him he had been in the front yard hitching up the traces on one of his prize paint horses for a parade during Eufaula's "Hawg Days" celebration. After this parade, which concludes with a bunch of roaring bikers doing wheelies down the main drag that runs north and south off of Highway 9, another relative, my Aunt Rosie, usually says, "I need a sedative." During the hitching, his horse had stood stock still, frozen like a statue, no matter how far or how long he went to fetch harnesses, and the horse's uncanny sense of his authority is the deepest thing I know about my uncle.

My uncle, propped up in bed in pajamas instead of his customary overalls or Wrangler jeans and roper cowboy boots, had an oxygen tube in his nose. His face was flushed and puffy, which made him look more like his siblings and less like himself—a short, wiry scarecrow of a fellow who steps inside his skin whenever he swings up into a saddle or takes hold of the reins in a wagon seat. My skateboarding and dirt-biking nephews in California love him on the rare occasions they get to visit Eufaula, and he must seem like something from another world to them.

My uncle, once my aunt jabbed him in the shoulder, hollered at the top of her lungs, and pointed my way, lit up when he recognized me standing on the other side of the bed. Though he kept grinning big as the lake itself, I quickly discovered he could hear hardly anything. He had me sit next to him on the bed, took my hand in both of his. Didn't let go. Holding hands in bed with a cowboy who won't turn you loose feels funny for the first few minutes. After that, I got kind of used to it.

His wife asked him if he could come into the kitchen and eat some lunch with us. He was hooked to an oxygen tube coiled up in the corner that must have measured the length of a football field. He agreed and rolled over on his side, pushed himself up, got his legs to the floor, and stood with the help of a walker. Pushing the walker down the long hallway, my uncle shrugged and told me, "We all gotta go somehow."

Seated at the table, he took me and my aunt by the hand and blessed the food, thanking the Lord for the time we had together. We ate and caught up as I reported on my parents' latest doings out in California and he did the same for our Eufaula relations. I expected to hear more about my staying away for so long but didn't. His wife, whose familiar voice he heard better than anyone else's, had to scream, jab, and point more, even after inserting a hearing aid that she said hadn't done him any good. Instead of going back to bed after lunch, he veered his walker over to a La-Z-Boy in the living room and got adjusted. He's short, but he'd never really seemed short before that afternoon. He perched with his feet tucked under his butt in the recliner, and I thought of the scissortails all around our country that balance precariously on strands of barbed wire, bobbing in the breeze, using their namesake as a ballast.

My uncle said, "I haven't played guitar in a year. Will you play for me?" I tried not to think too much about what his request meant, but I busted a string on the first guitar. Second one the machine heads on the tuners wouldn't turn. He had five, and I hit pay dirt on the last one, an Alvarez with a gaudy pick guard and an etching of a peacock on it. I used the shoulder strap, so I could stand next to the recliner and lean toward his ear. I sang like I was in a packed football stadium with no microphone. "Blue Eyes Crying in the Rain." "Swinging Doors." "Crazy Arms." "I Can't Help It If I'm Still in Love with You." "All Around the Water Tower, Waiting for a Train." "Wabash Cannon Ball." "Those Wedding Bells Will Never Ring for Me." "If You've Got the Money, Honey, I've Got the Time." "It Wasn't God Who Made Honky Tonk Angels." "Faded Love." I knew he could hear occasionally because he sang along now and then. He thumbed through his songbook, a binder he has full of hand-written lyrics of hundreds of country tunes. One of his specialties, "One Day at a Time," a pseudo-gospel song, is a tune he is known for singing around Eufaula, especially at the nursing home, his most requested number. He kept saying, "I just caint get nothing out," although he actually sang a couple verses. "Show me the stairway, I have to climb." I felt something of a usurper finishing it for him.

Guitar players, let's face it, like to show off their chops, but I didn't play jazz, classical, any of the technical stuff I normally would to let people know what I can do. Yet it felt exactly right for that afternoon east of Eufaula and north of the lake in my uncle's living room. I have a friend who says, "I love simple chords," and I always think, "Yeah, because that's the only kind you know." Yet what I played had more depth than any music I'd ever made, and something seemed right about open strings, first position, and lots of volume. That's what he wanted to hear even if he couldn't hear it.

My uncle put his hands above his head and clapped, sometimes with his eyes shut, while laying back in the recliner. My Aunt Rosie, who lives next door, had come over in the golf cart, and she added soft "amens," a dramatic contrast to my singing, which at that point had reached decibels that might daunt Sid Vicious. Other times it would be like my uncle was not there, his eyes staring vacantly ahead, and I knew the sound had faded out of his range or maybe other realities had caught his attention. One of the times I thought he'd zoned out he sat up, put his feet on the floor, and said, "Let me thump on that some." I handed him the guitar. He fumbled with the shoulder strap and his fingers made the shapes of the chords he wanted, but they made them in between the correct positions, over the fret wire, muting the chords. He played for a couple minutes and again announced, "I just caint get nothing out."

This went on as long as I could stand it, and I stood it a good long while. I came back the next day, an inferno of a July summer afternoon, and started all over again, singing when he was awake and walking around the lake while he slept, watching kids dive off a wharf and cast bass plugs from shore. The heat would drive me back into the house, and he'd have me sit right next to him in bed again. You might feel funny at first singing to a cowboy in his bed, but you get used to it. When I left for home my frazzled and exhausted aunt thanked me for keeping my uncle entertained for a spell. "Come back anytime" were his last words to me. He finally had to turn loose my hand. Or maybe I let go of his.

I write criticism to entertain and move people. Without a narrative sense it doesn't sound right to me, and my brain hollers, Whoa, wait a minute! After all these years, I no longer know if I am incapable of writing focused, thesis-driven criticism or if, as the saying goes, I would prefer not to.

For me criticism and theory is a practice whose larger purpose is to reduce human and nonhuman suffering in tangible and nontangible ways. I feel that if I divorce my criticism from the reality of pain—of those who cross my path or those whose paths I imagine—it will be to my detriment as a critic. I think it is important to imagine what it feels like for someone to hear music only in a far-off tunnel, and also to try to make it more audible. A goal of engaging in criticism is to make the world a better place, and I don't get embarrassed when someone makes fun of my naïve notions about intervening in the world for some kind of shared human or nonhuman decency. I am less concerned about the theoretical dangers of progressivism than I am about those of living in an intellectual bubble.

I have to admit this has not always worked out well. My criticism has sometimes caused suffering rather than helped alleviate it. Years back I took some hits for advocating a certain kind of "separatism" in my first book, and my response at the time was to step into the ring and hit back. These days I am more interested in holding hands with cowboys than I am in boxing. But I also have to admit the tone of my earlier work created some interest and benefitted me. A more restrained voice would have, I suspect, garnered fewer readers. In Native literature people were hungry for work that staked out claims. But now I'm convinced that one of our challenges is finding ways to speak strongly without closing down communication.

Let me tell you a different story, this one textual. Near the conclusion of his autobiography, *A Creek Warrior for the Confederacy*, G. W. Grayson, a late-nineteenth-century Creek politician, recalls an election so contested that the tribe had to go to Washington, D.C., and press the secretary of the interior to decide the results. Grayson's arguments and maneuverings won the day and the secretary decided on the candidate, J. M. Perryman, that Grayson's faction was rallying for. Although his faction prevailed, Grayson remarks that they lost a bigger battle. Grayson, an insightful political analyst (though sometimes a racialized thinker whose perspectives seem compatible with white supremacy), explains:

These nations were very jealous of their rights of self-government which had been solemnly recognized and even guaranteed by the terms of treaties with the government then in force. That would include the settlement of just such questions as that now before us; but for us to waive that right and ask the government to interfere and effect a settlement between us in a purely local question had the appearance of discovering incompetence for self-government on our part, besides creating a circumstance which might in the future be taken advantage of as a precedent that gave license for the United States to interfere in other of our national questions and render decision whether agreeable or not, thus in effect abrogating our cherished right of self-government.[1]

Lately, like Grayson, I have thought a good deal about the way in which we can make theoretical claims and "win" debates (in my case winning them mostly in my own mind!) but lose other battles, such as opportunities to listen, learn, and open up dialogue. When I responded aggressively to my critics, I helped to create a discourse in which writers listed the things they didn't like rather than engaging in creative, generative work—a kind of deficit criticism with its hands over both ears.

Contacting folks I've had the strongest disagreements with, I've asked them if we could just talk, inviting some of them to coauthor articles centered around listening rather than debating and bringing them to Emory to participate in forums that allow graduate students to see how we respond when we have to look one another in the eye. Before, I approached criticism the way people behave in their cars, screaming and throwing their hands around, insulated by a windshield that allows them to act in ways they wouldn't anywhere else. I'd like to spend part of my energy creating a different kind of critical community rooted in creativity and originality instead of looking for someone to take down. Recognizing my own deafness is at the center of my story lately.

A further aim of writing criticism and studying theory is to provide a philosophical basis for my activism. One of my colleagues, who is a strong activist and brilliant theorist, recommends keeping activism and theory separate. He notes that you can theorize your actions and still do stupid stuff, and, of course, history provides hordes of examples of well-meaning people with philosophical justifications for the havoc they've wreaked on the world. Still, there is a certain asymmetry in committing too much intellectual energy to thinking about theory and less to analyzing activism, hoping that blind luck will favor me with the right choices. Thus, for better or worse, I have tried to wed theory and activism in critical writings.

I believe in change, that this credo is a snapshot in time and a particular place, and that later, if I tell the story under a different tree, it might depart from, or even contradict, earlier work. And I believe that one of the most important and challenging aspects of criticism is trying to imagine how the people we represent in print might respond to what we are saying about them. I've addressed this in my writing, but I want to say something about it in relation to pedagogy.

Efforts to link my research in a dialogic relationship with the Creek community culminated in a class I taught in the spring of 2010 called Community Approaches to Academic Research. The class focused on helping grad students design projects that involved liaisons between academics and nonacademics by using our own interactions with the Muscogee Creek community as a case study. I cotaught the course with Creek citizens Rosemary McCombs Maxey and Ted Isham, live via video conference between Atlanta and Okmulgee, Oklahoma. Each meeting included weekly speakers who often lived within Creek jurisdiction in Oklahoma or Alabama, or occasionally were non-Creeks who had written books about the community. So the class was a beginning of a dialogue with Creek people that confronted the issue of what the people we write about might say about our representations of them. It was also an attempt to consider what criticism and teaching mean in relation to place and time. Not only is Emory located in the very heart of the original Creek homelands, but its founding, in 1836, is the same year as Creek Removal. My criticism and teaching, I feel, should address the history of the place I reside in.

Two moments regarding criticism have stayed with me from that course. While most of our visitors were Creek people involved in everything from holding political office to working on food-sustainability issues at a grassroots level, two non-Native academics spoke to the class. One of them was Ann Jordan, coauthor with David Lewis Jr., of *Creek Indian Medicine Ways: The Enduring Power of Mvskoke Religion* (University of New Mexico Press, 2002). In a fascinating exchange on the ethical issues involved in writing collaborative biographies, Jordan told about the agreement she made with Lewis, a medicine person who is the subject of her uniquely structured book, which includes Lewis writing in first person and Jordan in third. Lewis said certain things he told Jordan about his world could not be questioned or scrutinized. Jordan recalled for us how she recognized the long history of abuse associated with the fields of anthropology and ethnography and readily agreed to Lewis's request.

One of the most salient claims Lewis makes in the book is that he has a higher degree of training than any of the other medicine people in the Creek community. Even though Jordan did not challenge this, I asked the class how we might imagine the rest of the Creek medicine makers responding to such a claim. Any of us, in my opinion, has the right to assert that certain things are sacred and we don't want to share them. But what if we claim that some things we choose to share are absolute and unquestionable? Can a person write an academic book under those conditions? Jordan did, and it has a lot of merit, not the least of which is that she gives full credit to Lewis as her collaborator. I doubt, however, I could write under similar constraints. Might our university tradition, rooted in a sacred right to call things into question, also constitute a sacred tradition of its own? I think the answer is yes, and much of my work in Native critical studies has centered around the field facing its own particular reality of place: a Native studies department is housed in a university, and a university is committed to critical scrutiny.

Claudio Saunt also visited class to talk about the controversial stance he took in his study of the Grayson family, titled *Black, White, and Indian: Race and the Unmaking of an American Family* (Oxford University Press, 2005), an excellent, daring book that delves into Grayson's African American relatives and comments on the passages that the historian E. Everett Dale removed from the Grayson manuscript, which reveal Grayson's larger black family. Saunt juxtaposes a discussion of Grayson's history of participation in the American Civil War, various Creek political offices, and family relations with the contemporary situation of Creek freedmen who were disenfranchised when the Creek Constitution was rewritten in 1979. In short, he alternates between past and recent events. In one of the contemporary chapters on a freedman he interviewed, Saunt focuses on the derelict condition of the man's house in an attempt, I assumed, to show the force of racism the man faced at the hands of both whites and Indians. Some of the details, however, struck me as demeaning to the man. So I asked Saunt about this, and at first he provided a justification, saying he wanted to contrast his own middle-class values and reveal his level of discomfort in the encounter. Then he thought for a moment and said, "You know, that was a mistake. I shouldn't have done that." What a moment of grace! Especially for graduate students to hear an established critic say "I got it wrong." As intellectuals, we are trained in defending our positions and we're often quite good at it, so I admired Saunt's integrity in admitting a mistake when he could have easily provided convincing counterarguments.

My experiment interacting with the Creek community instead of merely studying it did not always go well. I know I am making progress in my teaching and criticism when it sometimes fails; failed experiments are often as important to the process of inquiry as successful ones.

NOTE

1. G. W. Grayson, *A Creek Warrior for the Confederacy: The Autobiography of Chief G. W. Grayson*, ed. W. David Baird (Norman: University of Oklahoma Press, 1988), 162.

6 |
LONG ISLAND INTELLECTUAL

JEFFREY J. WILLIAMS

B y the time I was fifteen or sixteen, I had decided I wanted to be a
writer. It wasn't, as some writers report, something I'd fixed on as a
small child; then I wanted to be a cowboy or, a little later, a pro basketball player. When I got to high school, I'd occasionally put "lawyer" in the
box marked "future occupation" on forms because I had verbal skills and it
seemed a natural default. I also saw the writing on the class wall—my father
worked at a cement plant, but since I was a good student I was being boosted
over that wall—and I had an uncle who was a lawyer, who took me on fishing
trips and drove a Lincoln. But I didn't have a passion for "The Law," as my
uncle would pronounce it, whereas I did for books.

During my junior year in high school, I began reading. I had conscien-
tiously slogged through my school assignments and picked up the odd novel
or sports biography in the summer, but I started shutting the door of my
room and reading for hours at a stretch every day. I found various lists of
books, from classics to contemporary novels, and pecked through them. I
kept a notebook in which I recorded the books I'd read and copied out quotes
that struck me. During a field trip to his house in Oyster Bay—I grew up on
Long Island, in a town called Centereach, aptly if prosaically named since it
was in the middle of the island, about fifty-five miles from Manhattan and
five or six miles from each of the ritzier shores—I heard that Teddy Roosevelt had read a book a day, so I aspired to that benchmark. It prompted
me to ferret out all the short novels I could find, although I abandoned it
for special cases, as when I embarked on Will Durant's *Story of Civilization*,

which one could get from the Book-of-the-Month Club. I got bogged down on volume 6, going back to novels. They were more entrancing and seemed to tell the secrets of the adult world. Now I'm less patient with fiction and keener about history.

Taking a break one night, I remember wandering out of my room and telling my mother, who always seemed to be humming around the kitchen, that I wanted to be an intellectual. I'm not sure what she thought; she asked if I wanted something to eat. Though my parents always encouraged reading and education, I suspect "intellectual" had something unseemly about it. It was the seventies, so it was probably better than saying I wanted to join a commune.

I've spent the time since figuring out what it means to be a writer and intellectual. George Orwell, in his credo "Why I Write," distinguishes four motives that writers have: sheer egoism, aesthetic enthusiasm, a historical impulse, and political purpose. I'm sure I started with a heavy measure of egoism: I didn't want to be a rock star, I wanted to have my picture on the dust jacket of a book on a table at the Dalton or Walden at the mall near my parents' house. I confess I still like to see my name in print, I hope not merely out of vanity but to have the work it took, like that of any craft, recognized.

I'm tempted to tell my story as an evolution from egoism or aestheticism to politics—which is Orwell's story—but that would not really be accurate. The truth is more fitful, and, as Orwell observes, one's motives fluctuate. Alongside ego, from the beginning I had some sense of politics, perhaps because of the time I grew up—the crash and burn of the Nixon years, Mao's red book on display at Dalton's—or because of my class background, seeing my father going to work at five in the morning for a lot less than a lawyer made or because of my family's religious leanings, Congregationalist (evangelical but a bit more refined than Baptists), which I turned away from but which gave me a sense of righteous indignation at some of the ways of the world. Or simply because I was the youngest and watched all the transit around me, as my sister's friends filled the house or my father told stories about work. Reasons don't necessarily answer why, but I had a sense that I wanted to tell their stories because they otherwise would not be told, and also to bring back to them what I had read and seen.

"Writer" seemed to cover politics as well as aesthetics. I had a vague idea that I would do different kinds of writing, as Orwell or Sartre did, ranging from philosophy to journalism, essays to fiction. I dabbled with fiction, though I liked the power of the essay to peg a point and to say what you mean without a mask. I was drawn to the way a writer might engage one's time, giving it words, chiding its excesses, drawing a future.

At first I thought my path was laid out for me. I got a scholarship to attend Columbia, where Kerouac and Ginsberg had gone and Trilling had presided (he died a year or two before I entered, in 1976, when I was seventeen). For an intellectual-leaning lad, the great books sequence was like nip to a cat, plus it was a natural path for an ambitious Long Island lad to the pulse of Manhattan. But a nineteenth-century novel might say that necessity impressed itself upon me, and an early marriage and child prompted my leaving college to get a job as a New York State correction officer. It was surely an unusual side step for a Columbia student, but I thought experience was like fuel to fill the tank of the things you'd write about, and I'd read Orwell on his time as a British imperial police officer. I also thought it would be a short intermission. But it turned out to be three years before I went back to college, and then I went to SUNY–Stony Brook because it was practically free and near where my parents lived, which helped with daycare. I had declared, when I was first headed to Columbia, that Stony Brook was beneath me; for my hubris I was returned.

Scrambling to make ends meet, I quickly finished my B.A.—in 1984, four years later than my class, so I always felt as if I was behind and hustling to catch up—and went directly on to the Ph.D. I'd considered getting my certification to teach high school, but the vacuity of the education classes I took dissuaded me and I thought being a professor would afford me more time to write. Though my graduate crew and I knew jobs were tight, those were the days, in the late 1980s, when predictions proclaimed a flood of retirements would open the gate of jobs over the next decade.

Graduate school funneled me into the world of literary theory. I had taken a good bit of philosophy so it was an easy step to make, and, during the 1980s, theory was where the action was. Though it was the sunset of theory, it was a colorful one, with the flaring of the culture wars, when it seemed that the "stakes" of deconstruction or postmodernism or the other isms could change the world. It seems a bit inflated now, but it was a time when George Will could say that Lynne Cheney, conservative director of the NEH, had a more important job than her husband, then secretary of defense.

Credos are as much about what you walk away from as what you walk toward. In some ways, after flirting with it in graduate school, I walked away from the mainstream of literary criticism. My first article, which started in a graduate seminar and became a chapter in my first book, was a reading of *Tristram Shandy* that used Gerard Genette's structural notations to make sense of *Shandy*'s notoriously disordered plot. The article also wheeled out some deconstructive points about reflexivity to show how the novel was a "narrative of narrative." (It was published in *MLN*, one of the prime homes of deconstructive criticism.) Looking back at it, I might dispense with some of the lines that channeled Paul de Man. But I think it is basically right about the plot of *Shandy*, and I still like my formulation of "narrative of narrative." However, I think there are more pressing issues that call our attention.

The article did what many critical articles do: it offered a reading of a well-known literary text, with some intricacy and difficulty; it drew on major theorists to authorize it; and it made an "intervention," albeit in an academic debate, proposing a modification of theory. There are definite rewards for doing that, and I could have had a fine academic career had I continued on the trail of readings. But I've chosen instead to spend my time on and write about more immediately relevant topics, in less narrowly academic and more writerly ways than I was trained.

One of the things I've focused on has been the state of American higher education, particularly the advent of what I've called "the post-welfare-state university" and its protocols of privatization, which have extracted greater profit from research under the public trust of universities, greater labor from its teaching force, and a greater pound of flesh from students, especially in the form of student debt. I feel there is a pressing need to expose the facts of the case of this institution within which we work and which runs through American life, to sort out the ideas and policies that inform its practices, and to publicize more just solutions. I can imagine a time when this would not be as pressing as it is now, but I find it unconscionable that, despite the radical claims of many theorists, few focused much attention or effort on the job situation their graduate students were facing or the draconian loan debt most of their undergrads were yoked to. Credos are not only about beliefs, since one can believe many things, but about choices. The key is not the beliefs you hold or espouse but what beliefs you act on.

Of course, the university is not the only issue that might call our attention. But it points to another plank of my credo: that we respond to the politics and culture around us. I think that we sometimes suffer from an exoticization of politics: we look to Kuala Lumpur rather than the everyday politics in front of us, in our time and place. It doesn't seem as impressive academically, but, as anyone who has been in a union would recognize, politics starts in one's workplace.

An adjoining plank is that we should extend our critical efforts to policy debates. In literary studies, we tend to spin out interpretations, spot contradictions, or "complicate" the typical view, but we rarely offer prescriptions or practical solutions. I think we should bring into our repertoire more pragmatic, practical proposals. One need not do this all the time, but sometimes it's called for: it is one thing to analyze the idea of the university, for instance, but another to propose ways to change it. Which is why I've not only written on the historical roots and ideological consequences of student debt but also thrown my lot with proposals such as the Labor Party's FreeHigherEd, or suggested that we institute a graduate student job corps. To paraphrase Noam Chomsky's credo, "The Responsibility of Intellectuals," we have the training, time, and resources to research and write on these things, and I think we have an obligation to throw our hat in the ring of concrete policy alongside theoretical analysis.

Some might object that this is not literary criticism: it is fine to do it, but it's sociology or union politics or journalism. This view relies on the narrowest of nominalisms, as well as a historically shallow view of criticism. Just because it is called "literary" criticism does not mean that it must focus only on literature. Historically, literary criticism refers to a range of commentary on culture and society as well as on literature, and literary criticism has a special role in the public sphere. Added to this, the university is a standard topic in the tradition of the humanities. Moreover, it is literary criticism because of the form it takes in the manner and mode of the essay rather than an article in sociology or communication. Or, as a compromise, one might call it cultural criticism.

Still, this is not to renounce the way that I was trained. The concern with reflexivity informs my looking at the university, and my training in theory has led to my writing on the institutional and material vectors of contemporary criticism. Though I would probably now bill myself as a historian of criticism, it might be more accurate to say that I do a *reflexive criticism*, oriented toward examining its conditions of production—which carries out Antonio Gramsci's credo in *The Prison Notebooks* that "the starting-point of critical elaboration is the consciousness [that] one is . . . a product of the historical process to date, which has deposited in you an infinity of traces."

The middle part of the twentieth century was known as the "age of criticism." I fear that our era will be known as an age of scholasticism. Sometimes accounts of contemporary criticism read as if we have made the kind of advances that they have in, say, medical science, assuming we have gone far beyond the leeches of the New Criticism to the sophisticated instruments of x theory. But our time might well be seen like that of medieval philosophy, when philosophers spent inordinate amounts of time on internecine debates and arcane issues and were absorbed in nominalist questions—for instance, what constituted a sign. A good deal of contemporary criticism is circular, slavish to authority (isn't it odd that a criticism that puts all things in question relies so heavily on a fairly narrow set of authorities, whom it intones with genuflection, "as Derrida says," "as Butler says," and so on?), and pretentiously ponderous. Sometimes the goal of criticism seems to be to make endless minor adjustments—we "complicate" and "problematize" texts, once again—that have relevance only to a rarefied coterie and function largely to keep the coterie going.

I believe that we have a modest but more consequential role to inform and educate. Over the past forty years, we've let that sense slip away as dull and dutiful, causing us to neglect general education and to lose a good bit of our audience. Rather than sophisticated or complicated, I think we should strive for a *useful* criticism, one that helps give people ways to think about our culture and figure out our, and their, worlds. I think we've gone down the wrong path to see criticism as "research," as if it were a technological advance rather than a comment on our culture.

One way I think that we can be useful is to do more "intellectual reporting," explaining intellectual issues to a wider audience, making sense of and assessing them and placing them in their histories. I have a good deal of sympathy for and admire Andrew Ross's turn toward "scholarly reporting" (in his credo in this volume), but my version is slightly different. His draws more on the investigative journalist; mine is a more translational role, reporting on intellectual history that we know and purveying it to those who do not. To that end, I've written a good deal on the history of criticism for both academic and journalistic audiences, and I've also conducted a great many interviews with critics that, I hope, fill out a more textured history of the past fifty years in criticism than we otherwise have. And I've reported on the history and vicissitudes of the university. I think that there is a need for this kind of reporting, particularly for students who are foundering in a sea of information, so there is a more accurate report than that offered on Fox News.

My migration since graduate school, or perhaps since my days of reading philosophy as a teenager, has been to see criticism as more pragmatic than idealist, shedding a romantic image of imbibing and dispensing large, earth-changing ideas and instead offering something more practical. Criticism should aim to reach people rather than reach the ineffable.

Another way to put it is that I have come to see criticism as a craft. It should simply be well made, which seems in short supply in much academic criticism, which piles on documentation and readings without much regard for pacing, measure, or any real consequence. We need to digest and distill rather than complicate and problematize. It is not simply that criticism should be accessible—and in fact one can imagine a well-crafted criticism that is not—but it is frequently difficult as a result of carelessness or windiness. Criticism should renew its domain as the essay rather than the academic article.

One line that has stuck in mind since I first read it when I was sixteen is the opening of Simone Weil's *The Need for Roots*: "The notion of obligations comes before that of rights, which is subordinate and relative to the former." I think that rather than a right that we exercise at whim, criticism confers an obligation, an obligation to those with whom we live, in our time and place, and an obligation to the needs of that time. Otherwise what we do is a self-interested hobby. Criticism can do more than that: if history is what hurts, criticism is what tells us which parts of it hurt and why and what we should do about it.

ACADEMIC LABOR

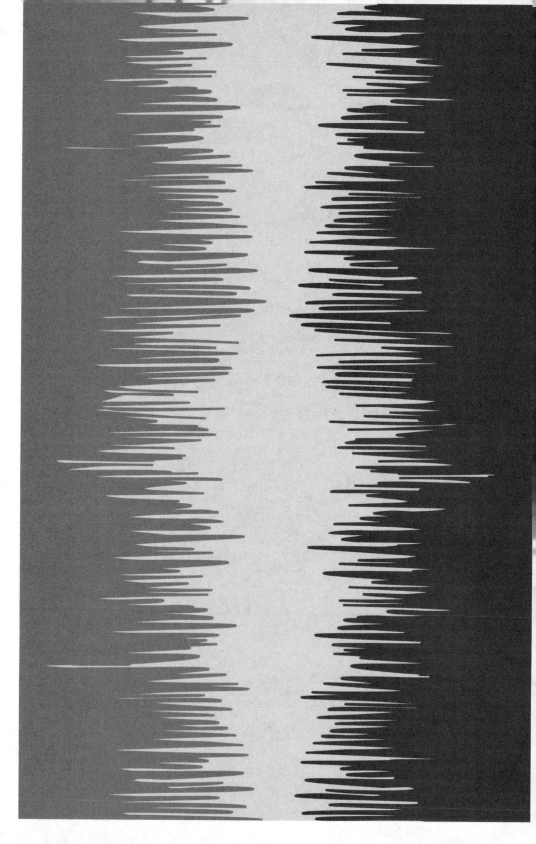

7 |
WE WORK

MARC BOUSQUET

I once shocked a colleague by responding to one of those newspaper stories about a prof "caught" mowing his lawn on a Wednesday afternoon by saying that many tenured faculty were morally entitled to think of their salaries after tenure as something similar to a pension. After all, in some fields, many folks will not receive tenure until they've been working for low wages for twenty years or more: a dozen years to get the degree, another three to four years serving contingently—and then, finally, a "probationary" appointment lasting seven years at wages commonly lower than those of a similarly experienced bartender.

In the humanities, the journey to tenure is often a quarter of a century and rarely less than fifteen years: if you didn't go to a top-five or top-ten graduate school in your field, you probably taught several classes a year as a graduate student, usually while researching, publishing, and doing substantial service to the profession—writing book reviews, supervising other faculty and students, serving on committees, etc. Call it, charitably, a mean of twenty years in some fields. Averaging the probationary years, contingent/postdoc years, and graduate student years together, you get an average annual take in contemporary dollars of $25,000 or less. The low wage is only the beginning of the story. There's the structural racism of the wealth gap, to which I'll return, and the heartbreak and structural sexism for families trying to negotiate childrearing during that brutal two decades. In most fields, most of those who begin doctoral study with the intention of an academic career fall away long before grasping the brass ring.

So at the end of all that, you have a person who is earning within ten or fifteen thousand dollars of $70,000 and has perhaps fifteen or twenty years of career ahead of them. All of the reasonable studies of faculty work suggest that this person will put in between fifty and fifty-five hours a week for most of those years, more or less voluntarily. There are plenty of enforcement mechanisms to make sure that most faculty will teach, serve, and do scholarship in some rough proportion to their abilities and inclination, but after a quarter-century of strict selection and socialization, it is rarely necessary to invoke them to get the faculty to do their jobs.

By comparison to the twenty-year probation leading to academic tenure, police officers, kindergarten teachers, and civil servants earn tenure or job security in a year or two, often less. During training, a high-school-educated police recruit in 2009 generally earns a salary of between thirty and forty thousand dollars, or about twice what a doctoral student earns during graduate school. Today's starting salaries for twenty- or twenty-one-year-old metropolitan police officers and state troopers are generally in the forties. They receive bonuses for completing two- and four-year postsecondary degrees, as well as tens of thousands of dollars in supplemental pay for overtime and special duty. In Cincinnati, for example, a recruit will earn $31,000/year during a six-month training period, and then begin work at $46,000. Five years later—at age twenty-six—they will expect to earn a base pay of $56,000, or about what junior faculty in many arts and sciences fields are being offered after their twenty-year apprenticeships, in their early forties.

The twenty-six-year-old police officer earning about the same base pay as our forty-year-old assistant professor can expect to work as little as another fifteen or twenty years, keeping up with inflation whether or not promotions are awarded, collecting additional fair compensation in such forms as the Cincinnati metro police site promises, "overtime earnings, court pay, certification pay, training allowance, and night differential pay." The Ohio Police and Fire Pension Fund estimator estimates that in 2009 a forty-eight-year-old retiree who had done nothing to save additionally and earned just under $70,000 in his final year as a twenty-seven-year veteran would receive a pension of about $42,000. That forty-eight-year-old would then be free to work another job—a corporate security position or a supervisory position overseeing poorly paid retail guards or real estate or whatever, earning, say, $60,000 a year, for a total annual income of six figures. Or the retired officer could work part-time, twenty hours a week or so, and still pull in about $80,000 or $90,000—likely quite a bit more than our largely fictional time-serving fifty-five-year-old associate prof is pulling in on the imaginary twenty-hour work week of just showing up to teach from old notes. Pension benefits for military service and certain civil service positions are similar: your average worker aged forty-eight to fifty-five without too many promotions but with a quarter-century or more of service will be eligible for pensions of between thirty and sixty thousand dollars, or the equivalent of between about $800,000 and $1,500,000 in your Fidelity or TIAA-CREF accounts.

No matter how you slice it, most public servants earn a better return on education and effort over the course of a career than most faculty, including those on the tenure track. It's hard to make a case that the rather unusual instances of lifetime associate profs who skate by on twenty- or thirty-hour work weeks are gaming the system. Instead, they are the unusual few who have refused to allow the system to game them. Whatever one thinks of these rare birds, one has to acknowledge the strength of character it takes to refuse the overwhelming appeal of the administration, the ideology of the profession, and the continuous hailing of their students and colleagues to give so much more than the standard set by other workers in the public service.

Furthermore, comparing professorial salaries to career patrolmen and high-school-educated infantry is bending over backward to prove the point. A more accurate and fair comparison would be to college-educated military officers. Someone who retires after just twenty years of service with the rank of captain (Officer-3 on a scale that rises to Officer-10) is eligible for a pension of almost $70,000 a year. Retiring at Officer-3 represents very few promotions over the years—possibly indicating a relatively undistinguished career.

So after twenty years, a low-ranking commissioned officer can cash in and collect a decent professor's paycheck for doing not a darned thing. If he does choose to exert himself, he can go to work as a corporate middle manager, earning about what a dean earns. Either way, after twenty years, it's his choice. He can work a bit and whack down a dean's salary. Or not—and still collect more than our hypothetical time-serving prof pulls in for actually working. Similar comparisons can be made in state or federal civil-service employment, in K-12 teaching, and in many private-sector careers.

When you get right down to it, considering the long years of preparation and strain, it's hard to find any position so poorly compensated as tenure-track college faculty—except, of course, most of the rest of college faculty, the majority of whom don't ever become eligible for tenure and earn even less.

Now you may well say that all of this tawdry consideration may not make for much of a credo. But we can take this line of thought in a number of interesting ways, many of which are fairly important for anyone thinking about the situation of culture and critique today.

One way to take this line of thought is toward straightforward observations regarding the social logic and policy environment of the United States: the low regard in which education is held, the possible virtues of greater rationalization of faculty careers, and so forth. I've already suggested that public institutions in the United States should treat faculty salaries like the civil service or military pay grades—winning some startled coverage in the mainstream press, though there are plenty of real-world precedents for this kind of rationalization, including in the United States, where many unions at public institutions have achieved step scales with excellent results for faculty retention and satisfaction.

Another route is analytical and psychological: we should probably pause to look at this irrational system of compensation and to ask, why does it function so well? Despite the injustice and impracticality of the arrangement, large numbers of young people continue to present themselves to the meat grinder of doctoral study. Most fall away, but a sufficient number persist, and of the persisting few, only the tiniest fraction take advantage of tenure to refuse steadily mounting demands. These are questions that corporate managers have been examining for decades with a keen sense of envy. How to emulate the academic workplace and get people to work at a high level of intellectual and emotional intensity for fifty or sixty hours a week for bartenders' wages or less? Is there any way we can get our employees to swoon over their desks, murmuring "I love what I do" in response to greater workloads and smaller paychecks? How can we get our workers to be like faculty and deny that they work at all?

An established analytical path on this question is the idea that in the great marketplace of labor, some of those who must sell their labor time in order to live will discount their wages for the more pleasant occupations—that in some professions the presence of a "psychic wage" encourages workers to accept a lower cash price. There are certainly problems with this observation: for instance, all too conveniently it is offered as an explanation of the lower wages of the workplaces and job descriptions in which women predominate. In the United States, the psychic-wage theory correlates less closely to variations in wages of comparably difficult positions than race and gender: other things being equal, the job description is likely to pay more if mostly white men are doing it.

Nonetheless, the notion of a voluntary discount of wages helps us to understand the group psychology of the professoriate. If a person can make mil-

lions as a tax attorney with less effort than they can impoverish themselves
for poetry, why do it?

At least to an extent, the foregone millions of the could-have-been tax
attorney inside the literary critic earning a bartender's wage gives us a sense
of just how much a human being values even a small degree of workplace
autonomy—or the chance of having that autonomy. Every year, thousands
of young people, having been warned about the poor chances of winning
a tenure-track job, nonetheless gamble their futures on the possibility of
spending their lives doing something for love (rather than for the hate and
greed that is parsing the tax code for the shareholder class). From the fact
that most people at some level refuse to even attempt to sell their labor time
in this way, we can probably deduce something hopeful about our common
humanity, that we collectively prefer not just autonomy but integrity, even
when tempted by a million dollars a year.

We can probably deduce something hopeful about the professoriate as
well. Despite our role in the reproduction of a class society, and the collision
of many of our highly educated tastes with those of the leisure class, we are
more like the mass of humanity in choosing as much integrity and dignity
as our circumstances permit over the false rationality of the highest possible
price for our labor time. If a willingness to give up wages to "do what we love"
is a marker of a broader refusal of capitalist inhumanity, it is something that
unites the faculty with most other people rather than divides them.

This human drive—toward integrity, autonomy, and dignity in our work—
is so powerful that capital's latest round of innovation depends on it, far more
so than it depends on "technological" innovation of the production process.
Contemporary management innovation in and out of the academy revolves
around creating workplace conditions that they hope will induce workers to
freely discount their wage. In the administration of higher education, this
means a delicate balancing act, in which management continuously tries to
seize control of institutional mission without killing the academic goose laying its golden eggs. The history of workplace change in higher education over
the past forty years is a slow, grinding war of position or culture struggle, with
administration continuously pushing to see just how partial or inauthentic it
can make the autonomy, integrity, and dignity of academic endeavor without
inducing the faculty to fall out of love with their work.

Likewise, the history of corporate management's effort to imitate the success of higher-education workplaces can be expressed as, "How can we adjust
our corporate culture to resemble campus culture, so that our workforce will
fall in love with their work too?" That is, the managers desperately want to

know, how can we emulate higher education in moving from simple exploita-tion to the vast harvest of bounty represented by super-exploitation? "Super-exploitation" is a term of art in materialist analysis, meaning "exploited more than the simple exploitation of regular wage workers," and usually implying some other, or supplementary, method for extracting surplus value than the putatively "free" transaction of labor time for a wage. There are any number of paths to super-exploitation, including various forms of forced, conscripted, or partly conscripted labor. Versions of forced donation of labor still exist glob-ally, in China, South America, Africa, and India, but also in the United States informal, fast-food, and personal-service sectors—in such forms as working through breaks, working after clocking out, refusal of overtime—not to men-tion prison labor, economic conscription into the military, and so forth.

But in the United States by far the major innovations in productivity im-provement all involve ideology, the highly inventive calling-forth by man-agement of voluntary, rather than forced, forms of super-exploitation. So far the most common examples for the average worker involve the donation of additional time represented by the ideology of professionalism. Workers not previously considered professional and not compensated like professionals now routinely donate countless hours to their employers: doing one's e-mail at six a.m., taking phone calls in the evening, writing reports on weekends, traveling and attending employer events on personal time, and so forth. Cer-tainly the massification of higher-education experience plays a role in this expansive professionalization-without-a-professional's-paycheck.

In turn the massification of faux professionalism works to erode the privi-leges of those who were formerly professional, such as higher-education faculty—initially in what Gary Rhoades describes as the emergence of "man-aged" forms of professionalism and, subsequently, as I would argue, in the gradual but steady conversion of residually "professional" positions (profes-sor, lawyer, physician) into ever more straightforwardly managerial positions. That is, the tenure-track faculty now retain professional status in at least partial relation to their managerial function—they manage a vast range of parafaculty (adjunct lecturers, tech support, undergraduate tutors, graduate teaching and research assistants). Just as much legal work is done by parale-gals supervised by lawyers, and physicians increasingly function to manage nonphysician medical practitioners, nurses of various grades, students, nurses' aides, technicians, secretaries, and other personnel.

Higher education legitimates the explosive growth of super-exploitation and casualization across the global economy in countless ways, especially the fact of its own practice, as I've already suggested in *How the University Works*.

In addition to collecting revenue from tuition, fees, grants, appropriations, and commercial transactions of all kinds, contemporary U.S. institutions and their partners are generally structurally reliant on the value they harvest from student time—not just time denominated "labor" but also time allocated to "leisure" and "education." Low-wage undergraduates, many of them filling positions formerly occupied by full-time staff, are often the largest workforce on campus, but the institution harvests value from their spending, their athletic activities, their blogging and journalism, even the time the dance team spends in practice and in tanning salons. The smoothly functioning campus is a post-Fordist company town, with a churning pool of self-subsidizing cheap labor that takes loans to spend in the company store, voluntarily poses for company marketing materials, pays for the privilege of serving as a "brand ambassador" for the campus, and so on.

The substitution of students for full-time workers, as facilitated over four decades by managerial "innovators" in university-corporate partnership, has ricocheted throughout an economy organized around the model of the full-time job (for health insurance, retirement savings, home ownership, etc). Low-wage campus work and cheerful building of the campus brand is just the tip of the iceberg—as low- and no-wage internships, service learning, and the economic conscription of rising tuition force students into more and more hours at low-wage off-campus employment. This arrangement is not just painful to the students; it displaces other workers, both staff and faculty, including other workers with college degrees and even graduate educations. The situation of the graduate student who has been teaching for a decade but can't get a professor's job after earning the doctorate (because new graduate students or former graduate students without a doctorate are doing the teaching) is parallel to the circumstance of the journalism majors whose reporting is published by a consortium of Florida newspapers who have fired staff reporters: the journalism student, despite having worked successfully as a student reporter, will have trouble finding a job in journalism because more and more of the work will have been allocated to other journalism majors (who in turn will have yet more trouble finding work, and so on). The super-discounted labor of students is ultimately, therefore, just as costly to the students themselves as to those they've displaced—in the end, they're displacing themselves. The super-discounting of faculty labor is similarly far more costly than it appears at first: one can reasonably ask, what harm is done if some book-besotted fools choose to work cheaply? One form of harm should be obvious: however enjoyable, the work pays so poorly that only those who can afford to subsidize their employer need apply; in many circumstances, the modesty of the wages simply does not support individuals without access to a secondary source of income, typically a professional-managerial spouse or family wealth. This has profound implications for the class, race, and gender of the professoriate and the curriculum they choose to teach.

Higher education has played a crucial, innovative role in the new order of the global workplace, trading on the willingness of most of us to discount our labor time in exchange for a little dignity and partial autonomy. It isn't just faculty work that's being spoiled; most people's work is being ruined in similar ways. There are certainly ways that the faculty's love for what they do is paradigmatic—hence "professing"—nonetheless, most people have similarly tried to find corners and pieces of dignity and autonomy in their working lives. Like the faculty, most other workers strive to protect their integrity and avoid the taint of administration. So what has happened to the faculty—because we love what we do, sometimes to the point of denying that our wages matter at all—is important not because the faculty are special but because we are typical.

8

WHAT IS CRITICISM ON ACADEMIC LABOR FOR?

KATIE HOGAN

B ooks, articles, reports, blogs, websites, and discussion boards focusing
on the dismal state of higher education have been appearing in rapid
succession over the past fifteen to twenty years, with each statement
attributing the current situation to decades of reduced financial and cultural
support for solid, analytic education. A stunning example of this criticism of
academic labor emerged eighteen years ago when Mary G. Edwards published "The Decline of the American Professoriate, 1970–1990." Edwards
outlined the all-too-familiar signposts: stagnant wages; the rise in contingent
labor and the evaporation of tenure-track positions; the feminization of the
professoriate; and the subtle yet profound disappearance of support for intellectual work and research. Today faculty are "free" to do research, but with
seven out of ten U.S. college and university faculty in non-tenure-track and
part-time positions, fewer and fewer faculty have the material support to
write and publish.[1] We are witnessing a dramatic whittling away of provi-
sions for academic energy, cultures, and workplaces. Except for a handful of
superstars, very few faculty are exempt from these systemic changes.

Given these vivid grievances, it is understandable that criticism on academic labor would primarily focus on unfair labor practices and economic
justice. But this new criticism could also include a more explicit statement of
its commitment to social justice for intellectual practices that create complex
academic insights and innovative ideas. Too often, this aspect of the criticism
is muted or left implied. Criticism on academic labor has the capacity to
argue more directly for the value of unhurried intellectual work and resistant

critical thinking in addition to issues of worker and student rights and justice. It can explicitly state that thoughtful education and intellectual practices are threatened and worth fighting for. The shrinking minority of overworked tenured professors underscores the need to argue for professors', and not only students', right to learn. Faculty at research institutions increasingly experience their right to grow intellectually as hijacked by the institution's fixation with prestige and image. Faculty at teaching- and service-intensive colleges and universities are experiencing extraordinary demands to keep institutions afloat while doing what needs to be done to earn tenure and promotion as well as keep abreast in their disciplines. Yet these diminishing opportunities to practice serious intellectual work are sometimes ignored or framed as less urgent than pressing economic realities.

Meanwhile, characterizations abound in the discourse on academic labor of tenured professors as selfish and useless individuals who could care less about students or their contingent colleagues; luxuriating in a world of books and articles, instead of entering the fray of labor activism, supposedly fills the days, weeks, and years of most tenured faculty. Even if such a group portrait is accurate in some instances, I find this kind of blaming language distracting at best and anti-intellectual at worst. I also think it contributes to the increasing expectation that professors prove their worth by being superserviceable, contributing to a service speed-up on many U.S. campuses. My professional experience at nonelite institutions suggests that many tenured faculty face enormous pressures to "do more with less"—a phenomenon that the majority of U.S. workers have been experiencing for years—and that many faculty are not aware of the connection between the adjunctification of the university and their difficult working conditions or the relationship between the misuse of contingent faculty and the decimation of genuine support for intellectual and academic culture and practices.

INTELLECTUAL ASPIRATIONS

Engaging in research and intellectual creative practices is often embroiled in the power of human ego and the lure of reward and visibility, and pretentiousness and self-interest are familiar traits among higher-education workers. Hollywood films are replete with images of burned out, self-absorbed, privileged professors who clearly don't contribute much to education or scholarship. But there is also an aspect of research and creative endeavor found in higher education that, while hard to disentangle from the self-interested achievement and advancement paradigm, is part of a larger project of intellectual dialogue, community, human rights, and freedom of thought and expression. Stanley Aronowitz captured this quality of the field when he proposed the idea that critics and scholars might present thinking as a useful and necessary full-time activity worthy of admiration and basic material support.[2] Admittedly, thinking as a full-time activity is a vague concept; it's more a process than a product, often elusive and only seemingly tangible when the long endeavor of research and revision results in a new course, article, book, or other cultural/creative work. Despite the challenges of pinning down thinking as a full-time activity, given that it is often not tied to money or a product, it is nevertheless one of the central reasons people gravitate toward academic careers, and it is a central reason that criticism on academic labor is potentially so meaningful and valuable. The right to practice intellectual work also brings to mind Robert Boice's vision of writing as a process of slowly emerging insights.[3] Slow thinking as a full-time activity is worth cultivating and preserving.

Thinking as a full-time activity also hinges on actively seeking out critical feedback, a process that is sometimes agonizing, but one that is crucial for creating ideas rather than shutting them down. Only through honest critique and dialogue with others can ideas, people, institutions, and cultures be transformed and expanded. Arrogance, mindless competition, and a compulsive fixation on career advancement are aspects of academic culture, but other dimensions of the profession point to the energy and purpose of engaging in challenging intellectual and creative work through teaching and research. These features are worth talking about—without embarrassment, sarcasm, or contempt. Pitting a focus on economic and political worker rights against this tradition of knowledge production is a losing strategy.

Remembering and restoring respect for intellectual traditions and practices can easily devolve into nostalgia based in an elitist idyllic past. As Andrew Ross shows in his influential article "The Mental Labor Problem," artists and academics are uniquely susceptible to allowing themselves to participate in their own exploitation, and they are routinely encouraged to see their labor in terms of an exalted, transcendent, sacrificial love. Ross's essay resonates profoundly with the vexed issue of gender, academic labor, and sacrifice. Sacrificing one's own intellectual and personal growth for the benefit of others, including the welfare of one's students, colleagues, and institutions is particularly expected of women, and the demand is often intensified when racial, ethnic, class, and sexuality dynamics are at play. However, in the downsized service economy of higher education, the self-sacrificing professor is increasingly an expectation for the majority of faculty workers, regardless of group identity. David W. Leslie and Ronald B. Head's article on part-time faculty rights illustrates this sacrificial ideology with a telling quote from a part-time faculty member who, in an ethnographic interview session, said that teaching was so meaningful that the instructor "would work for free, but don't tell the dean!" Although Leslie and Head's article was published in 1979, the notion of mental labor as morally superior and as beyond money, power, and tough negotiating has played a central role in the cheapening of faculty labor. Pleasure in doing intellectual academic work shouldn't mean accepting low pay, downsized contracts, or substandard working conditions. As Sharon Bird, Jacquelyn Litt, and Yong Wang assert: "[That faculty] enjoy the work [they do] is not why they are being paid for doing it."[4]

Prior to the emergence of the new strand of criticism on academic labor, critics such as Edmund Wilson and Adrienne Rich visited the issues of material conditions and intellectual culture in their work. Edmund Wilson's 1938 essay, "Marxism and Literature," is an intriguing framework for thinking about the purpose of criticism that addresses the economic and social struggles of academe. Rich's central preoccupation in all of her work, including in her poetry, is "conversations about justice, power, and what it means to be a [worker and] citizen," the very themes fueling contemporary theory and criticism on academic labor.[5] Both critics direct an intense focus on issues of social justice and creation of intellectual culture.[6]

Known for his supple and complex vision of the relationship between literature and the social, Wilson rejects any fixed or simple paradigm for analyzing politics and literature. Writers produce their best work not in times of social revolution or economic crisis but under social and economic conditions that nourish patient practice and support from what Wilson refers to as "long-enduring institutions." Wilson's essay also makes a distinction between short-range writing and long-range writing. Short-range writing is immediate, urgent, forged in the heat of the moment. He characterizes it as a form of pamphleteering and contrasts it with long-range writing, which builds from careful, thoughtful engagement in ideas, craft, and creativity in an unhurried world. Neither type of writing is set against the other; sometimes, as is the case now, the short-range immediacy of much of the discourse on academic labor is needed in the service of long-range writing projects supported by stable institutions. Literary and critical innovation can coexist with unflinching critical analysis of labor practices, and literature and criticism are not weapons but opportunities for continued exploration, clarification, and change.

Similarly, in a recent article in the *Chronicle of Higher Education*, "Why Today's Publishing World Is Reprising the Past," Jeffrey J. Williams echoes Wilson's idea when, in response to the oft-heard lament about the alleged paucity of creativity in current literary criticism and theory, Williams hammers home the point that intellectual and critical innovation require patronage, sustenance, and material support. Echoing Virginia Woolf's classic essay "A Room of One's Own," Williams speculates that the spotty support of the profession in the form of good, full-time, tenure-track jobs and money for publications, meetings, and conferences greatly affects the advancement of knowledge in literary criticism and theory. Even those who aspire to live the "life of the mind" must eat, and a starvation diet typically produces death or mere survival. A key factor in the rise of criticism that focuses on the various conditions facing faculty and students today has emerged because of what Williams calls the "pinched diet" of the humanities professoriate and the whittling away of support of long-enduring institutions.[7]

The gradual disappearance of support for long-range academic writing projects affects the majority of those in the profession, but such changes in support structures are especially poignant for women, queers, people of color, and academics from working-class backgrounds—the very groups whose participation in higher education has been relatively short when compared to dominant groups. There are more women in the academy today than ever before, but the work many female professors do is administration-imposed service or institutional housekeeping. Law professor Marnina Angel sees this pattern in the legal field, in which academic women are funneled into nurturing work that resonates with traditional ideas of women and femininity; "legal writing and clinical jobs that are intense, one-on-one handholding students through basic courses" are largely taught by women.[8] Similarly, in English departments, writing and introductory subjects in colleges and universities are courses overwhelmingly taught by women.

In several of Adrienne Rich's essays on education, she identifies the cultural customs and traditions that have resulted in women's uneven contributions to intellectual and creative knowledge. The expectation that women are involved in helping, assisting, serving, and guiding—meaningful and noble activities—interferes with their intellectual growth and exploration. Rich sounds a clear warning about the university's exploitation of women's socialization to perform altruism, a cultural dynamic that she says has been shrouded in silence, at the expense of women's own intellectual growth: "The extent to which [higher education] has been built on the bodies and services of women—unacknowledged, unpaid, and unprotected in the main—is a subject apparently unfit for scholarly decency."[9]

While altruism is one of the most formidable impediments to women's intellectual work, the other barrier Rich cites is the lack of affordable high-quality childcare on American campuses. Rich's insistence that women treat their intellectual work as a priority and resist being pressed into altruistic service, is matched by her argument that campus administrators should make childcare a top priority. These issues remain relevant today.

Rich's commitments to long-range writing and to the material conditions that make it possible resonate with assertions in Wilson's essay. Like Wilson, Rich makes a direct statement supporting the significance of intellectual growth. In "Claiming an Education," she opens with an analysis of the necessity for women's studies as a discipline, but the power of this piece is not its focus on women's studies; instead, it's the essay's delineation of the specific practices one needs to adopt in order to accomplish intellectual work: patience, the willingness to consider difficult texts and ideas, and, most important, the courage to seek out criticism. All of these elements are presented as the cornerstone of intellectual work, and all of them take time and patience.

Revisiting the work of Wilson and Rich is a humble acknowledgement that we can learn from those critics who came before us. They are resources for those of us who are thinking about, and tracking, changes in academic labor. Valuing solidarity, unhurried intellectual work, and resistant critical thinking, and demonstrating an active faith and commitment to changing the institutions in which we find ourselves, Wilson and Rich have much to offer us as we resist the egregious policies and injustices that are changing, and even corroding, the profession and higher education more generally.

While criticism on academic labor is rightfully suspicious of idealizations, nostalgia, and exalted abstract language, professors don't do their jobs for economic reasons alone or solely for opportunities to rebel, protest, and organize. Reasonable compensation and worker resistance are absolutely essential, but there is a current of desire for creative and intellectual exploration and community that motivates many of us in our teaching and research, and that should be cherished, not belittled or forgotten. Those faculty who are new to academe are in a precarious situation that is only aggravated by characterizations of professors as selfish and uncaring, as people more focused on their next book, article, or tenure than on the stewardship of the institution. For most professors today, finding time for practices that involve intellectual risk taking and creativity is a daily struggle. What's needed is a clear statement that restoring economic justice also means supporting academic intellectual culture for students and faculty alike. One solution is to value intellectual and creative work openly as the right of all faculty and students, regardless of the classification of their institution or their identity status.

NOTES

1. Mary G. Edwards, "The Decline of the American Professoriate, 1970–1990," *Anthropology of Work Review* 15, no. 1 (1994): 21–28.

2. Stanley Aronowitz, "The Last Good Job in America," in *Chalk Lines: The Politics of Work in the Managed University*, ed. Randy Martin (Durham, N.C.: Duke University Press, 1998), 221.

3. Robert Boice, *How Writers Journey to Comfort and Fluency: A Psychological Adventure* (Westport, Conn.: Praeger, 1994).

4. Andrew Ross, "The Mental Labor Problem," *Social Text* 63, no. 18 (2000): 1–31; David W. Leslie and Ronald B. Head, "Part-Time Faculty Rights," *Educational Record* (1979): 46–67; Sharon Bird, Jacquelyn Litt, and Yong Wang, "Creating Status of Women Reports: Institutional Housekeeping as 'Women's Work,'" *NWSA Journal* 16, no. 1 (2004): 203.

5. Michael Klein, "A Rich Life: Adrienne Rich on Poetry, Politics, and Personal Revelation," *The Boston Phoenix* (June 1999), http://www.bostonphoenix.com/archive/1in10/99/06/RICH.html.

6. Edmund Wilson, "Marxism and Literature" (1938), in *The Norton Anthology of Theory and Criticism*, gen. ed. Vincent B. Leitch (New York: Norton, 2001), 1243–1254; Adrienne Rich, "Toward a Woman-Centered University" (1973–74), in *On Lies, Secrets, and Silence: Selected Prose, 1966–1978* (New York: Norton, 1979), 125–55; Rich, "Claiming an Education" (1977), in *On Lies*, 231–235.

7. Jeffrey J. Williams, "Why Today's Publishing World Is Reprising the Past," *Chronicle of Higher Education*, 13 June 2008: B8; Virginia Woolf, *A Room of One's Own* (New York: Harcourt Brace Jovanovich, 1929).

8. Marnina Angel, "Women Disappear from Tenure Track and Reemerge as Caregivers: Tenure Disappears or Becomes Unrecognizable," *Akron Law Review* 38, no. 789 (2005): 3.

9. Rich, "Toward a Woman-Centered University," 135.

"ALL THINGS VISIBLE AND INVISIBLE"

BELIEVING IN HIGHER EDUCATION

MICHELLE A. MASSÉ

When Jeff Williams asked me to contribute to this reprise of the *Kenyon Review*'s "My Credo" series, my first association, like that of any other Catholic-trained child, was to the Nicene Creed. The years in which I intoned what's listed in my old Saint Joseph's Missal as "Our Profession of Faith" are long past. The structures of belief, however, remain in ways that can't be disavowed, even while I now parse that phrase as suggesting the often silent—and sometimes fatuous—faith that characterizes "our" profession, teaching in higher education.

Someone once asked me in some exasperation what I believed in. My answer was "feminism and psychoanalysis." That's still true. Both demand theory and praxis, faith and good works. Each also demands scrupulous attention to the conscious and the unconscious, the visible and the invisible, sins of commission and omission. Psychoanalysis calls for the movement from insight to action; feminism demands that that movement from the personal to the social be understood as political. And both are systems that require us to understand that the invisible, whether its traces be found in the workings of the mind or of ideological state apparatuses, leaves its mark.

What I did not articulate clearly as a part of my converted system of belief was that I was a worker. A first-generation college graduate on one side of my family and a first-generation high school graduate on the other, the shift from working class to middle class via intellectual vocation seemed a (paradoxical) no-brainer. Although I never doubted that I was indeed a laborer, I also never doubted (and still don't) that working in higher education would be a better job than the night shift at a local factory. So certain was I of that, so pleased at the melding of vocation and avocation, that I was slow to see that the "The University" I thought was sempiternal was closing its doors as surely as, even if more slowly than, that factory and the parish church.

That certainty also led to a certain purblindness, a not seeing the forest while I counted the trees. I still count: I automatically note, for example, the traditional all-male, all-white makeup of the *Kenyon Review* symposium, the pontificating references to "men of taste," "men of feeling," "man's task" that are as plentiful as grass seed throughout. While I smile appreciatively at Leslie Fiedler's brio and insight, I also ruefully see that no women can serve as priests in this church either, that the "our" to which I refer in my first paragraph always has to be in scare quotes because of its unthinking omissions of those cast into outer darkness.

A lot of my career has been spent redefining that "our": working to assure that women are present in the professorial workplace as teachers, students, and administrators, that women authors are in the curriculum, that gender inflects policy. In doing this, however, I increasingly wonder whether I am not, to paraphrase the title of Nancy Chodorow's groundbreaking text, *The Reproduction of Mothering*, reproducing professing in ways that are detrimental to my students and to my own goals. The mysteries of employment have come to seem more sorrowful than joyful. As tenure-track jobs placement for Ph.D.'s in language and literature fields shrinks to 50 percent after five years of job searching, as contingent labor swells to almost two-thirds of the faculty nationally, and as doctoral students express reservations about accepting jobs at what were once considered plum assignments because of the imbalanced lives and the increased debt loads they fear will result, I have to ask whether I'm warmly inviting students to an auto-da-fé that will ultimately consume them.[1]

Even while doubting the trinity of research, teaching, and service, I redraw it, invoking the ultimate salvation of tenured employment. In introductory graduate seminars, courses on pedagogy, and mentoring for national organizations as well as on campus, I talk to students and junior colleagues about what's "professional." Despite prayerful claims to the contrary, things seem not quite fair in the secular or the divine models of the trinity. God, the "Father Almighty," is clearly the ultimate patriarchal avatar of research. Christ, the Word made Flesh, parable drawer par excellence, the teacher. But isn't there something a bit defensive about the Nicene Creed's assertion that the Holy Spirit "together with the Father and the Son is no less adored and glorified"? And doesn't that mark the place of service in higher education, with its equality more asserted than demonstrated?

As Katie Hogan and I argue in our edited collection, *Over Ten Million Served: Gendered Service in Language and Literature Workplaces* (SUNY Press, 2010), service all too often remains a point of blind faith, a ritual in which many of us deeply believe, but which doesn't seem to be institutionally answered in the same way as research and teaching. Service can be an indulgence that we hope will remit the purgatorial sufferings of ourselves and others in community. It can be a penance imposed by others. It can be argued as a self-indulgence, freely undertaken time and again despite its lack of efficacy. Whatever service means at individual institutions, the volume and frequency of its litany marks an escalation of our labor. Exhorted to discipline ourselves for the greater good, we forgo pleasure for one more report, one more committee meeting. And, in watching us, our students learn to do the same.

I'd accordingly like to focus upon this least of the tripartite charge of the professoriate, service, in the rest of this essay. Much as I like the David Macauley–esque implications of Marc Bousquet's admirable book, *How the University Works*, which suggests that, in taking apart large structures, we learn "how things work," I think that talking about how the university works can potentially be a displacement and deflection from the actual agents of work: us. Schools of higher education—not all of which are universities—do not "work" in this sense of the verb. *We* do. We are the workers who are potentially so alienated that we no longer recognize our own labor as labor.

The power of service, like that of the Paraclete or Holy Spirit, hovers over everything but is rarely seen. Three decades ago, all too many of us assumed that effective teaching was simply the spontaneous overflow of powerful cerebration. Thanks in part to figures such as Paolo Freire, Henry Giroux, Ernest Boyer, and bell hooks, that presumption is no longer with us. Service, however, has not undergone the same reassessment. Texts whose focus is specifically academic "work" nonetheless often omit this crucial field of effort while emphasizing teaching. Yet service with a smile is part of the same quasi-monastic assumption about our unstinting dedication to our orders.

I am not positing sites of higher education as dark Satanic mills But I *am* saying they *are* mills: "knowledge factories," to use Michelle Tokarczyk's and Elizabeth Faye's phrase, in which we produce some very good things, mills in which many other things—including, sometimes, people—are ground exceeding fine, but also workplaces in which we *work*.[2] And much of that work, in particular service, isn't on the clock.

In our coedited collection, Hogan and I have built upon our experience and interest to bring together a collection of voices in which professorial workers struggle to articulate what "service" has meant in their lives. I say "struggle" because, despite the extraordinary collective acumen, experience, and achievements represented by these women and men, the majority display what Katie and I diagnose in ourselves and others as the "service unconscious." On a conscious level, our astute selves know that our behaviors sometimes damage ourselves and support organizational structures we don't want to reinforce. And yet we nonetheless persevere in these behaviors and articulate their value for the best of all possible reasons: the ways in which they *please* us, fulfill our deepest-held beliefs about the importance of existence in community, and support of our colleagues and students. Through splitting, we deny the contradictions between what we know and what we do.

For example, we all know that there is something wrong about our collegial definition of "work" as research, implicit in the question we routinely ask one another, "How is your work going?" According to the logic of this formula, teaching and service, which take up the brunt of our weeks, are time-absorbing distractions and not our "real" work at all. We all nod ruefully at the troubling inconsistency, but continue to ask the question.

Service has increased for all professorial faculty: there are fewer of us at the same time as there is more work to be done. At the same time as institutional service obligations have mushroomed because of changing accreditation criteria, outcome assessment, posttenure review, and an increasing reliance upon corporate management models, the number of tenured and tenure-track faculty who can do these jobs has shrunk by one-quarter to one-half at many schools. In addition, the exhilarating expansion of interdisciplinary programs and centers is often followed by the draining reality of no staff support. The challenging work of retheorizing the boundaries of knowledge and curriculum all too often also means finding not only one's inner secretary but one's inner accountant, one's inner fundraiser, one's inner IT specialist, and one's inner travel agent.

Doctors have "unbundled" their services in order to increase billable items. We, as faculty, have often *been* unbundled. At my own school, for instance, we have "Professors of Research"—scientists who do not teach. We had serious discussions about using "Professors of Teaching" for our full-time instructors, and I wondered if "Professors of Service" might not be next—or if, indeed, I wasn't perhaps already one. Service for most of us is surplus labor which we generate ceaselessly and unquestioningly.

Dismayingly like the clerks at Wal-Mart who "volunteer" to spend off-clock hours restocking, cleaning, or taking inventory, we all too often accept the right of our employers to demand our time and to impose penance. More dismaying still, in most instances the "associates" at Wal-Mart know they're being had: we, well-trained to see ourselves as disembodied rolling cerebrums, acolytes of the academy, often don't. Instead, clasping the ideologies of entrepreneurial self-sufficiency or purified merit to ourselves, we vigorously deny what that sage of our generation, Bob Dylan, noted, "You've got to serve some one." For undergraduate students that someone may nominally be UPS, as Bousquet so insightfully outlines, or Sallie Mae, as Jeff Williams cogently notes, but many Ph.D.'s refuse to believe there are any liens on them.

Even those who embrace service often do so semi-defiantly and semi-apologetically but, they believe, freely, knowing that they've violated the implicit hierarchy that descends from research and teaching to service. Although service has its own hierarchy, an exquisite sequencing of postulancy, it is, in general, a feminized mode of effort, as Hogan argued so well in "Superserviceable Feminism."[3]

We of course understand that female professors are not the only group who serve. We know that:

- Particular fields are service-intensive, such as composition, language instruction, and service learning
- Other ranks also serve: there are assistants, lecturers, instructors, and graduate students dedicated to institutional service. And they also serve who wait, and wait, and wait for tenure-track jobs
- There are individual men who are paragons of good citizenship; individual women who are shamelessly self-serving

Not surprisingly, however, institutional caregiving, like domestic, is heavily gendered. Women thus sometimes find themselves primarily responsible for doing the university's housework as well as the family's. This "housework," as Dale Bauer and others have called it, constitutes a silent economy that oils the gears of institutional functioning.[4] Like other kinds of work associated with caregiving, such as nursing and teaching, service work, particularly in its most necessary and standard forms, is often "feminized" and denied official recognition and compensation. Furthermore, the refusal to perform it, as evidenced in strike actions, means that one doesn't "really care": a criteria rarely applied to other forms of labor.

Such labor isn't sanctified by tradition, isn't performed by "stewards of the profession," that resounding Carnegie phrase. It's the work of caregivers. I hypothesize that, just as women fill the less-prestigious ranks of language and literature units, so too women and minorities are proportionately overrepresented when we start to tally who's doing the department's housework, who's making sure that the liturgy can take place. In a recent article in the *Chronicle of Higher Education*, Piper Fogg notes that "women have a harder time than men in turning away colleagues who ask them to contribute time and energy to a cause. Barbara Keating, a sociology professor . . . thinks that is because women have been socialized to be caretakers.⁵" We see that connection in far too many departmental cultures.

Professorial rank, as well as tenure/non-tenure-track designations, further modify the supply and demand for good institutional help. The demand for publication by junior colleagues, as well as their inappropriateness as committee members for many major committees, for instance, often leads to a lessened service load. And, as the number of associate professors listed as chairs, directors, and even deans suggests, it is increasingly difficult to recruit senior colleagues for positions of responsibility, such as chair, director of graduate studies, or director of writing, that were once assumed to be part of the rank's responsibility.

The Association of Departments of English (ADE) Ad Hoc Committee on Governance reports with a note of surprise that, in a discussion group made up of recently tenured faculty, "The self-descriptions of recently tenured participants revealed an extraordinary degree of administrative responsibility among faculty members who had held tenure only for a year or two. The group included a department chair, a director of undergraduate studies, and an associate dean, as well as many with heavy participation in important committees." The same schools that draw upon their newly tenured often will not promote them for performing the very tasks they're called upon to perform in order to maintain the institution: job description and actual tasks are bizarrely awry.

In addition, as the report notes, faculty members who are effective committee members and administrators are turned to repeatedly, which results in an "often uneven distribution of the load of departmental responsibility."⁶ Female—or feminized—professors' acceptance of above-average service loads can be forced by external pressure. It can also be embraced, or even sought after, because of the faculty member's own definition of professional commitments, internalization of institutional expectations, or naiveté about evaluation criteria.

Some of the authors in *Over Ten Million Served*, as well as some respondents to questions about service, rightfully praise the pleasure of service done well and rewarded appropriately. Others, however, have doubts about whether the rigors of their training have saved them and whether the orders they receive are holy. In discussing a recently completed study about graduate students' increasing reluctance to embrace the austerity academic orders demand, for instance, Mary Ann Mason quotes one apostate who exclaims: "Don't get a Ph.D.! Just don't do it: There are so many other things in life that you could do for a living." Such heretical misgivings don't go away with the beatification of tenure, as one of the comments Hogan and I got testifies: "How do I get a life??!! By this, I don't mean having children or a relationship. I mean a return to some semblance of the person I was before I got a tenure-track job, someone with interests, hobbies, leisure time, and the ability to think of something other than work and child-rearing."[7]

The ADE Ad Hoc Committee on Governance claims: "Service is governance, governance is service." In a good workplace that would be, to paraphrase Keats, all we know and all we need to know. That dictum can be a handmaid's tale, however, at a school in which female faculty members serve those who govern. If, then, rather than "changing the center of gravity in the institution," as Adrienne Rich charges us (128), I (and we) are assuring that our best and brightest are becoming the base upon which a crushing pyramid of privilege is constructed, then we must confess it.[8] But what possible penance and reparation can be exacted for such a sin? After such knowledge, what forgiveness? If the consolation of philosophy won't assuage the pangs of unemployment, will being a terrific close reader of texts and life? The very fact that this essay doesn't address The Book as central to all we do suggests a sobering loss of faith—or the need to put it aside for a while, not as one of the things of childhood, but as something that needs to be shelved temporarily, perhaps to preserve it.

I hear other communicants' voices talking about how we've sinned in the books I read. Some help to persuade me that there may be an end to a kingdom based upon exploitation. And so I mediate upon the insights of authors such as Marc Bousquet, Mary Burgan, Mary Ann Mason, Carey Nelson, Gary Rhoades, and Jeffrey Williams to help my growing disbelief in higher education.[9] I ponder in my heart the possibilities of unionization, collective action, and social justice. And I look forward to the life of that world to come.

NOTES

1. See George E. Walker et al., *The Formation of Scholars: Rethinking Doctoral Education for the Twenty-First Century* (San Francisco: Jossey-Bass, 2008); and David Bartholomae

et al., *Education in the Balance: A Report on the Academic Workforce in English*, report of the 2007 ADE Ad Hoc Committee on Staffing, Modern Language Association, 10 December 2008, http://www.mla.org/pdf/workforce_rpt02.pdf. Also see my "Higher Ed: A Pyramid Scheme," http://www.youtube.com/watch?v=TXHzzvWyKLQ; and "Ten Million Served!" http://www.youtube.com/watch?v=ig18SWw-h6g&feature=user.

2. Michelle M. Tokarczyk and Elizabeth A. Fay, eds., *Working-Class Women in the Academy: Laborers in the Knowledge Factory* (Amherst: University of Massachusetts Press, 1993).

3. Katie Hogan, "Superviceable Feminism," *the minnesota review* 63/64 (2005).

4. Dale Bauer, "Academic Housework: Women's Studies and Second Shifting," In *Women's Studies on Its Own: A Next Wave Reader in Institutional Change*, ed. Robyn Wiegman (Durham, N.C.: Duke University Press, 2002), 245–57.

5. Piper Fogg, "So Many Committees, So Little Time," *The Chronicle of Higher Education*, November 19, 2003.

6. Anne Breznau, Charles Harris, David Laurence, James Papp, and Patricia Meyer Spacks, "Report of the ADE Ad Hoc Committee on Governance," *ADE Bulletin* 129 (Fall 2001): 5, 6.

7. Mary Ann Mason, "A Bad Reputation: Why Are More and More Graduate Students Turning Away from Careers at Research Universities?" *The Chronicle of Higher Education*, January 27, 2009, http://chronicle.com/jobs/news/2009/01/2009012701c.htm; Michelle A. Massé and Katie Hogan, eds., *Over Ten Million Served: Gendered Service in Language and Literature Workplaces* (Albany: SUNY Press, 2010).

8. Adrienne Rich, "Toward a Woman-Centered University" (1975), in *On Lies, Secrets, and Silence: Selected Prose, 1966–1978* (New York: Norton, 1979), 128.

9. Marc Bousquet, *How the University Works: Higher Education and the Low-Wage Nation* (New York: New York University Press, 2008); Bousquet, http://howtheuniversityworks.com/wordpress/; Mary Burgan, *What Ever Happened to the Faculty? Drift and Decision in Higher Education* (Baltimore, Md.: Johns Hopkins University Press, 2006); Mason, "A Bad Reputation"; Cary Nelson, *Office Hours: Activism and Change in the Academy* (New York: Routledge, 2004); Gary Rhoades, *Managed Professionals: Unionized Faculty and Restructuring Academic Labor* (Albany: SUNY Press, 1998); Jeffrey Williams, "Renegotiating the Pedagogical Contract," in *Class Issues: Pedagogy, Cultural Studies, and the Public Sphere*, ed. Amitava Kumar, 298–312 (New York: New York University Press, 1997).

10 |
AGAINST HEROISM

JOHN CONLEY

Graduate workers have enough professional organizations—what we need are unions that win gains and exert collective worker power on the job. Organizing graduate workers' unions that can do these things also necessitates *re*organizing our relationships to our jobs, as well as the feelings, sentiments, and ideas about our work that probably seem more or less natural to many of us. Put frankly, although many grad workers may support having a union in the abstract, we should not underestimate some of the real and accumulated barriers that block the processes of unionization— not only the ones in the state legislature or in the specifics of a bargaining unit, but the ones that are reproduced daily in the common feelings and sentiments that are increasingly woven into the very fabric of our labor. One such barrier is the notion of politically committed academic labor. I contend that graduate workers can't afford—both literally and otherwise—to be radical pedagogues or politically committed academics. I believe that graduate workers need to intentionally and collectively develop a critique of politically committed academic labor and that this critique is internal to unionizing and in its interest. Hardly a detour from the "real work" of organizing, the critique of politically committed academic labor is in fact necessary for and at the same time a essential part of that work.

It turns out that in his famous essay on ideology, Louis Althusser has something to say about all of this:

> I ask the pardon of those teachers who, in dreadful conditions, attempt to turn the few weapons they can find in the history and learning they "teach" against

the ideology, the system and the practices in which they are trapped. They are a kind of hero. But they are rare and how many (the majority) do not even begin to suspect the "work" the system . . . forces them to do, or worse, put all their heart and ingenuity into performing it with the most advanced awareness (the famous new methods!). So little do they suspect it that their own devotion contributes to the maintenance and the nourishment of this ideological representation of the School.[1]

Written in January 1969, its not so far-fetched to imagine that Althusser has the "events of May" in mind, and he offers a nice starting point for coming to terms with some fairly common sentiments felt by graduate workers—with one important caveat, of course: today, any graduate worker knows that their teaching maintains and nourishes the ideology of the university and reproduces existing class relations. In my experience, it usually doesn't take too much time for this basic critique to coalesce. It doesn't always take the same forms, but does anyone really think that teaching "in itself" is a radical practice? And yet herein lies the problem: as a result, the so-common-so-as-to-be-structural response is to work all the harder, to put all the more "heart and soul" into our teaching, to squarely recommit ourselves to researching and practicing forms of radical pedagogy, to invest ourselves in the project of teaching our students to "think outside the box" and to "read against the grain." In other words, it is precisely because we understand so well how the university reproduces all kinds of hierarchies—class or otherwise—that we so strongly commit ourselves to teaching against it.

Whether about Darfur or Dos Passos, such teaching is indeed commendable and meaningful work. But isn't it interesting that Althusser says that this is, in fact, a *worse* position—in other words, a more exploitative and less empowered position—to be in than those that "know not what they do"? I think that this describes a lot of us who know very well the system that we work within but believe that, if we work really, really hard, maybe we can subvert it, if only in small ways and to meager effects. It's the old "if I can even get through to one student" argument. It is precisely this notion and precisely this desire—that is, to work within the "belly of the beast," to try to effect change in the world, etc.—that compels us to work so hard, to care and invest so much in our interactions with students, and to do so much of the extra work that is increasingly compulsory for graduate student workers. In this way, "politically committed" academic labor acts as a sort of ethical supplement to the pay we don't have in our wallets and the respect we don't get in our workplaces.

At issue here is the objective side of the critique of politically committed academic labor. By misrecognizing our labor as political work, our desires to participate in the construction of a better world are captured and effectively neutralized. What is more, by inducing us to work harder—whether quantitatively (grading more papers more quickly, holding extra office hours, providing more in-depth comments, etc.) or qualitatively (i.e., spending more time and energy building and maintaining affective and interpersonal relationships with students)—our power to act collectively to build a union is decreased. By this time, not only are we overworked, but our teaching has become overvalued and the highest political priority for us. It is this relationship to our work that, somewhat perversely, in fact ends up becoming a strong barrier to grad unionization rather than a conduit for it. In this way, perhaps politically committed academic labor is in fact the most thoroughly depoliticized form of our experience in the university and is robbed of any political efficacy in relation to our own working conditions.

Obviously, such a barrier takes slightly different forms with regard to research, writing, service work, and other forms of labor that graduate students perform with little or no formalized wage compensation—in other words, teaching is not the only way that graduate workers work, even though I focus mostly on teaching here. Let me try to explain what I mean by way of an example from the University of Minnesota. Over the last few years graduate workers there have not only tried multiple times to organize themselves formally but have repeatedly been put in the position of having to decide whether or not to cross AFSCME picket lines in order to teach. The AFSCME strikes generated a lot of discussions among us—productive ones, I think—about how to act ethically and politically in those situations. A number of positions were taken up by our fellow workers: some refused to cross picket lines and stopped going to work, some refused to cross picket lines and instead moved their classes off-campus, many dedicated themselves to "teaching the strike" as content in their courses, whether off-campus or on, and still many others crossed the picket lines expressly in order to continue teaching and mentoring students, considering that work to be politicized in itself to the degree that it was most important not to deprive the students of the opportunity to learn. I bring all of this up not to pass judgment on which response was best or most appropriate—there were a lot of extenuating factors (like threats of getting fired)—but rather because I think that future attempts at graduate unionization may be faced with similar kinds of conundrums if they are seeking formal recognition.

At the University of Minnesota, the administration maintains that unions set out to deprive the students of education. If and when graduate workers start acting like a union, it's reasonable to expect such discourse to be an early response from management. This is connected to the fact that, at the end of the day, management doesn't really care whether we take our classes off campus or not—and considering that they can use that opportunity to experiment with forms of "distance learning," maybe they would even be happy for us to do so! More immediate, however, is the fact that taking classes off campus traps us within a very limiting dialectic, and there's no point of escalation: if we go on to cancel classes, then we *are* depriving the students of what they deserve, and management says, "See? We told you—those damn unionists don't care about the university or the students, just themselves."

What is more, as the accumulating history of grad student organization tells us, gaining recognition for a graduate worker union may not be possible without organized work stoppages—and even then, winning is certainly not a slam dunk. Graduate workers will need to be ready not to simply move classes off campus but to withhold grades, cancel classes, and to otherwise collectively withhold labor. That sounds scary, but it may be true—and it's going to be a hard thing to do if *we ourselves* feel like we're depriving the students of their education.

Wouldn't the most radical pedagogy be to show our students that we, the workers, can exert power in the workplace? That we have better lives and work better collectively than we do as atomized individuals? That we need not be quite so enamored with power and so subjected by our jobs? This is how we need to reconfigure the concepts of radical pedagogy and politically committed academic labor if they are to have any positive content in our struggle. To realize such lofty rhetoric demands a developed and rich level of organization. In the meantime, grad workers may need more earthly, everyday tools. I think that a strong practical component of the critique of politically committed academic labor could be auto-reduction. Clearly our employers are not going to give us less work to do, so we're going to have to do it ourselves. We need to collectively develop ways that we can work less for the same pay—or, in what amounts to the same thing, develop ways that we can extricate ourselves from things like "student service" fees, inflated transportation costs, and other methods by which our employers systematically withhold our wages. Measures such as these should be done not in place of a union but as a priority and a function of the union itself.

I say this not because I advocate doing a sloppy job, and even less in defense of some kind of slacker utopia. Though there are a lot of good things that come out of "going on the slack," a union probably won't be one of them. Rather, I'm thinking of ways that we can take back the collectivization of our labor. This is hard work, too—as we know all too well, one of the prime forces against us is the kind of hyper-individualization of our work, the intense competition, and all of the bad feelings that go with it. We need to be better at sharing syllabi and resources, yes, but such things need to happen as an intentional and internal effort of the process of unionization so that we can put more time into organizing. Building a union is a tough, long process and we need to be clear about that—and unfortunately it isn't some kind of magically non-alienating labor, either. But we're so overworked—not only in terms of hours of the day, but emotionally and affectively as well—that it's really hard to find the time and energy for many of us to prioritize building a union, especially when we consider our work in the classroom to be so politicized.

We need to help each other work less—but not just so that we can go back to the "real work" of publishing, researching, or advancing our own career. Most of us have learned by now that we can't count on improving our CVs to change the world (much less our working conditions), but the fact is, neither does teaching our classes in a more "political" way. These days, it's a blind alley at best—but building a living, breathing critique of this problem need not be. Through auto-reduction, we can better sense the way that academic labor is increasingly depoliticized, as well as refuse a basic route by which our jobs impose on us. This is the subjective side of the critique, and the one that we should work on developing together. This critique is not identical with the process of unionization but it is essential to it.

NOTES

This essay is a slightly modified version of a talk given at the conference "Rethinking the University: Labor, Knowledge, Value" held at the University of Minnesota on April 13, 2008. Although some of what follows may apply to other cases, this essay is primarily concerned with the topic of graduate worker organizing and therefore is addressed to graduate workers.

1. Louis Althusser, "Ideology and Ideological State Apparatuses (Notes Toward an Investigation)" (1969), in *Lenin and Philosophy*, trans. Ben Brewster (New York: Monthly Review Press, 1971), 157.

11 |

PACK CONSCIOUSNESS

HEATHER STEFFEN

The history of the graduate student in America is a short one. We've only been around since the turn of the twentieth century, and we've only been used as TAs in large numbers since the 1970s. But our story (like that of adjunct instructors) is one of increasing reliance on our presence as the university's reserve army of labor. In the last few decades, much activism, organizing, and criticism has reflected the ability of graduate students to accurately (and angrily) read and respond to our position as academic workers. But alongside the sort of class consciousness built on the knowledge that "we work,"[1] we also need a way to think the articulation of our selves as workers and our selves as students. The line between these two positions is so blurry as to be nonexistent for many of us, and it's further obscured by the mystified way in which labor is divided at the departmental level: one ends up doing more work the better a student one is perceived to be, regardless of whether this work will draw on one's erudition. Having experienced the confusion and competitiveness created by this kind of labor system for six years now, my credo takes the form of a proposal for working against it. This essay is an argument for developing, as a counterpart to the class consciousness of the contingent (grad or adjunct) instructor, a graduate student "pack consciousness"—a mode of tactical and collective thinking meant as a heuristic for guiding day-to-day actions by cohorts of graduate students against exploitative labor practices at the level of the individual department.

Last semester I was asked by a faculty member from another department to list the committee positions that doctoral students in my program fill annually. She listened to the list and promptly declared that for graduate students this work isn't service; it's how we earn the "privilege of being represented." What is lost in this reduction of service to a form of representation is the fact that representation requires work. Committees and governing bodies involve all kinds of it: reading petitions, doing research, attending meetings, and keeping up with tidal waves of listserv e-mail. Saying that grad students are merely "representing" themselves in these instances obscures our labor and teaches that we must donate a steady stream of uncompensated hours in exchange for the right to work or to have a say in determining our working conditions. It's also a symptom of, and training for, the speed-up taking place at all levels of our profession.

Speed-up for grad students is often packaged in a language of opportunity, privilege, perk, or reward. The opportunities offered to add to our workloads come in the form of courses to teach, committees to sit on, and administrative work, including situations in which graduate students are responsible for managing and supervising their peers' labor. They usually include the chance to learn professional skills or to gain experience outside of composition teaching, but they can also interfere with students' plans for managing their time. Because refusing an offer might lead to being passed over for opportunities in future, an understanding of extra tasks and roles as privileges and perks can quickly become a coercive mechanism within the labor dynamics of a department.

Graduate students are vulnerable to this type of coercion in part because it plays on our belief that the institution in which we work and study is structured around meritocratic principles. We get into a graduate program because our academic records earn our passage there. We are chosen to perform special tasks because we have the special skills required or have proven ourselves a cut above our peers, even if we have no idea when or how or in whose judgment the comparison was made. There is a meritocracy at work in the university, but it is more often than not one of willingness and effective networking rather than any real system of accounting for skill or talent. Set in the world of work, debt, and service we live in, one function of the rhetoric of opportunity and merit is that it produces graduate students as super-flexible laborers.

Here is how the authors of a book on managing knowledge-based corporations define super-flexibility: "It means being 'agile,' able to move rapidly, [to] change course to take advantage of an opportunity or to sidestep a threat. It is also about being versatile, able to do things differently and to deploy various capabilities depending on the needs of a particular situation."

A super-flexible business (or graduate worker) will also ideally be able to do it all "without losing a sense of cohesion, identity and partial stability."[2] When we look at the situation of higher education at this juncture—reliant primarily on contingent, on-demand labor and hiring more administrators than full-time faculty—super-flexibility could be the best skill a newly-minted Ph.D. takes away from grad school.

But what is given up in trade for super-flexibility? Because labor conditions tend to condition the knowledge produced by those working within them, the experience of super-flexibility may be a defining force in the kind of research and teaching produced by future generations of scholars. What is lost for the super-flexible are the uninterrupted stretches of hours necessary for sustained reflection and intensive research on a topic, one's dissertation or otherwise. While the Internet has made research in the humanities faster, it hasn't erased the need for hours in front of the microfiche machine and the time-consuming multiple readings of a text upon which meaningful close reading depends. Students may therefore gravitate to supposedly "safe" or "marketable" dissertation topics, and ones that can be finished fast. Safety and marketability seem now to be mostly defined by a tendency to complicate and problematize others' ideas, contributing fresh theses only in the narrow sense of multiplying interpretations, rather than doing archival or historical research. Contributing to the pressure on graduate students to choose formulaic research topics and writing styles is the disheartening state of the academic labor system and the contraction of university publishing. Knowing all of that and scurrying about between meetings, student conferences, and our cubicles, there isn't much incentive for apprentice scholars to engage in challenging research or to spend extra time honing our craft as writers by authoring essays that won't appear in refereed journals—the kind of more public or controversial work that many of us hope we'll do as part of our professional lives and identities.

Super-flexibility may also teach us that our own teaching is a chore to be thought of as little and completed as quickly as possible. While most graduate instructors are no doubt thoughtful and dedicated teachers, it's easy to worry that hours spent carefully reading extra drafts, meeting with students, and designing new syllabi could be better used some other way. Long term, this can teach us that our teaching is not an activity to be valued—a lesson our students and the public are already learning from universities' continued use of underpaid non-tenure-track or graduate instructors for a majority of courses.

Perhaps the most damaging loss for the super-flexible is a sense of camaraderie or common cause among cohorts of graduate students. When a department sometimes assigns work and perks based on favoritism and sometimes through open application processes, it becomes almost impossible to see how cooperation could accomplish anything, since even demanding and getting nominal transparency for some positions doesn't prevent deus-ex-machina job offers for the chosen few. In this setting, grad students can develop a culture of competitiveness, worrying about remaining the favorite of one faculty member or committee rather than orienting toward other grad students. When some are left behind in the CV-line chase, these conditions add a further chill to the already isolation-producing quality of scholarly work.

To combat the inhumane conditions some departmental labor practices create and to reclaim the time to be excited about our intellectual production, it seems to me that what we need is more collective self-reliance. We should shift our orientation from faculty to fellow graduate students for mentorship, advice, and creative thinking about our position in the university. Union-ization is of course one way to do this and is the best and first answer to improving the conditions of graduate student work, but for many of us (in right-to-work states or at technology-oriented and decentralized universities like Carnegie Mellon) unionization is not a realistic or legal option right now. And even if it is, it requires energy that many of us simply don't have in our super-flexed lives. So I'd like to propose a heuristic for reorganizing our thought about our position in our departments: pack consciousness.

Becoming pack conscious might begin with analogizing the system that produces doctoral degree holders not only to a body producing excrement but also to an industrial dairy farm milking its producers for all their worth before consigning them to the dog food factory. We're the cash cows. For doctoral students confident in an advisor's protection and mentorship seeing them through to greener pastures, the factory farm image may not fit their experience of grad school. But rather than deny our precarity, we should value the solidarity, collectivity, and capacity for tactical alliance of the pack, over and against the domesticated individuation of the teacher's pet.

Pack consciousness means changing the way we approach our work and changing our working relationships with our peers, toward the goal of shap-ing our conditions of labor to be more equal and just. It has the potential, as a model and a metaphor, to help us see the tactical advantages of our position for several reasons. First, because the organization of the pack is one built for and defined by cooperation. While there will always be struggles for domi-nance and some in-fighting in a group, a pack comes together when it's time to get a job done. Second, the pack is, at least as a cultural image, the opposite of the unthinking dairy herd. Not drawing only from strength in numbers, a pack's coordinated activity is based on agility, responsiveness, and tactical thought. It has a corporate super-flexibility, using a common bank of experience to make intelligent decisions on the fly. And third, when opposed to a notion of graduate school as simultaneously enabling scholarly intellectual growth and domestication into the practices of academic labor, the pack as an idea from the wild is a heuristic for thinking against and beyond the ways our education is training us to reproduce the competitiveness and isolation of the academic world as it is. Beginning to think as packs of graduate students can facilitate communication between cohorts and enable practical actions currently prevented by the student-to-student interactions our labor conditions tend to produce.

In this volume, John Conley argues for slow-downs and auto-reduction strategies in "Against Heroism." Looking at the rhetoric of political commitment that surrounds teaching and acts as a balm for extra hours spent on it, he observes that to have the energy left at the end of the day to attend a union meeting, grad students need to find ways to work less: "Though there are a lot of good things that come out of 'going on the slack,' a union probably won't be one of them. Rather, I'm thinking of ways that we can take back the collectivization of our labor." Conley mentions sharing syllabi as one concrete way to slow down work, and there could be many others once we shed our domesticated fear of sharing. Syllabi, assignments, and other course materials could be kept in a library (filing cabinet), with the understanding that any piece of it could be used by any graduate instructor. That way, the time commitment of syllabus design is a reusable resource. We could help each other with new jobs and tasks by keeping practical information within the group, rather than asking each generation of grad students to learn it anew. This might be as simple as writing out and periodically updating data sheets on things like how to organize and publicize a lecture, the timeline for getting done what you need to when going on the market, or what to do if the university misreports your student status to your loan providers.

Packs of graduate students can also form reading and writing groups in order to broaden our knowledge of areas not taught in coursework or to improve writing skills when faculty take too long returning drafts. One particularly important topic for graduate students to educate ourselves about is the history and current situation of the university and any discipline's position in it. These groups could also perform the function of grassroots professionalization seminars, with advanced graduate students sharing experiences with newer ones. Perhaps the most successful example of tactical alliance in my department is a tradition of mock oral examinations. Before any student takes her qualifying exams, a group of people working in her area gathers to mimic the exam process. These mock exams preserve an oral history of how the exam process works and of what to expect from specific faculty examiners, as well as ideally helping the examinee prepare and gain confidence. Alongside self-help like this, a pack of graduate students could organize to refuse systems of perk or opportunity in their department and to demand more transparent and fair application processes without as much anxiety about individual repercussions. This could take the form of refusing to apply for jobs for which hiring criteria are not public or of forcing transparency by sharing information administrators would prefer to have kept quiet.

The actions outlined here include a mix of strategic and tactical suggestions for grad students to use in their departments. I think this mix is what's needed to continually put up a good fight against the tendencies of academic labor systems at the departmental, university, *and* professional levels to make us over as super-flexible workers. Because the situation of our labor can shift so rapidly with changes in budget or for no discernible reason at all, and because perks, privileges, and opportunities come up and disappear so quickly, a cohort of graduate students must have the ability to react just as quickly. Pack consciousness, by promoting long-term maintenance of the community through tradition building and by making possible temporary alliances, could help us see around and through our domestication to the tools we already have for making the conditions of our education and our labor more humane.

NOTES

1. For an analysis of "we work" as the central knowledge of the graduate student labor movement, see Marc Bousquet, "The Waste Product of Graduate Education: Toward a Dictatorship of the Flexible," *Social Text* 20, no. 1 (2002): 81–104; or Bousquet, *How the University Works: Higher Education in the Low-Wage Nation* (New York: New York University Press, 2008). In these places he also elaborates the excrement theory of graduate education mentioned later in this essay.

2. Homa Bahrami and Stuart Evans, *Super-Flexibility for Knowledge Enterprises* (New York: Springer, 2004), 5, 1.

DECLARATIONS OF POLITICS

ACTIVISM AND CURRICULUM

PAUL LAUTER

I was already thirty-one, with a Ph.D. and two children, when I became deeply involved in the civil rights movement in 1963. As an undergraduate, I'd briefly joined the NAACP, not an everyday event for my family in 1950, and I had been involved with my graduate school buddy, Allan Brick, a serious pacifist, in bringing A. J. Muste to speak about conscientious objection at Dartmouth, where I had my first full-time job. I'd passed out leaflets announcing "Dr. Spock is Worried" at the showing of *On the Beach* at the movie theater in Amherst, where I was shortly to be fired from the University of Massachusetts—perhaps for getting active in the union, perhaps for encouraging undergraduates to oppose ROTC on campus. Indeed, early in the sixties I'd organized a conference on nonviolence at Hobart and William Smith Colleges, where I'd been half of Citizens for Kennedy in the 1960 election. And I had gone to work for the American Friends Service Committee as director of peace studies. So I guess I was suffering from a mild case of movement activism before I began driving down from Philly to Chester in my little white Corvair convertible to participate in some of the nightly marches from one or another black church to the downtown stores that continued to refuse to hire "Negroes."

But it was only in Chester; in Montgomery, Alabama; and particularly in Mississippi that these impulses toward rebellion and political participation annealed into what might be called a credo. Before that, I simply shared the secular, liberal Jewish values, especially the commitments to civil liberties, that my parents had always maintained, even during the scariest time of

McCarthyism, when my mother worried that my father's job as a Supreme Court stenographer might be jeopardized by my NAACP membership. We read TRB in the *New Republic* (then an honorable magazine!), which was provided by a downstairs colleague active in Democratic Party politics. And it seemed only natural to applaud Norman Thomas when he spoke against compulsory national service in a debate at Bronx Science, as natural as rooting for the Brooklyn Dodgers.

What changed? First of all, I saw in practice the truth of Thoreau's remark about the impact of one person standing resolutely on his or her values:

> I know this well, that if one thousand, if one hundred, if ten men whom I could name—if ten honest men only—ay, if one HONEST man, in this State of Massachusetts, ceasing to hold slaves, were actually to withdraw from this copartnership, and be locked up in the county jail therefore, it would be the abolition of slavery in America. For it matters not how small the beginning may seem to be: what is once well done is done forever.

The Chester movement had been started by Mohammed Kenyatta, who had established and maintained a one-man picket of a discriminatory downtown store. In Mississippi, I had before me the many instances of SNCC field staff, who had carried the movement into the most benighted corners of Yazoo City, Greenwood, and McComb. I could see that one could not pass over one's individual responsibility for bringing about the change one desired.

At the same time, I began to understand the truth of Mao Tse-tung's observation in his pamphlet "On Practice," although I only came upon the comment later: "If you want to know the taste of a pear, you must change the pear by eating it yourself. If you want to know the theory and methods of revolution, you must take part in revolution. All genuine knowledge originates in direct experience." I thought I knew what was right and what was wrong, but I had no analysis of where malign practices came from, much less how one might help change them. So I followed people who, for one reason or another, I trusted: A. J., JFK, Allan Brick, Mohammed Kenyatta, my assistant at the AFSC, Martin Oppenheimer. Slowly, my experiences prompted the need to figure out why things happened as they did and also gave me the ability to do so. By participating in action for change one could come to understand why things happened as they did—an enormously empowering perception—and therefore where one might clog, as Thoreau said, with your "whole weight": "Let your life be a counter friction to stop the machine."

Or not only "clog," but act: "Action from principle—the perception and the performance of right—changes things and relations; it is revolutionary, and does not consist wholly with anything which was. It not only divides states and churches, it divides families; ay, it divides the individual, separating the diabolical in him from the divine."

Thoreau was obviously something of my guru at the time. I had written a piece, "Thoreau's Prophetic Testimony," arguing that he had designed his writing on the model of the Hebrew prophets to "awaken" his neighbors to the immorality of the slave system and to call them to their duty to end it. Such Thoreau essays as "Civil Disobedience," "Slavery in Massachusetts," and "John Brown" modeled a political approach to writing that, I saw, could be pursued in the pages of the *New York Review of Books* and elsewhere. Translate activism into prose, a night in jail or a day at the demo into an essay—and I tried to do so, often with my then partner, Florence Howe, and with friends like Dick Flacks, Noam Chomsky, and Louis Kampf. It was that intersection of activism and composition that I sought, and so I would align myself with the "action faction"—less talk, more action—of SDS, though I doubted the values of their fall into Weatherman street actions. In any case, my goal was not so much to "bring the war home" by shattering car windows along Michigan Avenue as it was to bring more and more Americans into engagement against the war, for peace and equality, and, not incidentally, into the deep pleasures of activism.

The book that Kampf and I edited, *The Politics of Literature* (1972), embodies that aspiration and defines a venue in its subtitle: "Dissenting Essays on the Teaching of English." While I had spent a number of years working full-time in the movement, finally I was a teacher, and the world I wished to change began in the classroom and campus. The question for me, then, was how to translate the lessons of movement politics into the lessons of the curriculum. The notion that classrooms are, or at least should be, neutral proving grounds wherein students simply hone intellectual skills has always struck me as fatuous at best, dishonest at worst. The choice of subject matter, texts, and authors, indeed of students, is deeply political. Who comes into a classroom, what they encounter there, and how they encounter it are fundamentally shaped by a priori political calculations about who and what are important in a society or culture. The segregated schools of Mississippi—and, indeed, of Washington, D.C., where I once worked—had at least one virtue: they were straightforward in their reckoning of who counted in America. You could calculate that by adding up budgets, inspecting facilities, evaluating teacher training, assessing expectations—and looking at the content of curricula and textbooks.

I turned to questions about curricula raised by the movement: Where are the blacks? Where are the women? They are questions about presence and absence, similar to questions about the absence of black people on voter rolls in Southern states into the 1960s. If there were few or no black voters who might hold a politician accountable, that said a good deal about Mississippi politics. If you were never taught by a woman in a college classroom, never read about one (perhaps apart from Abigail Adams) in a history text, and never read a female author apart from Emily Dickinson in American literature, that said a good deal about the "politics of literature." It was never our belief that the problems of racism and sexism would be solved by bringing black and female presence into curricula and textbooks; it was our belief that without that kind of presence such problems would not be substantially addressed. It is a necessary if insufficient condition of change, and I continue to believe that.

I need to be clear here: To argue that the classroom exists at the "dark and bloody crossroads" where literature and politics meet is not to promote the classroom as a venue for indoctrination. What a fruitless bore that would be. Students may not know their own minds, but they surely will resist efforts to tell them what to think: that's part of their indoctrination into American individualistic ideology. The politics of the classroom is not a function of what socialist, or liberal or reactionary teachers lay on their students, as if we could, godlike, mold them in our images. The politics have to do with what goes *into* the classroom long before we and our students first meet there; and that has to do with institutional commands. Let me use an instance from outside cultural study.

In 1964 when I was working for the AFSC, I had convened a substantial conference of college faculty working in a variety of disciplines on peace issues (from which I edited *Teaching About Peace Issues*). During the previous year I'd helped start a number of peace studies caucuses in academic professional societies, but it seemed to me that the proving ground was what we did in the classroom. We study conflict and wars, bombs and campaigns, and have whole institutions devoted to them, as well as many, many schools dedicated to teaching young people about the values of capitalism. But what if we decided instead to study how to end war and injustice? What institutions, what materials, what texts, what strategies would we need to do so? A similar calculus drove the initial insistence upon "multiculturalism." There was a dialectic between what was studied and what was considered to be of significance, so in committing myself to changing canon and curriculum I was applying what I had learned in the movement to the institutions in which I worked and which I felt I understood.

For me the primary strategy for change was embodied in the project we modestly named "Reconstructing American Literature." Founded at the Feminist Press, RAL was based on the premise that we could not work differently in the classroom if we did not have access to different texts, authors, and ideas. RAL was, first and foremost, an organizing effort, devoted to supporting and mobilizing those faculty and students desiring to give a new definition to "American literature," opening that category to the many female and minority writers who had almost entirely been relegated to the margins. Initially, we thought we would press existing anthologies and those who determined curricula to open them to a much broader definition, both of "literature" and of "American." However, it became clear that we would have to illustrate the principles of inclusivity by creating a wholly new anthology of American literature for use in classrooms across the country—and so came into being the *Heath Anthology*. (That is a story I have often told and so feel no need to repeat it here.) Doing an anthology was not a commercial enterprise (would it had much more commercial payoff!) but an expression of our values, and those, I think it is fair to say, were rooted in the civil rights and feminist movements of the 1960s. Reactionaries, such as those in the *New Criterion*, accused us of producing an "affirmative-action" anthology. That is true if one defines "affirmative action" as the effort to redress wrongs that express in cultural terms longstanding political arrangements.

The imperatives that drove the creation of the *Heath* look somewhat different with the election of a black man as president. But it's a little early to imagine that we can now simply relax back into teaching a canon supplemented by Toni Morrison and a dose of Bakhtin. For the questions of what we teach and whom we teach continue to place before us the issues of presence, priorities, and values. Multiculturalism has been transformed into—perhaps replaced by—what I've called "immigration shock." And the class treaty of the post–World War II period has been supplanted by the class warfare characteristic of neoliberalism. It thus seems imperative to reestablish what the social movements of the sixties were really about: marginalization, access, control, power. In short, politics. Yes, "politics" has been reduced in the United States to largely trivial choices between Tweedledees, whose seldom distinctive qualities have to be wildly exaggerated to make them appear as . . . Tweedledums. In the world in which I came of age, politics did not mean narrow contests for votes and for marginal modifications of an established system. Politics had rather to do with challenging fundamental definitions of priorities, and the incredible joy and pleasure in so doing. One does not put one's life or career on the line to determine just what kinds of derivatives can be regulated and which not. But one might, and did, to change the voting rolls, the seating on buses, how cops treat us, systems of hiring and unionization, who controls banks, what is manufactured and extracted, and whether we flush the lives of our youth and the treasure of our people down the sinkhole of endless wars—or stop. A movement is a political party—not the kind with names and symbols and candidates—but the kind in which people freely link arms, learn one from another, and stride forward into the pleasures of the possible.

13 |
REVOLUTIONARY CONSCIOUSNESS

CARY NELSON

Through all my work runs a reformist leftist impulse and at least a modest iconoclasm. As I contemplate potential projects—including books just begun on the poetry of hate and on the largely forgotten, elaborate American advertising poetry of the late nineteenth and early twentieth centuries—I typically gravitate toward the ones I feel will make the most difference in a particular cultural community or interpretive context. What project, in other words, will most unsettle a community's fundamental assumptions, lead them into thinking differently about the social and political meaning of cultural contexts in which they are heavily invested?

Recovering unknown or forgotten texts and voices is very much a vehicle for making that difference, for bringing to life historical realities absent from contemporary consciousness. A new past unsettles and remakes the present. The past can thus be transformative.

Repression and Recovery: Modern American Poetry and the Politics of Cultural Memory, 1910–1945 (University of Wisconsin Press, 1989) aimed to reconfigure the modern poetry canon wholesale while also adopting a poststructuralist view of the unstable and constructed character of all memory. The aim was to flood readers' consciousnesses with a wider range of interesting and vital poetry than any individual scholar had previously acknowledged. I adopted a fluid, nearly structureless narrative that simply hurled forward through time, rejecting fixed categories and placing poets in multiple classification systems. As Grant Farred demonstrates in his essay "'We Should Always Read What Other People Assure Us Is No Good'" (*Cary Nelson and the Struggle for the*

University, 45–58), the key theoretical influence on *Repression and Recovery* was Derrida. The book was successful in part because it was offered as a gift to other scholars, limiting itself to brief readings that left room for others to intervene and offering scores of notes designed to facilitate others' research.

Revolutionary Memory: Recovering the Poetry of the American Left (Routledge, 2001) has been much slower to take hold, in part because it is grounded in my large personal poetry archive and thus embodies research most other scholars could not readily emulate. While *Repression and Recovery* concentrated primarily on poetry in books and magazines, *Revolutionary Memory* embraces poetry on fliers handed out at public events, on broadsides displayed in public, and in scrapbooks assembled by individual readers—"poems written in trenches, tacked to trees, passed hand to hand in crowds, sung under fire" (136)—all of which gives deeper insight into the social and political functions poetry has served. I also began to search out poems by lesser-known writers that remained unpublished in personal archives. The revolution in consciousness available from documents never published, texts that had no historical impact beyond a few immediate readers, has an uncanny character of particular appeal. So in some ways I felt I had to go that route, even if it meant accepting a smaller fan club because it was research fewer scholars could emulate.

My new book, *When Death Rhymed: Poem Cards and Poetry Panics of the Great Wars* (University of Illinois Press, forthcoming), takes the personal-archive element much further. It is based on more than 20,000 wartime forms of poetry ephemera—cards, envelopes, letter sheets, postcards, and small broadsides—from some thirty countries that people presented or mailed to one another, often with messages inscribed. They give us access to what has been the holy grail of cultural studies: evidence of how ordinary people used a given cultural production in specific contexts. The archive on which the book is based, assembled over more than a decade, runs from the American Civil War to the present and includes a large number of poems distributed during World War I and World War II, with representations from Europe, Asia, and the United States.

Part of history is the record of the trees that fell when no one was there to hear them, like the anti-McCarthy poems Edwin Rolfe wrote but could not publish in the late 1940s and early 1950s, only now made available in his *Collected Poems* (University of Illinois Press, 1993). If you recover those trees and stand them up for view now, what is their status? They are a part of the present that is also at once unequivocally and marginally tethered to the past. They are in one sense a past that might have been—and was—but only in a state of largely unrealized potential. When they are recovered now, the present is transformed and left in possession of (and possessed by) a past that never quite was.

The connection between *Revolutionary Memory* and my massive coedited *Madrid 1937: Letters from the Abraham Lincoln Brigade in the Spanish Civil War* (Routledge, 1996) thus goes beyond the project of recovering the history of the American left, beyond even the subject of the Spanish Civil War that links them. For almost all the letters in *Madrid 1937* were never previously published. They were read by family members, often treasured intimately for decades, but otherwise often destined for obliteration unless children and grandchildren came to understand their value. They could have a place in family history but their authors might well leave no public trace in historical memory. Of course that has been the historical fate of most working-class people throughout time. These letters' writers for the most part were Communist Party members fighting for a historic cause; the letters grant these forgotten volunteers a human face widely denied them through the decades of the Cold War. For the first time, these largely forgotten voices from a frequently disparaged past speak to us with passion and conviction, describing details of daily life that make them more vivid and intimate than a typical historical account. And, of course, to urge a new view of the 1930s left is also, inevitably, to promote a different take on the contemporary left.

Much literary criticism begins with a felt necessity to alter the way a text or an author is understood, but too often no significant social or political impulse is at stake. Whether the projects above succeed or fail is for others to say, but they have been guided by wider motives.

One other large editing project, the *Oxford Anthology of Modern American Poetry* (Oxford University Press, 2000), follows somewhat the same logic. As the first comprehensive anthology of twentieth-century American poetry, it includes both the canonical figures of high modernism—T. S. Eliot, Wallace Stevens, Ezra Pound, William Carlos Williams, and Robert Frost—and a host of other poets. Some, like H.D. and Marianne Moore, were already established as major figures. Many others were not. The dozens of less familiar—and sometimes wholly unexpected—inclusions represent not only the fruits of writing *Repression and Recovery* but also a very specific cultural project: to demonstrate the centrality of an engagement with history throughout modern poetry. In an effort to discredit the professional ideology that insists on a separation between aesthetics and politics, I included scores of poems that were formally and rhetorically inventive but also deeply engaged with historical analysis, witness, and representation. My aim was to alter not only readers' sense of the modern tradition but also to transform common understandings of the social function of poetry.

Nowhere other than in poetry, I believe, is historical witness more productively entangled with the problematics of representation. No other form of discourse can do as much with as little, encapsulating an event or a period in a stanza while honoring its importance and its complexity. No other form of reading so thoroughly foregrounds the intellectual and emotional dynamics of reception and puts it into an intricate and ongoing relationship with what we take to be historical fact.

Perhaps unsurprisingly, my work on higher education is driven by similar impulses. With *Manifesto of a Tenured Radical* (New York University Press, 1997), I sought to gain a place in our understanding of higher education for the invisible and frequently marginalized graduate student and part-time faculty teachers who increasingly do the majority of college and university teaching. Although the focus in *No University Is an Island: Saving Academic Freedom* (New York University Press, 2010) is more structural, to account for and theorize the forces that have overtaken higher education as a whole over the last generation, it is also an effort to convince readers that they must reevaluate their personal, institutional, and generational histories so as to live differently in the present.

I believe scholarship always—though with varying intensity, relevance, and self-awareness—negotiates the relationship between past and present. Indeed, one of the virtues of cultural studies is that it urges us to accept this as a necessary and desirable condition of all scholarly work. That means confronting the matter reflexively and amplifying, not suppressing, its effects.

The goal of getting faculty to examine their assumptions about their personal experience and historical understanding of the profession and its institutions is, to be sure, daunting. For all their claims to be able to think critically, many faculty members are deeply invested in maintaining, rather than interrogating, the status quo. They have been socialized to believe their interests lie in personal achievement unhindered by reflexive political critique.

As my writing on higher education evolved from *Manifesto of a Tenured Radical* through the two books I coauthored with Stephen Watt, *Academic Keywords* (Routledge, 1999) and *Office Hours* (Routledge, 2004), to *No University Is an Island*, the pressure I was placing on faculty members to reform not only their thinking but also their behavior steadily increased. By the time I completed *No University Is an Island* in 2009 I had become convinced that the power relations on American campuses need to be radically reconstructed. With power increasingly receding from faculty senates and departments and flowing toward the central administration, academic freedom and shared governance are steadily being undermined. Meanwhile both the number of largely disenfranchised contingent faculty members and the cohort of career administrators who have never taught or done research are growing. Faculty members need to intervene in campus governance in a systematic and forceful way. I am urging faculty members to accept that community responsibility is a central part of their identities.

I have always been engaged in activism, and I would insist that writing can always be a valid form of activism, though many scholars who claim political impact by way of rereading texts are deceiving themselves. Such self-deception has been a persistent pitfall for cultural studies in the United States. The impact of activist writing, however, is almost always more modest than one might hope.

I am, no doubt, a product of the 1960s. A veteran of numerous anti-Vietnam demonstrations, many of which included poetry readings, I immediately began teaching anti-Vietnam poetry when I became a faculty member in 1970. My second book, *Our Last First Poets: Vision and History in Contemporary American Poetry* (University of Illinois Press, 1981), dealt extensively with protest poetry. When I was writing most regularly about the Spanish Civil War, I also served as vice chair of the Abraham Lincoln Brigade Archives and helped promote contemporary recognition of 1930s activism. These have always seemed productive rather than disabling interpenetrations of writing and activism.

As I began to write about higher education and the profession in subsequent decades, I became active in professional organizations, most notably the Modern Language Association and the American Association of University Professors. I have sometimes blurred the line between writing and organizational activism, to the distress of my colleagues, especially as I have written about both my department and my university. I have also written extensively about both the MLA, whose executive council I served on, and the AAUP, whose leadership I have served in for fifteen years, moving from its national council to its executive committee to its presidency. *No University Is an Island* includes two long chapters about the AAUP.

Notably, I have written about institutions and organizations while I was still very much active in them, since that seemed the best way to provoke discussion. There have been a certain number of "we don't like to see our dirty laundry aired in public" complaints, some very hostile. There have also been efforts to silence me or censure me. The MLA executive council, for example, discussed censuring me for comments I made in *Academic Keywords*. By then

I was off the council, so the discussion took place without me. As it happened, I would have been more than happy to have them censure me since it would draw attention to my critique of the organization, but they decided silence would best serve their desire to preserve the status quo.

Such writing is itself at once a form of public disclosure and a call to internal organizational reform. Both are sometimes necessary to get a bureaucracy to accept change. A leadership role blurs these distinctions further since you typically have to write large numbers of letters, memos, press releases, and public statements.

When I began my career, with the 3/3 teaching load that was typical then, I always had to work to carve out time to write. As I moved up the academic ladder—something today's contingent faculty are never able to do—and my teaching load evolved to 2/2 and then 2/1, more time became available, and writing gradually became a part of daily life. I commonly write drafts of essays every day about events that are still in process. In some ways, writing is a form of therapy. Committed to the essay form, I use it like a diary. Indeed, I have full-length essays on various subjects that I know I cannot publish for years, if at all.

The mix of scholarship and activism that shapes my academic life is not without conflict and contradiction, but it is central to my credo. No disabling lack, no aporia, falls between the activist deed and the activist word. There are different registers of action, but they are fraternal forms of ironic play. The evolution from speaking at Yale GESO rallies to editing *Will Teach for Food: Academic Labor in Crisis* (University of Minnesota Press, 1997), which covered the grade strike and the history of labor relations at Yale, was natural and fulfilling. The act of getting arrested in a 2006 demonstration at NYU dovetailed with the brief talk I gave at Judson Memorial Church beforehand, with the chants we performed in the street, with "Why We Were Arrested" and "Paddy Wagon Politics," the short pieces I wrote for *Inside Higher Ed* and *Academe* shortly thereafter, and with the detailed analysis in *No University Is an Island*. I joined the building occupation rally that won recognition for graduate employees at Illinois then wrote up the experience in *Academic Keywords*. The list could go on, but the point is clear: these overlapping, mutually reinforcing commitments enhance one another and lead to a more unified life.

14 |

GEOPOLITICAL TRANSLATORS

DAVID B. DOWNING

I n the fall of 1957, I was a young boy watching the grainy screen of our
family's first television set when images of an odd, spherical object with
whisker antennae and the word "Sputnik" flashed across it. A month
later, they (and "they" were pretty bad folks) sent a dog, Laika, into orbit,
without even a thought that they might actually try to bring the creature
safely back to earth. I was astounded. I certainly couldn't imagine sending my
own dog into space knowing that was the end of her. None of the watered-
down explanations about what was going on here made any sense to me, but
I laughed when they called it "muttnik."

I didn't then understand it in terms of Cold War politics, but the 1947 Tru-
man Commission on Higher Education for American Democracy (which
later spurred the 1958 NDEA) provided the political discourse to translate
these events into U.S. funding for science education. These federal resources
would propel me (and my generation) right through grade school and on into
college. If any of these events did get translated into simple terms, they were
Manichean views of us versus them. None of the imperialist features of U.S.
history got translated into any meaningful venue in my (or most anybody
else's) primary and secondary education in the 1950s and 1960s. Most of us
white, middle-class baby-boomers growing up in the shadows of the Second
World War never learned an intelligent word about socialism or Marxism in
our formal schooling, and what we did learn about communism was a conge-
ries of evil, fear, and inhumanity.

By the time (1961) Yuri Gagarin stepped out of his capsule, the first man who had ever been in "outer space," as we called it then, I was completely hooked. The sciences went wild, and I went with them. The only literature that mattered to me was Tom Swift science-fiction. I left for college to major in biology, funded with a scholarship from Hewlett-Packard, one of the post-war start-ups from California that opened a large facility in the emerging tech corridor along the Route 128 beltway outside Boston, only a few miles from my home. Now it is easy for me to see why my grad school teacher and mentor, Leslie Fiedler, had focused his 1950 *Kenyon Review* "Credo" as an attack on "scientific criticism," the culturally dominant but deadly effort to convert literary study into a field with scientific credentials.[1] (1950 was also the founding year of the National Science Foundation.) Back then, Vannevar Bush's influential 1945 book, *Science: The Endless Frontier*, had set the stage for translating the dwindling frontiers of U.S. geographical colonialism into the sociopolitical landscape of "Big Science" with a nationalist fervor, and Fiedler was beginning to mount his career-long critique of those myths. But as we entered the 1960s, I had hardly a doubt in the world about a ready-made path into a career in biological research.

Well, something happened along the way. You could call it politics, economics, culture, or perhaps the 1960s. America changed, and so did many of my cohort in the baby-boomer generation. Something got translated between culture and politics, art and society, science and the humanities, and the social effects of those translations reverberated around the globe.

My own turn towards the humanities was partly because I became acutely aware of all that my science-based education had deprived me of, and partly because it was relatively easy to do. All of higher education was riding the wave of the postwar boom—the GI Bill, NDEA, and deep investments in public education—even if it was driven by aggressive government favoring of science education so we could get to the moon first. The good thing was that the nationalist project of investing in competitive science carried along with it a surplus: the "soft" fields expanded right along with the "hard" disciplines. The growth of public higher education became a huge experiment as a growing majority of an emerging generation was allowed to be college and university students for a prolonged period before they became workers.

The experiment produced a lot of dissent. Indeed, the demographics of higher education changed: more women, minorities, working-class, and non-Western cultures swelled student ranks. And those of us who were white men could (until the 1969 draft lottery, at least), get student deferrals so we could protest the Vietnam War rather than fight in it. Many of us became part of what we called the "Movement," the broad-based amalgam of human rights, women's rights, gay rights, civil rights, ethnic rights, cultural rights, worker's rights, student's rights. The New Left, SDS, SNCC, NAM, NOW, GBLT, Amnesty International, the Third World Liberation Front (TWLF), the Free Speech Movement, and many other left-leaning organizations emerged on the scene. Even though relations between the different sectors of the movement didn't always work in harmony, they certainly couldn't be ignored.

When in November of 1968, the Black Students Union and the TWLF led a student strike at San Francisco State College (where I earned my MA a few years later), it turned into the longest strike in the history of higher education, and the credo then was pretty clear: a university had to have as priorities equity and social justice. Knowledge was not "neutral" or "disinterested" since it was always produced by human labor, and it should serve the broadest possible sense of human needs, not just the increased power of an elite few. "Liberation" became an educational mission, and it had tangible consequences for the university. For example, as part of the strike settlement agreement, the College of Ethnic Studies was established, the first of its kind, and many more would follow as area studies set up programs across the country. At San Francisco State University, Ethnic Studies celebrated its fortieth anniversary this past year, and now more than 70 percent of the student body there are people of color (and this from a student body that was once almost entirely white and middle class, like most of U.S. higher education up through the 1950s).

The Movement joined hands on the basic credo: equity and social justice. Even if there was little practical expectation that it could be realized, social justice certainly seemed a worthy goal. When we marched on Washington or got tear-gassed in Madison as National Guard armored vehicles lined University Ave., it was hard not to have a sense of solidarity that we were part of a changing world and that solidarity in the movements all around us could indeed have positive effects on bringing about those changes. We were young, idealistic, and sometimes just plain wrong, self-centered, or stoned-out, but right enough in large numbers that our commitments to social justice would not go away, even as the reactionary defunding of the humanities got underway in earnest in the 1970s.

The last thirty years has largely been the story of how the party crashed for many reasons: the right-wing backlash, the oil crisis, free market fundamentalism, structural adjustment, spiraling maldistribution of wealth. The economy went sour along with the U.S. balance of trade, the huge rise in reactionary neoliberal and neoconservative think tanks designed to shape and influence public policy, the attack on organized labor, and the rise of unilateral militarism. It seems historically accurate to say the social-welfare state has been mostly dismantled, and we now work within the "post-welfare state university."[2]

This period of contraction accelerated during the 1970s, when I moved through graduate school. The academic job market collapsed. Whereas I had listened to my professors' stories of getting jobs ABD in the 1960s by selecting first the area of the country where they wanted to settle, I and those in my cohort have stories that resonate more with current circumstances. In the fall of 1978, I applied for seventy-five jobs and got three interviews, one where there were 900 other applicants in the pool. It was a tangible task to survive, let alone flourish, in these kinds of working conditions. And I was one of the lucky ones, since I slipped into a tenure-track job in 1979. Anyone wondering why politics, economics, and the social entered the profession with a rage about that time only needs to consider the many stories of my less-lucky peers who became the intellectual migrant workers, rushing between temporary and adjunct positions, many of them ending up leaving the profession altogether.

There were some pretty intense translations between the academic and the political. Those of us on the political left were often in the humanities and social sciences because those were the fields where we felt we could most directly address social and political issues in education and culture to make the world better. That was a pretty generalized, if sometimes vague, version of a credo, even though careerism sometimes eventually blunted those ideals. The old rhetoric of disinterested research and knowledge for its own sake seemed like ideological pipe dreams from the start of our careers.

For the past thirty years transnational capitalism has been translating profits for wealthy corporations into pockets of geopolitical power at rates not seen since the age of robber barons. How different peoples in different parts of the world can recover from the damage of this project requires the utmost skills of what I call "geopolitical translators." This term reflects one of the two key dimensions of my own credo: all of us are engaged in the inevitably social and political struggle to translate between different discourses, different histories, and different geographical places where the local and global intersect. My credo thus has two interrelated components: the task of translation and the ethos of social justice. Especially for those of us in the humanities—our training is in language, discourse, representation, and rhetoric, so we bear field-specific skills as geopolitical translators. Our work may differ in focus, content, and institutional circumstance from nonacademic work, but we have considerable social obligations to translate between those different circumstances as shaped by the global economy.

One important task immediately before us is to rewrite and translate a viable credo in our age of turbo-capitalism. We ought to ask now some basic questions: what can we do, how should we organize, and what kind of hopes can we have as we enter what no doubt will be a difficult time of global depression? My own credo for geopolitical translators bearing a social ethos has its personal roots in the 1960s (and we should not forget some of the organizational models of the 1930s), but we must accept that such a task is inevitably a project of critical utopianism, imagining visions of a more just world even as we organize in our unjust world.

A problem we have often had in our mantras about justice is that invoking such an abstract concept can often seem like an intractable problem if pursued with all the philosophical rigor it deserves. After our affair with postmodernism and poststructuralism, it can be a risky venture to even imagine, let alone articulate normative claims about global justice. The historical archive, however, is pretty resourceful on this score. The traditions of socialism, Marxism, and the left have offered the most provocative visions of social justice. At root is a simple principle: the value added to any raw materials in the process of production need not be maldistributed to an elite group of owners and employers—it can be redistributed to all citizens.

In this tradition, social philosopher Nancy Fraser offers a theoretical model of justice that I believe can be adapted for our everyday lives and our professional concerns. For Fraser, any consideration of justice involves both issues of recognition and redistribution. In simple terms, recognition involves issues of status, and redistribution issues of class; the former focuses primarily on attitudes, beliefs, and identities, whereas the latter focuses on material resources, wealth, and economic inequalities. Of course, any sociocultural situation or event involves both recognition and redistribution. There are good reasons, however, to keep the analytic separation because in many instances the two dimensions do not always point in the same direction. All the social movements I named above have had more success at the level of recognition than redistribution: area studies, ethnic studies, multicultural, transnational, transgendered processes have too easily been tied to liberal versions of diversity that don't always call for substantive kinds of economic change. Thus recognition without redistribution conceals the class struggle and fuels material inequity. Fraser argues that this "general decoupling of the cultural politics of recognition from the social politics of redistribution" has become the main dilemma of our "postsocialist condition." Her goal (like mine) of a credible vision for the left calls for the creation of "another 'postsocialism,' one that incorporates, rather than repudiates, the best of socialism."[3]

There is sometimes a vexed calculus of recognition and redistribution in higher education. For instance, one can recognize composition as a separate discipline but defund salaries for those "service-oriented" writing faculty. A credible alternative to this kind of institutional decoupling of recognition and redistribution requires a conception of justice willing to invoke normative claims: that is, the goal of justice is to achieve "participatory parity."[4] As normative ideals, they are not difficult to conceptualize. Recognition parity would mean that all (adult) participants in a given social situation have equal rights and recognition to participate in decision making that affects the social body (shared governance); likewise, for such recognition parity to even be possible also means that there must be relative parity of economic, material resources.

The ethical impulses for recognition and redistribution also have a relatively empirical basis best represented in the work of some of the capabilities theorists of social justice. To speak of human capabilities is an attempt to name the cross-cultural conditions for human flourishing. This is a necessary phase of the process of articulating and translating some of the crucial normative conditions we hold as a credo to guide our work for human dignity, participatory parity, and social justice for all human beings. Martha Nussbaum offers ten "Central Human Capabilities" that include basic needs for bodily health and integrity (including reproductive health, food, clothing, shelter, etc.) but also capabilities for emotional attachments, love, care; the capacity for reason, imagination, thought, and sensual experience; the capabilities for affiliation, identity, respect, dignity (thus nondiscrimination); opportunities for play, laughter, enjoyment; and political and material control over one's environment.[5] Without elaborating on them here, what should be clear is that these are substantive, outcome-oriented goals for human well-being and are very close therefore to the human rights movement. They are not just procedural stipulations, however, and you can't have them without substantial kinds of both recognition and redistribution.

The social ethos I have just outlined needs to be combined with the tasks of geopolitical translators. "Geopolitical" emphasizes the global and the inevitable socio-historical significance of all our translations; "translators" combines the literal and metaphorical meanings of "translation" and emphasizes the interpretive dimension of carrying meaning ("trans") from the general to specific circumstances and vice versa. Our translations invariably cross political borders and disciplinary divisions. Our rhetorical performances must be accountable to academic and public audiences so that the virtues of academic enclosures from profit are a public good and not a private enclave.

With respect to higher education, the basic principle of academic freedom that we prize so highly has generally been cast in a humanist light as the necessary condition for "knowledge for its own sake." But another way to think of it is socialist in nature: a protection of inquiry and the labor of creating new knowledge in a public domain relatively free from direct capital control. Creativity, imagination, and play are human capabilities calling for recognition and distribution of social resources to sustain them for all peoples, and thus work in the humanities calls for a social contract that secures such spaces of freedom from exclusive focus on profit/loss ratios. The humanities are not just luxuries to be had once we get a surplus, but one among many other domains crucial to human flourishing and global justice. Education itself becomes a socialized necessity as a precondition for serving basic human capacities to learn, know, and imaginatively interpret our complex worlds.

The task of all humanities workers is therefore inevitably historical: we all need self-reflective translations among the histories of our specialized disciplines, the histories of the many different kinds of higher education, and the complicated histories of global capitalism. This often means we have to create and clarify our choice of the historical frames by which we make intelligible the crucial links between local and global contexts.

In the crucial coming months, with President Obama putting neoliberal gurus like Paul Volcker, Lawrence Summers, and others at the head of his economic team, those of us on the left more than ever need to communicate the alternatives and thus to renew an anticapitalist critique that creates solidarity across disciplines and across various public domains, with as much rhetorical clarity for a wider audience as we can muster. And we need to do this without nostalgia for the 1960s. Translating between these and other domains and discourses in such a way as to further the project of social justice seems to me like a worthy credo. So far as I can see, the more geopolitical translators doing this kind of work in and out of the academy, the better the world will be.

NOTES

1. Leslie A. Fiedler, "Toward an Amateur Criticism," *The Kenyon Review* 12, no. 4 (Autumn 1950): 561–74.

2. Jeffrey J. Williams, "The Post-Welfare State University," *American Literary History* 18, no. 1 (Spring 2006): 190–216.

3. Nancy Fraser, *Justice Interruptus: Critical Reflections on the "Postsocialist" Condition* (New York: Routledge, 1997), 3, 4.

4. Nancy Fraser and Axel Honneth, *Redistribution or Recognition? A Political-Philosophical Exchange* (London: Verso, 2003), 36–37.

5. Martha C. Nussbaum, *Frontiers of Justice: Disability, Nationality, Species Membership* (Cambridge, Mass.: Harvard University Press, 2006), 76–78.

15 |
CRITICAL CREDO

BARBARA FOLEY

My critical credo—or what would become my critical credo—was formed in the crucible of 1968 and 1969. Tens of millions were in motion to transform the conditions in which life is lived. It was imaginable that exploitation and its accompanying oppressions might be abolished, that people might create a social order in which it was possible to be human. The capitalist world order seemed anything but eternal: it had come into being in history and could go out of being in history. The understanding that communism is necessary, desirable, and possible became lodged in me as I came of age. While the world has changed in significant ways over the past several decades, my Marxist view of historical necessity has not. Indeed, in many respects—given the vast and spiraling inequalities to which the drive to capital accumulation gives rise, as well as the threat it poses to the future of the planet—my conviction that humanity must free itself from the yoke of class society is if anything more urgent than ever.

Although I harbor no illusions that literary criticism constitutes any kind of front line in the global class war, my commitment to the revolutionary transformation of society has over the years definitively shaped my scholarship, pedagogy, and citizen participation. At first the gap between my leftist activism and literary interests was close to schizophrenic: my graduate training at the University of Chicago in the early 1970s turned me into a neo-Aristotelian of sorts even as my political engagement drew me into both the antiwar movement and the struggles of black working-class people on Chicago's South Side. An enduring benefit of my exposure to the Chicago neo-Aristotelians, however, was my appreciation of both the propositional and the rhetorical power of works of literature. In my first book, *Telling the Truth: The Theory and Practice of Documentary Fiction* (Cornell University Press, 1986), I attempted to situate the novel's changing ways of rendering cognition within a Marxist analysis of changing modes of production.

I have placed increasing importance upon recovering and critically analyzing traditions of literary radicalism that have been unfairly derogated and dismissed because of the enduring influence of anticommunism, whether in its Cold War, postmodernist, or ethnic studies guises. My 1993 book, *Radical Representations: Politics and Form in U.S. Proletarian Fiction, 1929–1941* (Duke University Press), constituted an effort to understand and evaluate the scores of leftist novels produced in the Depression-era United States. In subsequent projects I have investigated the dynamics of African American literary radicalism. *Spectres of 1919: Class and Nation in the Making of the New Negro* (University of Illinois Press, 2003) explored the radical origins of the movement that would later be known as the Harlem Renaissance. My recent book on Ralph Ellison, *Wrestling with the Left: The Making of Ralph Ellison's Invisible Man* (2010), examines Ellison's early journalism and short fiction, both published and unpublished, as well as the thousands of pages of drafts and notes that were abandoned, augmented, or rewritten as Ellison struggled to create his now-classic 1952 novel. My current project, provisionally titled *Jean Toomer and the Political Unconscious: Race, Revolution, and Repression in Cane*, builds upon *Spectres of 1919* by situating Toomer's 1923 masterwork in the aftermath of the postwar revolutionary upsurge and studying the text's rhetorical maneuvers as symbolic acts suturing irreconcilable historical contradictions.

While these book projects indicate that my interests and emphases have shifted somewhat over the years, a fairly consistent critical credo forms a figure in the carpet. To begin with, as a committed leftist I have believed that it is crucial to try to get it right about the left, as it were. In writing *Radical Representations*, I found it necessary to do a good deal of ground-clearing about the early-twentieth-century communist movement, both in the United States and international, before I could even begin to encounter proletarian literature on its own terms. Original archival work was essential—I had to get past a host of continually recirculated untrue truisms about writers and the left—but so, too, was a dialectical assessment of the historically specific strengths and limitations of the Depression-era left. My feeling that the 1930s literary radicals were, in a sense, my own ancestors helped me to formulate an often stringent critique of their shortcomings—and of the political consequences of these shortcomings—without resorting to such labels as "Stalinism" or "class reductionism," which obscure far more than they explain.

A central concern in this effort to "get it right about the left" has been the recovery and renarration of the relationship of African American writers to communism, a relationship that (despite the vitally important work of a new generation of "black red" scholars) to this day remains one of the best-kept literary-historical secrets of the past century. My abiding conviction that the United States—no matter what the hue of its president—remains a deeply racist country and that far-reaching social transformation will be impossible without a forthright struggle against racism in all its forms has strongly influenced my decision to devote scholarly attention to both movements and individuals embodying the dialectical interplay of race and class. It is only when class analysis is caricatured as economic determinism that it is possible to dismiss anticapitalist critique as irrelevant, or only marginally relevant, to the situation of people of color. The history of the Marxist-inflected New Negro Movement, which shaped the consciousness of Jean Toomer, and of the U.S. Communist Party, which defined the outlook of the young Ralph Ellison, reveals that leftist ideas and programs have exercised a significant influence upon these and many other African American writers. I have found that intersectionality theory—currently popular among scholars interested in teasing out the connections between and among gender, race, class, nation, sexuality, and other identities—has limited utility in accounting for the phenomenon of black redness. Indeed, this theory guts the anticapitalist analysis of racism by promulgating the liberal pluralist notion that all oppressions can be mapped as crisscrossing lines on the plane of social life, with each possessing its distinct causality and none exerting primacy over another. Recovering the history of African American radicalism, literary and otherwise, enables us to move beyond the notion of identity as subject position and to grasp the relationship between oppression and exploitation within the structured totality of capitalist social relations.

My close examination of the process by which Toomer's *Cane* and, especially, Ellison's *Invisible Man* came into being has sharpened my awareness of an important theoretical dimension to the project of biographically informed literary criticism, namely, the usefulness of reading forward to a text's published version, rather than backward from a standpoint that views the published text as a well-wrought urn. While this challenge to New Critical formalism might sound like a deconstructive maneuver—and, indeed, shares deconstruction's radical skepticism about the notion of textual fixity—it differs in that it locates the text's slippages and ambiguities not within a crisis in signification endemic to all language but within a historically specific dialectic. Texts like *Invisible Man* and *Cane* are, upon close examination, radically un-well-wrought because of their structured silences, inconsistent characterizations, and overdetermined symbols. If, as is the case with *Invisible Man*, the archive reveals that the text's narrative elements were repeatedly inserted, withdrawn, rearranged, and thematically reinflected, the text loses its aura of inevitability. It emerges as a series of historical acts that are themselves inseparable from the historical world in which the author was living as he wrote and rewrote. The published text of *Invisible Man* interpellates the reader as a coherent and self-aware anticommunist subject, and many a literary critic has answered its red-baiting call. But an examination of the novel's coming-into-being shows that Ellison himself had to struggle hard to subdue recalcitrant political elements threatening to disrupt the rhetorical patterning for which the novel has become famous. To read forward through *Invisible Man*—and, I believe, through many a text whose creative process can be traced—is to follow the author's travel along a series of taken and untaken roads that are simultaneously aesthetic, political, and historical.

Where my work on Ellison has stressed the archival dimension of reading forward, my work on Toomer—who left letters detailing the inspiration and composition of *Cane* but no drafts—has emphasized the author's struggle to represent a historical reality for which he possessed inadequate explanatory paradigms. *Cane*'s overwrought tropes and indeterminate narratorial interventions reveal its author's repression of historical contradictions that defy containment within the nationalist and aestheticist categories in which, in the wake of the failure of the revolutionary upsurge of 1919, he took refuge. As the proposed title to my book suggests, in this project I revisit Fredric Jameson's abidingly valuable notion of the political unconscious. What I hope to demonstrate, however, is that the status and function of the "ideologeme"—which for Jameson functions as the hazily defined structure of feeling mediating between the Real, the "history that hurts," and the text's symbolic acts, which continually struggle to suture the irreconcilable contradictions produced by the Real—vary widely with the historical experience and political positioning of a given author. Writers who, like Toomer, have been influenced to one degree or another by left-aligned political movements are likely to be more fully cognizant of, or at least sensitive to, the ideological freight borne by their own guiding conceptions than are the more "bourgeois" writers (Balzac, Gissing, and Conrad) whom Jameson treats in *The Political Unconscious*. The "ideologeme," in other words, is more explicitly ideological. What I explore in my current project on Toomer, then, is the grounding of textual silence, ambiguity, and overdetermination in the specific pressures—both potentialities and limitations—operative in a given conjuncture. The unconscious is political, I argue, in historically specific ways.

What I have been describing to this point is the work I do when cloistered with my computer on nonteaching days. Resituated in the classroom, especially the undergraduate classroom, this critical credo undergoes some reemphasis and mutation. As frequently and in as many contexts as I can, I include on my syllabi works of proletarian literature and African American literature that, in various ways, introduce students to the red line of history or at least invite them to destabilize the apparent fixity of the capitalist social relations in which we all are compelled to live our lives. Favorites (in a very long list) include Jack London's *The Iron Heel*, Richard Wright's *Uncle Tom's Children* and *Native Son*, Arna Bontemps's *Black Thunder*, William Attaway's *Blood on the Forge*, Anne Petry's *The Street*, the radical poetry of Langston Hughes, Tillie Olsen's *Yonnondio*, Myra Page's *Moscow Yankee*, Dalton Trumbo's *Johnny Got His Gun*, Mike Gold's *Jews Without Money*, John Sanford's *The People from Heaven*, and John Dos Passos's *U.S.A.* Recent works that continue in this tradition include Steve Yarbrough's *The Oxygen Man* and Toni Morrison's *A Mercy*.

Even as such texts display the power of literature to defamiliarize the status quo and grasp the necessity for far-reaching social transformation, I stress equally in my teaching the power of literature to occlude, fetishize, and legitimate capitalist social relations. Here is where my training in the rhetoric of fiction decades ago at the University of Chicago—compounded by Louis Althusser's notion of interpellation, Pierre Macherey's theorization of structured silences, and Kenneth Burke's work on ideology and symbolic action— has come in handy. Examining texts that I consider to one degree or another affirmations of dominant ideology (ranging from T. S. Eliot's *The Waste Land* to William Faulkner's *Light in August* to Ralph Ellison's *Invisible Man* to Cormac McCarthy's *The Road* to Barack Obama's *Dreams from My Father*) I ask my students to consider how these texts position their readers to embrace without interrogation hegemonic assumptions about art, race, gender, family, nation—indeed, the meaning of life. Literature, I hope to show, has the capacity both to afford radical glimpses of an unalienated future world and, conversely, to affirm idealist propositions that—whether in liberal or reactionary form—serve to naturalize existing structures of inequality and exploitation. Literary texts fight out the class struggle in the realm of ideology; through the juxtaposition of texts possessing different political valences I try to bring the class struggle—if in somewhat etiolated form—into the classroom.

Finally, my commitment to an unreconstructed sixties radicalism has led me to put my shoulder to the wheel of political activism. In recent years this has meant marching in the streets alongside students, colleagues, and members of NOW-NJ to protest the invasions of Iraq and Afghanistan; the horrific government response to Hurricane Katrina; and (more locally relevant) the refusal of the Rutgers administration to condemn "shock jock" Don Imus for his sexist and racist verbal assault on the Rutgers women's basketball team. It has also meant working within the Radical Caucus of the Modern Language Association to support the struggles of graduate students and non-tenure-track faculty against their super-exploitation and to pass resolutions contesting the false division between our professional activities as scholars and teachers and the larger political and historical context in which these activities occur. While one could readily engage in any or all of these forms of political practice without being a Marxist, I have endeavored to bring to my involvement, here as in the classroom, an analysis of the ways in which capitalism is the root cause of most of the problems that humanity faces, as well as a vision that another world (here I do not hesitate to use the c-word) is possible.

My critical credo, as both a thinker and a doer, was formed in the crucible of history. It is my hope that, in however modest a way, my scholarship, teaching, and activism have contributed to sharpening the contradictions of our time and hastening the day when humanity may exit from the kingdom of necessity and enter the realm of freedom.

16

THIS I BELIEVED

MICHAEL BÉRUBÉ

Sixteen years ago, in the summer and fall of 1993 when I was writing *Public Access*, I described myself as "a lefty middle-innings pitcher, keenly aware of living in a time when New Deal liberalism marks the leftward border of the thinkable in the United States, and committed to a pragmatic politics of the most fairly regulated markets this society can produce or imagine." The end of that passage marked me as Not Left Enough in some quarters, but it's the beginning of the passage that I'd like to explain. The middle-innings pitcher is the guy who shows up when things have gone badly awry. He's not the closer, who shuts things down in the ninth, and he's not the setup man, who takes care of the seventh and eighth so that the fireballing closer can face the absolute minimum number of batters and live to throw heat the next day. He's the schlump who appears when the starter has coughed up one hairball after another or when the starter has coughed up hairballs and his hapless replacement has followed suit. The job of the middle reliever is to stop the bleeding and give the team a chance to rally. If they can.

At the time I wrote those words, I was thinking of the spectacular, thrilling, world-historical media extravaganza known as the PC scare, in which the hardened culture warriors of the right faced off against the mostly befuddled and muttering legions of academic liberals. Two years earlier, as a second-year assistant professor, I had stepped up and written a response to Kimball, D'Souza, et al., out of sheer frustration—frustration at my senior colleagues for not taking the right seriously, or for taking the right seriously but having no clue how to respond in a public forum. Needless to say, I didn't have any idea how to respond in a public forum either because I had never done it; but I thought, in 1991, that the starters and their hapless replacements were coughing up hairballs, and I didn't think I could do any worse.

That was arrogant of me, perhaps, but . . . well, there is no but. It was arrogant, full stop. I'm still glad I did it, because I was right in one respect: my senior colleagues were coughing up hairballs whenever they tried to reply to the right's shock PC troops. But the conditions of my response had some deleterious effects on me over the short term. Because one of my desires, in intervening in the PC debates, was to explain literary theory to people who thought it was (a) a tool of leftist indoctrination, (b) nothing but obfuscatory jargon, or (c) a scary thing that might hurt literature, I wound up thinking—for at least the next few years—that I was, or should be, in the business of defending every variant of theory from every kind of attack. In my defense (which I can't help but undertake, even at this late date), I was working at a time when curmudgeonly and anti-intellectual senior faculty in English, some of whom had produced little or no scholarship in decades, could (and did!) vote against hiring or tenuring brilliant and promising junior colleagues who identified themselves as deconstructionists or feminists or queer theorists (or all of the above). That is, I took part in the PC wars not only to bear arms against the dishonest and ignorant hacks of the American right but also to engage in side skirmishes with the theory-backlashers in my own discipline—and I did so with glee, for I knew very well who the angels and demons were.

I say this now with a mixture of irony and nostalgia because the terrain has shifted so dramatically since then. In the early to mid-1990s, it was quite easy to give in to the temptations of side-choosing, good Us against evil or clueless Them; indeed, at times it was actually imperative. When exactly? At hiring time, for starters.

One evening when I was dining with three of my senior colleagues at Illinois, I heard one of them say that the job crisis was overblown: you write a dissertation, he said, and you get a Ph.D. and a job; you revise it into a book, and you get tenure. It was a good deal thirty years ago, and it's a good deal now. Aghast, I blurted out, "Oh, come on—in the 1960s, back when there was a *shortage* of faculty, people got tenure for being carbon-based." I meant, of course, to call attention to the disparity between the achievements of some senior faculty and the demands these faculty were now making of junior scholars. But I realized immediately that the three people to whom I was speaking (a) were all pretty distinguished senior faculty and (b) had been hired prior to 1970. One of them was my department head. So I added, sheepishly, "Present company excepted, of course." The next day, I asked one of those colleagues, Cary Nelson by name, whether I had shot myself in the foot or perhaps some place more vulnerable. We proceeded to have a long talk about the job crisis and the changes in the profession over the previous thirty years. Over the ensuing months, a number of decisive things happened: Cary got a call from someone at another department, asking him for a tenure evaluation for a promising junior feminist who had, at that point, published two books; Cary said he assumed the tenure-and-promotion was a slam dunk but would be happy to write a letter for a young scholar whose work he admired—whereupon he was informed that the review was *not* a slam dunk because some senior faculty at this institution (Nameless College, if memory serves) were dead set against tenuring a feminist. Cary proceeded to relay this exchange to me, and I did not fail to say, "Yep, I told you so." At the same time, Illinois's multiyear hiring freeze came to an end, and we advertised a junior position in American literature; neither Cary nor I served on the search committee, but we heard from committee members that 772 people had applied for the job. Many of them had books in hand; some had more than one. And then one of my senior colleagues refused to do an *internal* review of a young female professor on the grounds that he didn't consider feminism a sufficiently scholarly subject. Long story short, that was the semester when Cary and I started to write about the job crisis, to call for a combination of early retirements and reduced graduate admissions, and to criticize business as usual in English. And if we demonized some of our senior colleagues, we had good reason: they *were* demons. We simply -ized them.

That same year, the editor of this fine journal had a similar experience and wrote about it for his local alternative paper. Jeff was teaching at East Carolina at the time, and even though he had given *the minnesota review* a national profile in only a few short years, he had some senior colleagues who weren't too happy with the way things were going in their discipline. Jeff responded by writing an essay explaining the academic job-search process for a general audience. In it, he described a terrific campus visit and job talk by one of the finalists for a junior position—a visit and talk that unfortunately met with much *what's-all-this-then* harrumphing from the senior faculty who thought of theory as a scary thing that might hurt literature. Jeff then proceeded to narrate his disbelief that anyone would respond negatively to so intellectually engaging a job candidate and admitted that he could not restrain himself from surmising that the "no smoking" prohibition in his department building had less to do with public health than with the possibility that the high percentage of deadwood in the building constituted a fire hazard. Jeff sent me a copy of the essay; I admired his lucid description of what search committees do and why and was duly impressed by the chutzpah of the "no smoking" quip—since he was still untenured at the time, and even though his deadwood colleagues were indeed very dead wood, they were nevertheless capable of reading Jeff's work in the local alternative paper. I remember thinking, "Wow, this guy has even less sense of self-preservation than I do."

I tell these tales because now that fifteen years have passed and the energetic young firebrands have become middle-aged guys sitting around telling heroic stories of their impolitic youth, it sounds silly—no, absolutely crazy—that anyone could ever have believed that the angels and demons were so neatly aligned. *Theory = The Left = Intellectually Curious Scholars v. Anti-Theory = Reactionary Politics = Deadwood and Dinesh D'Souza.* All good things v. all bad things. How could that be? It was easy enough (for me, anyway) to show that Dinesh D'Souza didn't know the first thing about Marxist criticism, but it was impossible (for me, anyway) to dismiss Tony Judt's devastating 1994 takedown of Louis Althusser as the work of a know-nothing right-wing hack—because it was in fact the work of a sophisticated and widely read leftist intellectual. And yet we weren't crazy, and we weren't simply self-flattering, either. Back then, we really did have senior colleagues who got tenure for being carbon-based, who hadn't changed their lecture notes in decades, and who, we believed, needed to step aside and enjoy retirement so that lean and hungry new Ph.D.'s could take their place. All we wanted to know from our distinguished older colleagues like Frederick Crews and Morris Dickstein was, *Which side are you on?* And every time Crews or Dickstein (or figures like them) wrote something we didn't like, we knew that they were the enemy of the people—and that the people, united, would never be defeated.

Then, in 1996, three things happened. In February of that year I finished writing *Life As We Know It*; in May the Sokal Hoax rocked the academic left; and in June I read in the pages of this fine journal a review essay of my book *Public Access* in which it was decided that because I had noted (correctly, by the bye) that postmodernism had its critics on both the right and the left, I had somehow reinforced the "left-right equivalency thesis" that underwrote the Reagan administration's support for Central American death squads. Thanks to the Sokal Hoax and that review, suddenly I no longer thought of myself as a middle-innings reliever for the left. I realized, as I certainly should have realized earlier, that there are dozens upon dozens of professional franchises on the left, some of which I wouldn't pitch for if you paid me. And thanks to the experience of writing *Life As We Know It*, I began to think and write more about disability and public policy—learning, in the process, that one rarely knows ahead of time where one will find one's political allies and enemies when the subject is disability rights.

I took the Sokal Hoax personally, even though I was not involved in it, for two reasons. First, because in writing about my son Jamie I was also trying to write about the intersection of disability, genetics, and social policy; accordingly, anything that worked to delegitimate humanities scholars as analysts of the sciences seemed to have ominous implications for my attempt to intervene in (for example) bioethical debates over prenatal screening and selective abortion. Second, because the Sokal Hoax happened—at least on my reading—partly because the editors of *Social Text*, some of whom I count among my friends (and one of whom, Bruce Robbins, I consider a dear friend indeed), read Sokal's essay not for its merits but for its (apparent) side-taking in the Science Wars: *for* Stanley Aronowitz and Andrew Ross, *against* Paul Gross and Norman Levitt (who are duly chided as "right-wing critics" in one of Sokal's footnotes). I never believed that the publication of Sokal's essay implied that *Social Text*'s editors were radical relativists who believed that gravity was just a "social construct," whatever that might mean, but I did believe, and continue to believe, that it testified to the existence of an academic subculture in which pledges of allegiance take precedence over intellectual rigor. Philosopher David Albert noted this in a 1997 discussion of the hoax. Disputing Sokal's post-hoax claims to have found something deeply rotten at the core of cultural studies or theory or postmodernism or any of the other targets of his parody, Albert suggested instead that the hoax worked on "another level":

> The character of the opposition (if there is one) between mainstream analytic philosophy of science and science studies or cultural studies attitudes towards science doesn't seem to me to be helpfully characterized in terms of a disagreement about the philosophical propositions like realism or anything like that. You can find people indisputably within the standard mainstream analytic philosophy of science position, people like Nelson Goodman, whom no one in the poststructuralist camp is going to beat for anti-realism, or relativism, or social constructivism, or what you will. I think the way most people reacted to Sokal's piece was on another level. For them the article pointed to something alarming about standards of scholarship in certain quarters, and standards of argument, and highlighted how much could be gained by simply declaring allegiance to certain kinds of agendas. There was an enormous gap between what he presented himself as doing and what was actually interesting about what he was doing.[1]

The Sokal Hoax got me to brush up on my astrophysics and start reading more widely in science studies; it also led me to think about how much can be gained, in the world of contemporary criticism, simply by uttering pledges of allegiance. And I kept thinking that thought all through the long aftermath of the hoax, in which many people pledged allegiance to Sokal not because they knew anything about science or science studies but because they believed he had confirmed their darkest suspicions about cultural studies, theory, postmodernism, jargon, the academic left, or whatever was most bugging them at the time. It was, in retrospect, a festival of side-taking.

But to return to my first reason: in writing *Life As We Know It*, I was hoping not merely to contribute to the nascent field of disability studies and to offer a compelling account of my son's life; I was a bit more ambitious—or arrogant—than that. I hoped, as I explained in a follow-up essay on the Sokal Hoax, to show that Down syndrome is at once a matter of nature and of nurture, or, in John Searle's terms, both a social fact and a brute fact—and that it might serve as a demonstration case for why we should think of "brute fact" as an observer-independent realm that gradually gets carved—by us humans, working in the dark as best we can—out of the realm of social fact. I took sections 43 and 44 of Heidegger's *Being and Time* as my starting point for that argument, but I had more immediate goals: I was trying to reply to *The Bell Curve*, taking Steven Jay Gould's *Wonderful Life* and *The Mismeasure of Man* as my models, hoping to show that if the lives of children with a chromosomal nondisjunction could be vastly improved by policies of "early intervention" and "full inclusion," then surely the same could be said, a fortiori, for every nondisabled child born into poverty or a racially discriminatory society.

Over the next decade, the lessons of the Sokal Hoax turned out to be invaluable—even when the issues at stake had nothing to do with the issues that animated Alan Sokal. In the Balkan crisis, for example, there was no way to predict where one's political allies and enemies would be. When the United States and NATO finally intervened in Kosovo, long after the siege of Sarajevo and the massacre in Srebrenica, I initially opposed the war—until I heard the lunatic arguments of some of my nominal allies, who were not merely opposed to dropping bombs from 30,000 feet (as many reasonable people might be) but were actually convinced that Milosevic was being persecuted by the Western powers because he was Europe's last socialist. Or that the Serbs were the victims all along, valiantly struggling against a terrorist Kosovo Liberation Army, Islamist allies of Bosnian Muslims, and agents provocateurs sneakily blowing themselves up and staging massacres of their neighbors so as to provoke the intervention of Western Europe and the U.S.

After reading a few of Diana Johnstone's accounts of the war, I decided that even if supporting intervention put me on the side of Madeleine Albright, John McCain, Margaret Thatcher, and the editors of *The New Republic*, it was better than dithering in the face of mass murder and ethnic cleansing on the side of Tom DeLay, Noam Chomsky, Phyllis Schlafly, Pat Buchanan, and far-right Russian nationalists. I have since decided that the Balkans are the place where the time-honored tactic of guilt-by-association died, because everyone in that conflict had deeply unsavory allies; accordingly, it was impossible—or merely irresponsible—to choose a side on that basis.

I experienced a sense of déjà vu all over again in the run-up to the U.S. war in Iraq: though I opposed that war on the grounds that it would shred international institutions and devastate millions of innocent Iraqis, I acknowledged that the removal of Saddam Hussein was a desirable and legitimate goal that could not be accomplished by the Iraqis themselves, and if there were some method of overthrowing Saddam that did not shred international institutions and devastate millions of innocent Iraqis, I would approve of it. I also approved of the no-fly zones that protected the Kurds from genocide, and of the renewed UNSCOM inspections that would determine whether, in fact, Saddam possessed the weapons of mass destruction recklessly attributed to him by the Bush and Blair governments. That position put me at odds with the leadership of the antiwar movement, which held the inspections and no-fly zones to be imperialist incursions on Iraqi sovereignty, and which was willing to countenance opposition to Saddam's distinctive brand of fascism only when, in the 1980s, the U.S. seemed willing to tolerate it in the pursuit of realpolitik. In the dark days of 2002–03, some of my friends advised me sternly that it was madness to criticize "our side" as the Bush-Cheney administration made its plans for war. I replied that insofar as the antiwar leadership was opposed to war in Iraq, it was on my side; insofar as the antiwar leadership opposed no-fly zones and inspections, and dodged the question of whether Iraq would be better off without Saddam and his psychotic progeny, there was no meaningful sense in which it was on my side. After Saddam was toppled, insofar as the antiwar leadership argued that the war was illegal and fought on false pretenses, it was on my side; insofar as it actively cheered the Baathist, Islamist, and Shi'ite "resistance" and likened it to the French Resistance in World War II (as in Susan Watkins's essay, "Vichy on the Tigris"), it was most certainly not on my side.

The problem with thinking of yourself as a middle-inning reliever in such circumstances is obvious: you run onto the field and you realize that no one called you out of the bullpen in the first place. Indeed, you're not even on the team; you're in the wrong ballpark; you might even be in the wrong sport altogether. There is no "I" in team, as the cliché has it. More to the point, there is no "team" in criticism.

But I don't draw from this the conclusion that each of us can speak only for him- or herself. Though I have grown allergic to pledges of allegiance, I have not developed any taste for declarations of independence. On the contrary, the more I work in disability studies the more I see independence as simultaneously indispensable and inadequate. Indispensable, because the disability rights movement is built on the desire that people with disabilities might lead more independent lives in more accommodating environments; inadequate, because even in the most accommodating environment there will be some people with disabilities who cannot live independently—and some who will always require surrogates and guardians to represent them.

My son represents himself quite well in many situations and needs help in others; though he works on "independent living skills" in high school, his parents work on the assumption that he will not live independently as an adult. I mention this not to ground my remarks in the details of my life but to remind myself that although independence is indispensable to criticism, it is not a modus vivendi; and its overemphasis—in public policy, in Rawlsian social contract theory, and even in little essays like this—can lead us to overlook the mundane and inescapable facts of dependency in our daily lives. So I now think I was foolish and mistaken to suggest, even half-jokingly, that my critical work is that of a lefty relief pitcher. I don't pitch for any team—neither the ones that want me nor the ones that don't. But all the same, I'll continue trying to represent people like Jamie as best I can, in whatever medium I have at my disposal. Although I work in a discipline that is exceptionally wary of the indignity of speaking for others, I have learned just enough about disability to try to respect the dignity of others who cannot speak for themselves.

NOTE

1. David Z. Albert, John Brenkman, Elisabeth Lloyd, and *Lingua Franca*, "*Lingua Franca* Roundtable," in *The Sokal Hoax: The Sham That Shook the Academy*, ed. *Lingua Franca* editors (Lincoln: University of Nebraska Press, 2000), 254.

17

"HOPE DIES LAST"

CULTURAL STUDIES AND STUDS TERKEL

VICTOR COHEN

s an undergraduate, I was drawn to the world of literary studies. Though I also pursued a degree in political science, it was in my literature classes that I learned about left politics. In spite of their Arnoldian framework, these classes trained me in a unique form of empathy that could be carried on throughout a lifetime and productively applied to situations, people, histories, and even things. How (let alone why) they accomplished this is something of a mystery to me, though Leslie Fiedler, in his own credo published in the Autumn 1950 *Kenyon Review*, provides a clue. He wrote that "the general failure to come to terms with works of literature is often a failure to *connect*".[1] Though I'm confident Fiedler would be nonplussed by much of my academic training, I find it uncanny how his point describes my undergraduate experience as an English major in the late 1980s. I was trained to connect.

After graduation and a subsequent master's in English, I became even more interested in the relationship between left politics and culture, helped along by writers such as Raymond Williams and Stuart Hall. They pointed towards a vision of social transformation that relied on an analysis of culture that held to the spirit of Fiedler's legacy while overcoming its Cold War animus. After looking hard for places to read more of what Williams and others engaged with, I landed in a cultural studies department, one of the few that still provided a venue for reading in that tradition. Though I'm not sure what I expected to find when I began my doctoral work, I vividly remember discovering a much more confusing academic practice and professional landscape than I could have imagined. We read widely in left cultural and social theory, but I found it challenging to connect these movement-oriented analyses of culture to the pressing concerns of the moment. For my dissertation, I studied popular representations of mid-twentieth-century American mass politics. In retrospect, it seems a project more appropriate for an older generation of academics who came up against Fiedler and his cohort, who generally saw their role as providing the official opposition to the popular culture and mass politics of that era. How my project came out of the late 1990s intrigues me.

I'm not having a backhanded laugh at this kind of work, which I still find useful, or my department at Carnegie Mellon University, which has its own noteworthy spot in the history of cultural studies in the U.S. Instead, I've been struck by the degree to which, when I began my studies, I was unaware of the relationships between cultural studies and the complicated if hopeful legacies of the New Lefts, both British and American, and in turn, their relationship to older left formations. The fraught existence of these (New) left political traditions, in an era and institutional setting that has more generally obscured the role of organized lefts both New and Old, helps explain the challenges cultural studies faced. Yet I rarely heard this history discussed or referenced at conferences, within my department, or in the articles I read. In fact, the questions I'm left with have as much to do with the nature of these challenges as with how (and why) people from my generation were drawn to cultural studies in the first place.

When I find the time I work on answering these questions, though not in the way I was trained to carry out a task like this. As I completed my doctorate, I stumbled across the story of the New American Movement (NAM), a 1970s socialist-feminist organization that based its political practice on Antonio Gramsci's analysis of civil society. NAM formed in the aftermath of the breakup of Students for a Democratic Society, had chapters across the U.S., and grew throughout the 1970s. As the 1980s arrived and Ronald Reagan was elected for his first term, NAM attempted to grow exponentially by merging with the Democratic Socialist Organizing Committee (DSOC), an older socialist organization whose roots went back to the Debsian Socialist Party. Together, NAM and DSOC formed the Democratic Socialists of America, the largest socialist organization in the U.S. today.

I came across this group's history while in casual conversation with a professor in my department. He had helped organize NAM's flagship school in Los Angeles but had not talked about this experience for decades. I found NAM's history strikingly relevant to cultural studies, said so, and in response, he helped me get in touch with other NAM members. As I interviewed them about their work in the school, and then the organization, many of my questions about cultural studies and my place in its history became legible. I began to see how Williams and the people involved with cultural studies after him were preoccupied with the same problem NAM faced—how to develop a utopian political project in an era that saw support for (or even interest in) utopian politics evaporating in an unprecedented way. Williams, in "Notes on British Marxism Since 1945" (first published in the Nov. 1976–Jan. 1977 *New Left Review*), has a useful description of the immediate prehistory of cultural studies that illustrates these conditions, and also provides a fascinating account of the contradictions of bringing Marxian theory into academia that remains relevant today.

One of the most curious of these contradictions that continues to make itself felt, and which is a telling indication of the nature of the political atmosphere Williams and NAM were working against, is the persistent interest in radical politics and thought that are oddly removed from their context in social movements. Many of us are familiar with Walter Benjamin's "Work of Art in the Age of Mechanical Reproduction," but I wonder if we are as aware of its publication in the U.S. in *Studies on the Left*, a journal of the U.S. New Left that ran during the 1960s. The journal is seldom referenced today. (I first heard about it from a NAM member.) Part of the reason has to do with its topicality—it published reports on the movement and timely debates around issues of organizing and politics. But it also presented to its audience of American radicals central theoretical texts from the Frankfurt School, including an early translation of Benjamin's essay.

I imagine many of Benjamin's current readers would benefit from understanding this context of the American reception of "Work of Art." Certainly, Benjamin's utopian critique of mass culture was very important to a generation of radicals for whom mass culture—rock-n-roll, for example—provided a venue to express their ambitions for a different social order. I also find it telling how I came across the essay—by accident. While many left academics of the 1960s and 1970s actively contribute to their disciplines and departments today, and carry forward the history of the New Left (and Old) in thoughtful and productive ways, my experience suggests that unless one attends to the lived connections between radical politics and cultural studies, these bonds remain invisible.

Since that first conversation about NAM, I've left behind the criticism of cultural forms and instead begun to speak with the generation of people who were radicals first and academics second (if they were academics at all) to try and recover these connections. It troubles me that cultural studies is no longer the academic movement it once was.

I am also motivated to do this work because this is not a problem unique to cultural studies. The obituaries that followed the death of Studs Terkel illustrate this quite well. Terkel was a talk-show host and well-known author of numerous collections of interviews with people regarding their experiences of the social structures that determine our lives: work, race, war, death, economic scarcity, and the dream of economic security. Terkel's ambition to represent in interview form the lived experience of these determining forces would suit many who come out of cultural studies. At least that's true for me. However, the roots of Terkel's "ambition" were generally missing from many of his obituaries, no doubt because of their origins in the political movements that helped shape him.

As a young man, Terkel took part in the radical left culture and anti-fascist/pro-Communist politics that characterized the 1930s and 1940s. He was a member of the Chicago Repertory Group, originally a workers' theater troupe, and with them he performed many of the era's key proletarian dramas throughout the city, from soup lines to union halls. The day after the Memorial Day Massacre, he and other members of the theater group met with the steelworkers who, as they were having a picnic while taking a day off from their strike against Republic Steel, were beaten and shot by Chicago police. Terkel eventually became a radio scriptwriter for the WPA Writers Project and helped raise money for the Soviet American Friendship Committee and the Anti-Fascist Refugee Committee. Though never a member of the Communist Party, USA, like many others he was blacklisted from getting work for sharing their politics—from the Red Cross first, and, after World War II, from television as well. His TV show, *Stud's Place* (begun in 1949) was canceled in 1951 when Terkel's prewar sympathies were pointed out to NBC.

Terkel was luckier than most who were blacklisted—he continued to find work that suited his interests, and he retained control over the radio program that he hosted for most of his life. In a way that would make Benjamin proud, we should note that Terkel's literary legacy is a product of the radio, that central institution of twentieth-century mass culture. Its format taught him his craft. He honed his interviewing skills on-air, talking to people from all professions and of all ages, for almost an hour every day for forty-five years. It was only through the suggestion of editor Andre Schiffrin that Terkel came to the book projects he became famous for, such as *Hard Times*, his oral history of the Great Depression, or *"The Good War,"* his collection of interviews about people's experiences in WWII, which earned him the 1985 Pulitzer Prize for General Non-Fiction.

While the writers who composed Terkel's obituaries had no difficulty describing his contributions to our collective memory of the twentieth century, his connections to the political matrix of the Popular Front and the 1930s were less visible. He was often grouped with other Chicago writers whose lives and work were shaped by that moment and movement, such as Nelson Algren and Richard Wright, but the connection seemed primarily geographical and generational.

One of the few writers who attempted to characterize Terkel's politics was the *New York Times*'s Edward Rothstein, who did so in a feverish and prurient fashion but at least brought up the word "Marxist" and correctly identified Terkel as an abiding communist at heart, if not affiliation.[2] Like most red-baiters, Rothstein drew false connections between criticizing capitalism and enabling the horrors of totalitarianism, and faulted Terkel for holding to a dogmatic idealism as opposed to looking at the world "the way it really is." Rothstein added that he failed to connect with any of Terkel's work, but, thanks to Fiedler's observation, we know the fault more accurately lies with Rothstein.

Obituaries in *The Nation*, including Howard Zinn's response to Rothstein, were much better about claiming Terkel as a member of the left. Gary Wills, in the November 2008 *New York Review of Books*, provided a fuller account of Terkel's politics and those of his wife Ida, who had stood vigil with other concerned women outside the Chicago apartment where Black Panther Fred Hampton was murdered by police. However, Wills, though sympathetic to Terkel, did not attach a name Terkel's politics. To his credit, he pointed out that Terkel not only acted in a version of *The Cradle Will Rock* (Marc Blitzstein's iconic proletarian drama of the 1930s), but had interviewed four of the actors who performed in the original. Wills also noted how Terkel's blacklisting from TV stemmed from his refusal to sign a loyalty oath and that he took his nickname from the poor Irish protagonist of James Farrell's proletarian trilogy, *Studs Lonigan*. However, what particular vision of social justice could motivate Terkel, or his wife, was left unspoken.[3]

There is a similar disconnect between the political movements that shaped Terkel's life and worldview, the way his work and life were represented on the occasion of his death, and the political roots of cultural studies and the way departments, universities, publishing houses, and bookstores represent cultural studies to us today. In his autobiography Terkel recounts his admiration for the elderly Wobblies who populated his parents' boarding house and his work with the Popular Front that caused his blacklisting from TV. He was neither ashamed of the blacklisting nor the politics that got him there. Cultural studies could use a few memoirs like this, such as Stuart Hall's recent "The Life and Times of the First New Left."[4]

If it seems a meaningless term because of its ubiquity in academia today, when it got underway in the U.K., most people understood that "cultural studies" was a euphemism. As someone who attended the Birmingham Centre for Contemporary Cultural Studies told me, the term was the best anyone could do to replace "socialist-feminist studies," which is what the school was really trying to put into practice. I like to think that anyone who spends time trying to connect with the bulk of art, history, and political thought of the twentieth century and doesn't become a socialist and a feminist is by default executing exactly the task Fiedler imagines bad readers perform. As he puts it, such a critic "aggravates an endemic weakness of our atomized world" (564). I remain committed to looking for the connections between the history of the left and the possibility for future social change, and it is in this context that I find the fate cultural studies still most relevant. I also take inspiration from Fiedler's sense of what constitutes good criticism. In his credo, he characterizes a bad reader as someone who "chooses to deal with the work in isolation" (564); I agree, and imagine the best of our work as critics can bring together people, their work, and its contexts to help others connect with what has come before them in the best possible sense.

NOTES

1. Leslie Fiedler, "Toward an Amateur Criticism," *The Kenyon Review* 12, no. 4 (Autumn 1950): 564.

2. Edward Rothstein, "He Gave Voice to Many, Including Himself," *New York Times*, 2 November 2008.

3. Gary Wills, "He Interviewed the Nation," *New York Review of Books*, 18 December 2008, 53–54.

4. Studs Terkel, *Touch and Go* (New York: The New Press, 2007); Stuart Hall, "The Life and Times of the First New Left," *New Left Review* 61 (2010): 177–96.

PEDAGOGICAL MOMENTS

18

CREDO OF A TEACHER

GERALD GRAFF

My credo as a teacher: do whatever it takes to turn students into compulsively analytic intellectuals like yourself. It's never mattered to me what *kind* of intellectuals my students become—Left, Right, or Center—as long as I do something to help them become intellectuals I feel I'm a success. And if I do something to help them become really good intellectuals I'm even more of a success.

Of course, if all or most of my students became followers of Ayn Rand or Charles Krauthammer I'd worry, but that hasn't happened yet. I've been on the warpath for some time against "radical pedagogy," "the pedagogy of the oppressed," "teaching for social justice," and other descendants of sixties political pedagogy that expressly aim to turn students into radical Leftists. This strikes me as a terrible idea, both because it doesn't work—more students rebel than become converted—and because even if it does work it's unethical and unprofessional.

Instead of seeking to radicalize students, the goal of political education in my view should be to expose them to controversial political issues while equipping them with the intellectual tools for forming their own conclusions, bringing them into the conversation of intellectuals rather than trying to convert them to the intellectualism of the left. My point has been perceptively summarized by David Shumway, who distinguishes my "teach the conflicts" pedagogy from the oppositional pedagogies advanced by Henry Giroux and others. Shumway writes that "Graff wants to make use of opposing points of view to make the significance of having a perspective clear to students, who he believes frequently do not understand the arguments Giroux's conception takes for granted. . . . Giroux fails to consider that Graff's goal might be a necessary step if students are to come to see [social] transformation as possible and necessary."[1] Precisely: until students grasp what it means to "have a perspective," trying to inculcate radical left perspectives puts the cart before the horse.

Since my writing began to focus entirely on educational issues in the mid 1980s, then, the credo behind my published work has been that the function of schools and universities should be to turn the highest possible percentage of students into intellectuals. Measured by this criterion, I'd have to say colleges and universities do about as bad a job as possible, in large part because we not only don't collaborate in our teaching but actually undermine and cancel each other out through what I've called the "mixed message curriculum" and the cult of teaching as a solo practice (which I've recently called "courseocentrism"). Since I don't think we can make any kind of transformative impact on students unless we work together (as workers do in almost every other complex enterprise besides college teaching), I've spent an inordinate amount of time trying to get the whole institution to change by getting faculty members to work together to create a curriculum that would make coherent sense of the intellectual world for students and thereby draw a higher percentage of them into it.

I'm still at that project of trying to change the institution—see my 2008 MLA Presidential Address entitled "Courseocentrism" (a condensed version of which has appeared in *Inside Higher Ed*), which may turn out to be my last bullet or last gasp, as the case may be. But several years ago I got tired of the slowness and improbability of trying to change the whole university and hit on a shortcut method of turning students into intellectuals, which for me is the slightly sneaky aim of the two "Critical Controversy" textbooks I've done with James Phelan on *Huckleberry Finn* and *The Tempest*, and above all of the most recent one co-written with my wife, Cathy Birkenstein, entitled *"They Say/I Say": The Moves That Matter in Academic Writing*. This last book has a secret behavior modification agenda, giving students templates that they have to become intellectuals of sorts in order to fill out very well:

In the debates over _____, a controversial issue is whether _____.
Whereas some argue that _____. Others reply that _____. My own view is that _____.

This book has been by far my most successful publication (it's now used in over 800 colleges in many different disciplines) and allows me to feel that I'm accomplishing my goal at the grass-roots level while I'm waiting for universi-ties to change in the ways I've urged.

This brings me to the last part of my credo, which is that the distinguish-ing mark of intellectuals is dialectical debate or what our textbook calls the "They say/I say" game. Our premise is that John Stuart Mill and Kenneth Burke got it right: intelligibility is hooked to controversy, contradiction, dia-lectic. We never do anything just to do it but only as a counterstatement or response to something, if only a lack or absence. In teaching I believe there's no viable way to organize a course or any kind of intellectual material other than as a debate or controversy; the failure to do this at least partly explains the abysmal state of education around the world. If students are given no controversy to enter, as generally they are not, the only thing they can do is regurgitate information or make smart or true statements in a vacuum—which is what the ACT and all the other tests ask them to do.

NOTE

1. David Shumway, "Graff and the Left," *Pedagogy* 3, no. 2 (2003): 261.

19 |

OF CREDOS AND CREDIBILITY

WILLIAM GERMANO

On a recent trip to Salt Lake City I made the visit to Temple Square, where I was greeted by two sisters, as Mormons style young female missionaries. One was from Berlin, the other from the Marquesas, and they were the politest people I'd ever met outside Japan. What was more remarkable? That missionaries had gone past Hawaii and Tahiti to a barely inhabited island Melville first told me about, or that Mormons had reached cosmopolitan, agnostic Berlin? The sisters asked me where I was from (Manhattan) and why I was in Salt Lake (conference). Neither of them had ever been to the States before; all that they had seen of this country was Salt Lake. I tried to discuss their homelands—they were amazed that I had been to Berlin and to the Society Islands—but what they wanted to talk about was belief.

"What do you believe?" they asked me. This is not an easy question for an academic, who will tend to have long and complicated answers, full of conditionals and escape clauses about agency and subjectivity. One of the sisters pointed to a passage from a well-worn volume and invited me to contemplate its meaning. I read it over. The text was vaguely familiar (I heard the echoes of the Jewish prophetic books) but also familiarly vague. If you wait long enough prophecy will be fulfilled, she said. She was young, but her tone was grandmotherly ("Just you wait . . ."). We spent an hour talking about what belief might mean. I went into teaching mode, trying to import into the conversation ideas about belief and how they have changed, but we had different senses of change and very different senses of what time means. My interlocutors had come from a dynamic European capital and a South

Pacific archipelago, drawn into yet one more imagined community not by nationalism but by the persuasive force of a religious movement. Their sense of history was based on miracle and the resolution of prophecies while mine was based on change and persistence, violence and accommodation, contact and culture. There we stood, three international visitors to Temple Square, living in the pancake-flat, miracle-poor twenty-first century. They studied texts as the basis for belief. I studied literature, a business often involving texts but that is much messier than it sounds. Globalization was part of my hosts' world, but history? History, it seems to me, wasn't much on their minds. I was bound to the our-story-so-far world; the sisters—and in their way they were like students everywhere—were part of the just-you-wait world.

There are two kinds of belief: belief as persuasion, based on logical argumentation (I believe you when you say you didn't eat the last piece of cake, and I believe you because I saw the frosting on the dog's whiskers), and then there is real belief belief. It may be the trace element of a Catholic childhood, but for me a credo conjures up 318 Fathers gathered in council in fourth-century Nicaea, brokering a declaration of Christian faith. The point, of course, is that the Nicaean creed is a belief in what cannot be known. Anything less is a guide to the good life or a set of operating principles, somewhere between Marcus Aurelius and a book on car repair. But what would a critical credo—crisp alliteration aside—have to do with my belief belief? Academics concern themselves with credentials (their own, other people's), which in turn establish their credibility as interpreters. Underlying all this is some bedrock of ideas that makes thinking-in-the-world possible. Is an academic credo a belief? If so, it's a belief with footnotes, and maybe a few Heideggerian dashes, just to be on the safe side.

I teach historically, culture as our story so far and literature as part of its documentary evidence. My job as a teacher is in part to make those texts speak twice—in their own time and voice and in mine. I can't do that without a sense of the text's un-neat lives over time. (I am fond of un-neat categories, and "literature" is an un-neat category.) My scholarly interests lie mainly in earlier periods—Shakespeare, Herbert, Milton, seventeenth-century writing and the culture of the book, and sometimes the musical culture of mid-nineteenth-century Europe—what they are, how they mean, how those meanings link to other forms of meaning across time, how those meanings get reinvented by us today. These are knowledge questions but also belief questions. You can't teach literature without believing in it.

So what might a credo mean for me? A credo is what one takes to be true: not only how one does what one does but what is at stake. In the heyday of theory, explanatory models jostled one another to offer the hungry reader new and rigorous tools for reading. Many were misread as the key to all mythologies. Some were more trouble than they were worth. But theory was systemic and systematic, a big Refresh button poised smack in the middle of the humanities curriculum. One of the unintended consequences of theory, now that the fever has broken, has been to refocus attention on one's own tool kit. Before it jammed, theory's compass was pointing to philosophy, and we have read philosophies of all stripes since then. Even if one is not a self-identified theorist, one's work as a critic and scholar derives from something, and all things being equal it's good to know what that something is. But it is not an easy thing to do. One can argue endlessly on behalf of literature or the humanities or, more broadly, what the French call *sciences humaines*, but there is a point at which the ideas of which we speak and to which we devote our working lives must in turn speak directly to others as they have spoken to us. If you're asked to prove literature's value, you discover that literary study is in some sense a faith-based initiative.

When I enter a classroom I find myself wondering if students believe what I tell them and, if they do, why. What capacity do I have, aside from the authority of the grade book, to affect their engagement with literary texts as part of the human imaginary? of the history of ideas? Do I dream or wake when I think that it is possible to teach something called literature and make it stick? On one hand, we often say that we want to teach students "how to think" or how to "think critically" and, specifically, how to think about and with the materials of humanistic discourse. We want them to have cultural capital and to value it. Nothing is simpler than to complain that one's students are ignorant of a particular literary text or even of an entire historical epoch, but nothing is as important as developing a student's desire for knowledge about these things. The goal of teaching isn't to dole out knowledge as a set of cognitive collectibles (get them all, trade them with your friends) but to make students hungry for the unfamiliar. Drum roll please: We want students to learn so that they can become vivid participants in their own world making.

I teach my students, and believe when I do, that everybody makes the world up. Some people work hard at making up their own worlds. Others passively accept third-party reductions of complex questions. But the world gets made, person by person, and no two worlds look exactly alike; it's the ordinary work of organizing reality, something that literature takes as its principal task. The arts and the humanities are complicated and usually slow engagements with those worlds. Those of us who care enough to want to spend our time on these questions, and lucky enough to have the jobs that give us that time, work to make the student's world deeper and thicker than it might otherwise be.

This is how we would like students to envision what we do for and with them, but I don't think students—or anyone else—can be blamed for regarding the study of the humanities with a naïve instrumentalism. American society grapples anxiously with issues of purpose and outcome, with the costs of education and its relation to future employment. When it comes to higher ed, Americans want the ocular proof of its utility. Four decades ago, when I was the first in my family to go to college, such a development seemed like the gift it was. A liberal education was tacitly understood as being "of value," not only to the adolescent on campus but to the larger society to be enriched by the adult that adolescent would become. The now ascendant acronym STEM—science, technology, engineering, medicine—represents a dynamic educational system as constitutive of technical and professional training, apparently taking place outside the "soft canon" inhabited by the squishy nonquantitative social sciences, the humanities, and the arts. That seems to me wrong for many reasons but primarily because it evades the philosophical, social, and creative issues that lie at the heart of humanistic discourse and because those issues—those unanswerables—are what make our little human machines tick.

As a teacher, I try to wear lightly the lessons of the theoretical explorers, but one constant in my own classroom is the necessity of showing the curious dynamic within reading. The artifactuality of the literary work (or the historical document or the philosophical or theoretical tract) is a function of its rootedness in its time and social production. And that artifactuality is always in tension with the work's afterlives—the readings, interpretations, and remediations that later readers bring to a text. We are always those later readers, and we have no choice but to make old texts our contemporaries. And as we do that we shift them, sometimes a little, sometimes a lot. At the same time, we create new tools for understanding the then-ness of a text; we discover new archives and invent new analytic tools with which we reimagine the time and social process that yielded the work under scrutiny. As professional readers—and that's what we do for a living as critics and historians and theorists—we are constantly recalibrating the pastness of literature. Each recalibration in turn adjusts further the literary work's then-now dynamic. A work's reunderstood past creates for us, its readers, new possible ideas of the present.

"What do you believe?" I believe in questions more than answers. When I was an editor I once asked a philosophy professor what questions she was working on. "What questions?" she replied, "We haven't answered the first one yet." As they say on game shows, good answer. Teaching literature means teaching ideas, and if you don't like dealing with philosophical questions, at least some of the time, you're not going to be happy with literary texts and a room of smart, inquisitive students. But if philosophers haven't solved the First Problem yet, the rest of the humanities can't feel superior. The humanities don't solve problems—the social sciences are much better at solutions. But the humanities bring problems more sharply into focus, making them clearer even if that means making them more complex and more difficult to solve.

For the record, I am unpersuaded that "humanities" and "social sciences" are labels that describe separable arenas of inquiry. It seems clear to me that narrative and data are the poles of contemporary inquiry and production and that much of the social sciences and almost the entirety of the humanities are narrative-driven enterprises. Sustaining narrative—as an art, as a critical act—is an essential task of the scholarly life and one never more worth thinking about than now.

I begin a freshman course asking students whether they are modern and, if so, how they know. Over the course of the term we read together texts by More and Machiavelli, Shakespeare and Locke and Rousseau, and we end asking ourselves how we might respond to one of intellectual history's most famous survey questions—"What is Enlightenment?"—a query to which Kant provides a short and very complicated answer. Behind the course is my interest in the seventeenth century as a laboratory of art and invention. The 1600s produced the most remarkable and diverse technes upon which we ground modernity: Dutch microscopy, Italian telescopy, Continental optometrics, Newtonian physics, and the English forays into cardiac research. To those mechanical and clinical achievements of the age, I would add the Spanish novel and the Italian opera. All are tools and imaginative projects with which we measure and construct the modern self.

One of my favorite writers is the mid-seventeenth-century Norwich physician Sir Thomas Browne, the man who became famous for his spiritual autobiography *Religio medici*, in which Browne laid out the unresolvable uncertainties of a wondering physician's belief system. Browne was a learned physician but one with a taste now and then for mystical rapture. Browne was happy to lose himself, he says, in an *altitudo* rather than neutralize the unresolvable conflicts of subjectivity. What would *Religio professoris* read like in the twenty-first century? Would it have room for *altitudos*? I turn to three very different strands of human endeavor to ground my own responses to "literature," however broadly considered that sign may be: first, history, because the work of reading and writing is grounded in specific cultural formations and conditions; second, religion, because theological tenets and the cultural dimensions of religious identity have been determinative for almost everything we teach; and finally, music, which of all the arts seems to me most powerfully to demonstrate the expressive and communicative capacity of nonlexical sign systems. Music is irresistible on its own, but it performs another function for the study of literature in showing us just what cannot be said with words.

Can I take undergraduates who are busy pursuing careers as artists and chemical engineers, architects and computer scientists—not one of whom is pursuing a degree in the liberal arts—and show them how culture produces and is sustained by imagination and contemplation as much as by formulas and structures? Show them and make them want more? It seems to me that that's the function of teaching, within which one's private world of science and history and art, of pedagogy and belief, makes any kind of teaching possible. And that, for me, is nothing if not critical.

20 |
TEACHING FRICTION

ANN PELLEGRINI

Debates over the relationship between education and democratic citizenship have a long and often contentious history, from Plato's Republic of philosopher-kings (and a few queens) to the contemporary and bipartisan hand-wringing of U.S. politicians over the failure of American students to keep up with their international peers—a failure that is held to threaten the economic future of the United States. At a moment when money is the measure of everything, this economic peril constitutes an existential threat to the future of America and the vaunted American Dream. As President Obama put the matter in a March 2009 address "on a complete and competitive American education" to the Hispanic Chamber of Commerce: "The future belongs to the nation that best educates its citizens—and my fellow Americans, we have everything we need to be that nation." After this Olympian puff of nation-building spirit, the president expended a considerable amount of his speech detailing why the United States has fallen behind despite having everything we need to win that future. One of the reasons we lag, according to the President, is that other nations (and he specifically singled out Singapore) are "spending less time teaching things that don't matter, and more time teaching things that do. They're preparing their students not only for high school or college, but for a career. We are not."[1]

With educational success equated to "career" preparation and placement, who needs critical thinking, let alone the liberal arts? There is already a considerable literature arguing in defense of liberal arts education and for its democratic value.[2] I won't rehearse those arguments here. Instead, in this brief essay I want to focus explicitly on the critical matter of teaching. What does it mean to matter in the classroom and for the future—whether our students' future, our own as teachers, or some ideal polity's? How do things come to matter, and how might they matter differently between two people or across an individual's own lifetime?

These are large questions for such a small essay, and I can hardly hope to answer them by the end. But I do want to raise them as matters of critical/ criticism's practice. Perhaps a concrete example will help. I have been teaching a lecture class called Religion, Sexuality, and American Public Life at New York University since 2004. Religion and sexuality are a volatile mix in American public life, and this holds true for the classroom, too, especially on an avowedly "liberal secular" campus like NYU's. I love teaching this class. The class size is usually capped at sixty, and the students are uniformly engaged and always manage to surprise me—an experience that is not always comfortable. But I don't think comfort and safety are the same thing. Indeed, one of my hopes is to create a classroom atmosphere where students are willing to risk their own discomfort by opening themselves to encounters with positions and subjectivities different from their own (though perhaps less different or at least differently different than they think).

Some significant share of the students major in religious studies or gender and sexuality studies, but the majority take the class as an elective. Their motives are diverse. Some are drawn by the chance to investigate the intersection of religious and sexual politics; others, both queer and straight, are struggling with the place of religion in their own lives. There are avowed atheists in the class as well as students who are religiously engaged. Among this latter group, some (but scarcely all) of the Christian-identified students are trying to sort out their own feelings about homosexuality. The diversity of academic backgrounds, political commitments, and religious and sexual self-identifications makes for fascinating and sometimes frictive conversation as students' assumptions—about others, about themselves—rub up against one another. I'll come back to this point.

I adjust the syllabus each time to reflect changing issues "in the news" (and also to keep the class fresh for me). But within any given semester, I also find myself changing the syllabus as we go along; my outline for the class is frequently overtaken by the day's newspaper headlines—something that is guaranteed to happen given the combustible mix of the course's three keywords: *religion, sexuality, American public life*.

I have many ambitions for this class. One big take-away is the limits of tolerance: I want students to understand just how cramped the frame of tolerance is as a way of making room for social difference, not just for "being" different in public life but for "doing" difference. In this class, legal debates over religious freedom—and, in particular, what happens when the Supreme Court protects freedom of belief but not freedom of conduct—are one major way to illustrate the limitations of tolerance and how these limitations are connected to specifically Protestant understandings of religious *and* secular subjectivity. In turn, the distinction between belief and conduct connects to debates over what sexual freedom, as opposed to sexual equality, might look and feel like in public life (the course rests in large part on the arguments Janet Jakobsen and I make in our book *Love the Sin: Sexual Regulation and the Limits of Religious Tolerance*).[3]

I also want students to grapple with the question of framing: how the kinds of claims we can make in public debates and the kinds of subjects we can be in private or in public (and the course historicizes and opens up the public/private distinction) are limited in advance by assumptions about what religion "is," what sexuality means for "everybody," and the proper boundaries between public and private for sexual identity and for religious identity, too. Of course, the kinds of claims we can make also differ across discursive contexts or speech communities: what we would argue before a judge, as we make our pitch to and through legal tradition and precedent, is not the same as what we might be able to dare in a different forum, in debates within a particular religious community, say, or over dinner tables with family members or friends. I am especially eager for them to come out of the class able to engage with media critically.

One of the ongoing challenges for me is developing assignments that fit the critical goals and ambitions I have for my students in this class. I am not interested in some sort of "skills assessment," if by that is meant determining whether or not they can write coherent essays. Yes, I want them to be able to do this, but this is a generic goal and one that has no specific relation to the three keywords of my class. Rather, if I want the students who take this class to come away able to critically analyze the limits of tolerance in practice and not as some abstraction, I need assignments that do more than just give them an opportunity to show they have done the reading and can regurgitate the arguments.

One such recent assignment, in fall 2010, was an option for students to make their own It Gets Better videos. If students chose this option, they also had to write an analytical paper, in which they drew on articles assigned for the class, explained the choices they made in their video, specified who was their imagined audience (gay teens, for example, or the friends and family of gay teens), and considered how the particular space of YouTube or the framing of the It Gets Better Project did or did not delimit what they could say in their video. This particular assignment was connected to a larger unit in the course that was specifically focused on media, tolerance, and the construction of "the" general public. (Students uploaded their videos directly to YouTube, but my teaching assistant Katie Brewer Ball also made a YouTube channel for our class videos so that students could find and see each others' work more easily: http://www.youtube.com/user/RELIGIONSEXAMERICAN.)

My goal with this particular assignment and throughout the class, really, is for my students to come away with an awareness of the ways mediatized grids of intelligibility shape what any of us can say, know, or experience as "true." Another way to put this is to say that I want them to rub up against some "inconvenient facts." The term "inconvenient facts" is Max Weber's from his 1918 lecture "Science as a Vocation." The larger passage in which the term appears bears repeating here:

> The first task of a competent teacher is to teach his students to acknowledge *inconvenient* facts. By these I mean facts that are *inconvenient* for their own personal political views. Such extremely inconvenient facts exist for every political position, including my own. I believe that when the university teacher makes his listeners accustom themselves to such facts, his achievement is more than merely intellectual. I would be immodest enough to describe it as an "ethical achievement," though this may be too emotive a term for something so self-evident.[4]

But it is precisely what is self-evident that may occasion the deepest surprises. This pedagogy of surprise is also an ethics of suspended certitude and critical reimagination. *Surprise!* The world is not as you thought it was. Or *surprise!* The world may well be as you think it is, but is this the only version of it or of your own being in the world that you can imagine?

Weber does well to underline that such encounters with inconvenient facts are not only on the side of the students. For both students and teachers, the classroom is a space of as-if, a transitional space (to use Winnicott's terminology) for practicing the messy, inconvenient, but also necessary endeavor of sitting down with difference—perhaps two or three times a week for a semester—and learning that it won't kill us. Such experiences of living with, alongside, and through difference rather than spit polishing it out of view are good practice for the messy work of living agonistic democracy. It is also a vital task of living, not just teaching, criticism.

NOTES

1. Barack Obama, "Remarks by the President to the Hispanic Chamber of Commerce on a Complete and Competitive American Education," 10 March 2009, http://www.whitehouse .gov/the_press_office/Remarks-of-the-President-to-the-United-States-Hispanic-Chamber-of-Commerce/ (accessed 18 June 2011).

2. See, for example, Michael Bérubé, *What's Liberal About the Liberal Arts? Classroom Politics and "Bias" in Higher Education* (New York: Norton, 2007); and Martha C. Nussbaum, *Not for Profit: Why Democracy Needs the Humanities* (Princeton, N.J.: Princeton University Press, 2010).

3. Janet R. Jakobsen and Ann Pellegrini, *Love the Sin: Sexual Regulation and the Limits of Religious Tolerance* (Boston: Beacon, 2004).

4. Max Weber, "Science as a Vocation," in *The Vocation Lectures*, trans. Rodney Livingston, ed. David Owen and Tracy B. Strong (Indianapolis: Hackett, 2004), 22.

21

COERCED CONFESSIONS

BRUCE ROBBINS

I begin with two anecdotes. I would like to think that the genre of the anecdote offers at least a thin layer of protection against the threats of self-importance and self-righteousness. Self-importance and self-righteousness become significant hazards from the moment you even think about answering an invitation to produce a credo. Don't be afraid, go ahead, tell us: how seriously do you take yourself?

First anecdote. About ten years ago I was asked by a well-respected publishing company to consider working on writing a textbook in collaboration with an even better-respected authority in the composition field. The idea was to combine the teaching of writing, which she does, with the teaching of literature, which I do. As I was an admirer of hers and not averse to contemplating the small fortune that might come my way, it was hinted, should the book "take off," I said a tentative yes. At the first meeting, however, I discovered the plan the editors had put together for the textbook. I already knew that our theme was to be "community," and this seemed initially plausible to me as a way of emphasizing the social nature of writing and inducing students to think of writing as learning to enter into a conversation. What I didn't know until I arrived, or perhaps resisted knowing, was that this would entail organizing the readings around the communities that our students were assumed to belong to: the family, the school, the church, and so on, presumably up through the nation. In other words, the literary works that were my responsibility were to be classified according to the presumed primacy for each of a community pertinent to today's students. So *King Lear* would illustrate membership in a family—or was it a state? *Othello* would illustrate belonging to a race—or was it a state again? Or a family? It suddenly struck me—a bit late in the game, given the investments in time and airfare that had gone into this meeting—that this was not only different from any way of looking at literary texts I was used to but was at odds with basic beliefs that until that moment I had not been aware I held. By way of explaining that I really couldn't go forward with this project, I found myself saying, in a hesitant but emotionally charged way, that when I tried to think of literature and community together, I thought of my daughter's experience of watching the first film version of *Frankenstein* at about six or seven years old. She knew that the monster was the bad guy, but when the crowd of outraged villagers arrived with their torches to put an end to him, she burst into tears and cried inconsolably right through the ending. Pretty much the same thing had happened when she saw *King Kong*. In both cases, you might say, community is defined by the expulsion and destruction of a kind of monster. What seemed "literary" about these narratives (though of course they're films) was the impossibility of not identifying with the monster, the impossibility of feeling good about belonging to the community that expelled the monster, the sort of dividedness in her identifications and loyalties that would properly leave even a six- or seven-year-old sobbing in front of the TV.

A second anecdote. I gave my first lecture at Columbia on the twelfth of September, 2001. The events of the previous day were very much on everyone's mind. I asked the class whether they wanted to talk about the attack on the World Trade Center or to try for business as usual. By a very large majority they opted for business as usual. But consulting my own feelings, I found I could not avoid some sort of segue. The text on our syllabus was Tayeb Salih's novel *Season of Migration to the North*. *Season of Migration to the North* reverses Conrad's *Heart of Darkness*: a dark-skinned Arabic-speaking African travels up the Thames to London, and in that northern heart of darkness he commits several unspeakably violent acts against white women, women who end up dead. This came too close to the horror of September 11 to pass unremarked. So I invited the students to imagine a secretary in the firm of Cantor Fitzgerald who was at her desk in the World Trade Center bright and early the day before and who therefore lost her life in a way that we would be tempted to describe as utterly meaningless. By "meaningless" I meant, I said, that the attack that ended her life seemed to have nothing to do with her life—nothing to do with who she was, her history, her personal relationships, her character, with her life in the sense that life is what novels are made of. And then I told the students that one reason for paying attention to the novels we were going to be reading was that this is the challenge they set themselves: to produce something like meaning out of historical materials that, like the planes that attacked the World Trade Center, seem to come from nowhere and thus seem to defy the whole project of novel writing.

This was an unrehearsed and somewhat desperate gambit. The fact that it's what I said on that day doesn't make it true. The fact that it comes close to what I had said five years earlier at the composition textbook meeting doesn't mean that I necessarily believe either one. I offer both statements as potential answers to the question of why I do what I do in part because I didn't really have time to think about them seriously—because they were forced out of me, as a stressed disciplinary subject, by acute pressure from external events, and thus might be seen as expressions of a sort of disciplinary unconscious.

On the evidence of these two moments, I (and perhaps "we") would seem to believe that literature is worth teaching because it offers a distinctive experience of living with ethical and emotional contradiction. (For the 9/11 story, I ask you to imagine for yourselves how even that act of monstrousness could and should elicit some degree of dividedness.) One obvious thing to say about this living-with-contradiction idea is that it's not new. On the contrary, it's a recognizable version of the "romantic imagination," seen as an ability to hold opposing views in focus simultaneously, to resist resolution, to live in uncertainty. For me personally, this credo seems entirely plausible, if not very flattering. It would reveal me as falling back, in a moment of high anxiety, on what I learned in college from the New Critics. But romanticism works a little better for the *Frankenstein*-and-my-daughter anecdote than for the September 12 anecdote. In what I said to my students on September 12, the problem would be the hinted promise of "meaning." If "meaning" suggests that the novels are going to say something commensurate with what the loss of a single life means to the one who loses it or to their loved ones, then it's clearly setting the bar too high. But there's also the old business about poems being rather than meaning. Haven't we learned to say that what's distinctive about literature is *resistance* to anything so crude as meaning? Perhaps it would have been better if I had said the following: Thinking about the secretary at Cantor Fitzgerald, you may well feel that life is meaningless. The novels you are about to read will be more honest with you than the government or the newspapers or the churches. They will show you that you're right. Instead, I seem to have been channeling Matthew Arnold, another figure from my earliest training, who famously saw literature as doing much the same redemptive, meaning-affirming work as religion.

In his book *The Meaning of Life*, Terry Eagleton makes a distinction between two senses of the word "meaningless": 1) that the world is full of "meanings in plenty, but they are specious"; and 2) that life is "unintelligible."[1]

He is ready to grant the first but not the second. This seems right to me, and worth insisting on. What I don't want to say, in other words, is that for the world to be in a state of contradiction is for the world to be unintelligible. Or that the world's resistance to intelligibility can be happily embraced or surrendered to—that we can repose happily in the presence of the ineffable and even feel we've done our duty by showing once and for all that things *are* ineffable. I would like to think that the question "Why teach literature?" can be answered without in the process making a case for religion, or for what is now being called the postsecular condition. This is not obvious. To cultivate paradox, learning to hold two irreconcilable ideas in the mind at the same time, opens a royal road to religion, for (like Cleanth Brooks talking about the paradox of the Incarnation in Donne) it insists on fundamental and irreducible mystery. In this sense, my anecdotal credos can look as if they are saving the literary only by turning it into a life preserver for religious thought. This is something about which I do not feel comfortable. We're in a moment when the old "everything is" formulas—everything is language or discourse or narrative or rhetoric—are in danger of being supplanted by an equation that they will arguably have done much to facilitate: everything is belief, or (worse) everything is faith. This equation, too, is a way of living with emotional and ethical contradiction—living with them so as to *enjoy the insuperability* of the contradictions. Which leaves me to reflect that when I chose "meaning" over "meaninglessness" on September 12, 2001, one thing I hope I was trying to choose was a more secular attitude to contradiction.

What would that be? Among other things, one that could be aligned with Edward Said's notion of "secular criticism." And one that had more room for information. What I was trying to tell the students on September 12 was that providing information was indeed part of what these novels were doing. This information might seem extraneous, but it was information about how we are connected, and it was information that ought to change how they *felt* that connection. If feeling in a state of contradiction is a traditional answer to the question of literature's value, what may be slightly less traditional here is feeling in a state of contradiction that is created by and dependent on seemingly extra or extraneous information, that is informed in part by looking away from what is in front of it. I have written elsewhere about novelistic representations of atrocity which enrich the reader's emotional response precisely by looking away from the atrocity. In a formal embodiment of contradiction, I suggest, the looking away both spares the feelings and at the same time augments them by adding information that doesn't seem to fit.

Information is also a way of reframing one of the most widespread and maybe indispensable answers we have to the "why teach literature" question. According to the National Council of Teachers of English, "Literary response and expression are aesthetic acts involving complex interactions of emotion and intellect. The acts of responding to, interpreting, and creating literary texts enable us to participate in other lives and worlds beyond our own and to reflect on who we are." This may sound a trifle embarrassing—in fact it gets worse—but putting "intellect" there next to "emotion" is a plus, as is "worlds beyond our own." When the NCTE statement goes on to affirm that literature enables students "to discover how literature can capture the richness and complexity of human life," I can't say this statement is incredibly informative. But the point that literature *is* informative needs to be made. I think we find it embarrassing even when it is better made—for example: literature as a vehicle for the preservation, transmission, and interpretation of the experience of people distant from us in space or time. (And, of course, for the self-reflection that contact with such experience encourages.) This position is embarrassing, in part, because it seems to suggest that literature is simply instrumental, merely a vehicle; in part, because it seems to suggest that the experience of others is open to more or less reliable interpretation; in part, no doubt for other reasons. But for an answer to the question "Why teach literature?" to avoid becoming a backhanded case for religion, I think some version of this dry, rational position needs to be articulated. Yes, oh dear yes: literature . . . represents.

At more or less the same time that I was having my misadventure with the textbook publisher, the National Council of Teachers of English was trying to come up with national "standards" for the teaching of English in secondary school. The draft that was initially circulated made no provision at all for teaching literature. It was all critical thinking, ability to understand and use language effectively, and so on. There was an outcry, much of it from people like us, and literature got put back in—literature understood as enabling us "to participate in other lives and worlds beyond our own and to reflect on who we are." The fact that literature only made it in by the skin of its teeth suggests that this case is far from well established in the minds of ordinary practitioners. I'd like to see it better established, in spite of its multiple embarrassments. It would have been good, in September 2001, if more people had been able to remain in a state of emotional irresolution, mourning the dead innocents and at the same time holding the country itself far from blameless and therefore hesitating to seize what the government offered as resolution. Making the acquaintance of the subjectivity of others is good for you, even (or especially) the subjectivity of monsters. Being forced to realize that the monster is like you in some way, is connected to you in other ways, is a useful thing. These are banalities we can't afford to be afraid of. And in the future, a future that is sure to have increasingly sharp confrontations over immigration, that is sure to see anti-Chinese racism recurring on a larger scale as the U.S. faces the unaccustomed experience of losing out, economically, to a rising competitor, it will be good if people are able to think about "aliens" with some of the emotional intelligence that my daughter brought to the film version of *Frankenstein*. It will be a step toward a world that will have fewer monsters.

NOTE

1. Terry Eagleton, *The Meaning of Life: A Very Short Introduction* (Oxford: Oxford University Press), 70–71.

22

ON RACE AND LITERATURE

KENNETH WARREN

I began my career as a scholar at a moment when many of us were buoyed by the belief that it was imperative to align our scholarly practices with our political beliefs and that some of the literature we studied, especially the literature written by black, Latino, and Asian American writers, could contribute significantly to that effort. But I quickly came to see problems with this belief. As I wrote in my first book, *Black and White Strangers: Race and American Literary Realism* (1993), when it came to left politics, "the assumption implicit within much contemporary African-American critical practice—that one's pleasures were necessarily on all fours with one's politics—could not serve as an effective guide."[1] Since then, the prospect that left political ends could be served by attending to the racial dimensions of literary production has not brightened. Rather, as the contours of the neoliberal economic order have grown more salient, it has become clear that the reverse seems more likely. Indeed, Walter Benn Michaels has argued, given that elite college campuses have gotten more racially diverse while poor students of all races find it ever more difficult to compete for admission, "African-American and Asian-American studies are two of the very many ways in which an elite (predominantly white, increasingly Asian, and still only a very little bit black) represents to itself a vision of social justice that has less and less to do with the great social injustice—economic stratification—from which that elite benefits." And with respect to black studies in particular, Adolph Reed Jr. and I have recently observed that the discipline does not "help advance a practical program or critique." Instead, its "hortatory message fails to go beyond hollow calls to combat racism, and, often enough, the burden of its monotonic narrative is to reinforce the notion that no significant political change is possible."[2]

To be sure, these assessments are attuned to the present moment, and any assessment of the politics of literary and intellectual work must be alive to historical change. It is fundamental to literary inquiry to articulate text and context dynamically. Neither can be grasped fully without the other, nor can one be reduced entirely to the other. In addition, one must be aware of contingency because, even as the scholar-critic finishes producing an account of the mutual constitution of text and context, the world that the text sought to apprehend, to critique, and perhaps to resist may have changed in ways that leave the textual gesture—like the wave one gives to an acquaintance who has already rounded the corner—out of sync with the moment. Or maybe the text itself worked upon its context in ways that have altered not only its world but also its own role as a text within that world so that what it had once accomplished, whether with eloquence and grace or insult and outrage, remains beyond its capacity to sustain or repeat.

My early orientation to this problem came through one of those constellations of texts that, both by design and by accident, often forms in the head of a graduate student. One point in this constellation was Wallace Stevens's "The Noble Rider and the Sound of Words," which, in tracing the idea of nobility, placed the poetic project within history's vicissitudes, insisting, on the one hand, that "the imagination loses its vitality as it ceases to adhere to what is real" and, on the other, that at the present moment a "possible poet must be a poet capable of resisting or evading the pressure of reality." Even as Stevens dismisses "the social, that is to say sociological or political obligation of the poet," with the terse declaration, "He has none," he nonetheless argues that the poet's "role, in short, is to help people live their lives." Taking care not to say that the poet's role is to help people change the world—which would sound too much like politics—Stevens does say, in a phrase that has become paradigmatic of his work as poet-critic, "what makes the poet the potent figure that he is, or was, or ought to be, is that he creates the world to which we turn incessantly and without knowing it and that he gives to life the supreme fictions without which we are unable to conceive of it."[3] So if one way to understand poetry's nobility is that it helps create ways of flourishing in an inhospitable world (without necessarily changing that world), another might be that it gives us the fictions that assist us in conceiving of the world differently than we do at present.

The other points in my constellation were provided by Jane Tompkins's *Sensational Designs: The Cultural Work of American Fiction, 1790–1860* (1985) and Philip Fisher's *Hard Facts: Setting and Form in the American Novel* (1986). Rather than focusing on literary texts associated with nobility, they addressed texts that were more likely to be regarded as trite or banal. Recuperating the power of sentimental fiction associated with the likes of Harriet Beecher Stowe, both Tompkins and Fisher helped alert me to the ways that what one could no longer feel, or feel only with embarrassment, may have indicated a certain kind of artistic success rather than artistic failure. A sentimental novel like *Uncle Tom's Cabin* may have done the work of transformation so effectively and thoroughly that what was once "unimaginable becomes, finally, the obvious."[4]

My sense was that much of the literature by nonwhite writers then coming to the fore of critical study wanted to have it both ways, performing social change while retaining a recognizable literary nobility. To illustrate, several years ago I directed (or, more correctly, participated in) an independent study on Asian American literature with Patricia Chu, author of *Race, Nationalism, and the State in British and American Modernism* (2010), who was then a Ph.D. student at the University of Chicago. We read a range of works by Asian American writers, among them Janice Mirikitani's poem "Why Is Preparing Fish a Political Act?" Consisting of five stanzas of varying length, the poem opens with the speaker describing herself as unsuccessfully trying to "capture the flavors" of the Japanese New Year's meal that her grandmother used to make. The poem's next stanza contrasts the grandmother's use of the whole fish—"guts, eggs, head"—with the "immaculately gutted" fish the granddaughter buys in the first stanza, and then focuses on the knife, with rusted "handle screws" and the "pot, dented, / mottled with age" with which the grandmother once prepared the meal.

The granddaughter then focuses on a specific moment of racial condescension that explains why the grandmother continued to use the old knife and dented pot rather than purchase new utensils. The granddaughter tells us:

Someone once tried to sell her
a set of aluminum
pots, smiling too much, called her
mamasan.[5]

The grandmother responds to the salesperson's condescension with a silence that expresses both her refusal to give up her old pot and knife and her repudiation of the stereotypical disparagement of Japanese women. The old pot and knife are tokens not of poverty but of cultural resistance.

Among the many things one might say about this poem is that while the grandmother is reticent (even if eloquent in her reticence), the poem is comparatively voluble, spelling out its key points. For example, not only does the second stanza tell us that the grandmother "saved each part" of the fish for cooking, but the final line repeats the point with the two-word sentence "Nothing wasted." Similarly, the poem elaborates the grandmother's silence with series of comparisons with the meal she prepares. Her silence is "thicker than / steaming shoyu, / whiter than sliced bamboo root / boiled with fish heads." And, lest we miss her point, the speaker concludes the poem by re-phrasing the title's question as a declarative sentence: "Preparing fish / is a political act."

While one might be tempted to view the poem's explicitness as an aes-thetic mistake (after all, doesn't the grandmother's silent refusal to buy the new pots speak for itself?), it might be more accurate to see Mirikitani's de-clarative sentences as an aesthetic choice consistent with what the poem is attempting to do. The poem was written at a moment when many Asian American women writers were insisting on the importance of challenging their stereotypical depiction as silent, mysterious, and indirect. Indeed, the title of Mirikitani's 1987 volume of poetry is *Shedding Silence*, and "Why Is Preparing Fish a Political Act?" not only attempts to make the grandmother's silent behavior legible as political speech but also illustrates the granddaugh-ter's refusal to countenance the expectation of either silence or indirectness. The poem speaks straightforwardly.

Yet if the poem's explicitness is not a mistake, the poem's title may include an error. (As I recall it, that formed the center of the discussion Pat and I had about it.) What the poem demonstrates is not exactly *why* preparing fish is a political act but rather *when*, or the conditions under which, an individu-al's preparation of a meal become politically expressive. In highlighting the scene in which the presumably white salesperson addresses the grandmother as *"mamasan,"* the poem locates the instant when the dented pot and rust-handled knife became politically significant. Before that moment their value may have been simply personal or purely utilitarian. In fact, it seems that the grandmother may have even wanted to buy new pots and knives. But as the recollection unfolds in the poem, it is only in response to the expression of bigotry that the grandmother's ritual preparation of the *oshogatsu* meal and the utensils she used become luminous with political meaning. To be per-fectly accurate, the poem's final declaration ought not to be "Preparing fish /

is a political act" but perhaps something like, "Under the right circumstances preparing fish / is sometimes politically expressive"—which is admittedly less forceful and resonant.

Beyond its representation of the grandmother's act, the poem suggests two further questions: "Why Is Writing a Poem About My Grandmother Preparing Fish a Political Act?" and "Why Is or Is Not Critiquing a Poem About the Politics of a Woman's Grandmother Preparing Fish Also a Political Act?" I noted that Mirikitani's substitution of "act" for "expression" might be an error, but, rather than seeing it as a moment of confusion or carelessness, it may be more helpful to understand Mirikitani's goal as identifying expression with action, a reading that becomes clearer when we consider the poem's context. "Why Is Preparing Fish a Political Act?" and *Shedding Silence* as a whole were framed in part by the hearings of the Commission on Wartime Relocation and Internment of Japanese American Civilians in 1981. Japanese American citizens who had been interned and had property confiscated during the Second World War were able to give testimony about the personal costs and humiliations they suffered at the hands of the United States government. Another poem in Mirikatani's collection, "Breaking Silence," is dedicated to her mother and composed of excerpts from testimony her mother gave to the commission. The testimony of surviving internees helped move the commission to issue a report to Congress recommending apologies to and reparations for those Japanese citizens who had been unlawfully detained. The report paved the way for the passage in 1988 of the Civil Liberties Act of 1987, which acknowledged the injustice done to Japanese citizens as a result "of racial prejudice, wartime hysteria, and a failure of political leadership."[6] That the passage of the Civil Liberties Act and the publication of *Shedding Silence* were roughly coincident helps Mirikatani make her point about a politics in which expression and act are also coincident.

This convergence also helps bring into view the terms through which such a politics could succeed. These poems emerged within a Civil Rights and post–Civil Rights era framework in which various groups and constituencies could put forward claims for recognition and redress by demonstrating that prejudice and discrimination had denied them the rights otherwise due to them as citizens and, in the case of the Commission on Wartime Relocation, property owners. The testimony of Mirikitani's mother in "Breaking Silence" recounts the loss of property suffered by internees:

the U.S. Army Signal Corps confiscated
our property . . . it was subjected to

vandalism and ravage. All improvements
we had made before our incarceration
were stolen or destroyed.

The mother's testimony then makes it clear that the incarceration of Japanese
citizens was an act of discrimination:

it seems we were singled out
from others who were under suspicion.
Our neighbors were of German and
Italian descent, some of whom were
not citizens. . . . It seems we were
singled out.[7]

To the extent that the coherence of the nation's social order was perceived
as depending on subordinating some citizens to others on the basis of racial
identity and then silencing and discrediting them, a politics of testimony
and speaking out could mount a fundamental challenge to that order. But
if the stability of that social order rests on the right to accumulate property
and wealth, the testimony given by Japanese internees could hardly count as
a fundamental challenge. In calling for redress of the obvious wrongs per-
petrated against Japanese Americans, its function would instead be that of
ratifying the existing order. Mirikatani's poem emerges, then, in a context in
which racism rather than a differential accumulation of private property and
wealth is understood as the fundamental injustice. "Why Is Preparing Fish
a Political Act?" makes us see the problem of inequality in terms of racial
discrimination rather than in terms of economic inequality.

To make this observation is not to suggest that Mirikatani's poems should
have taken up something other than what they do. The signal achievement of
work like Mirikatani's is that it manages to convey the urgency of a politics of
antidiscrimination while remaining a work of serious literature. Even as racism plays an ever-diminishing role in determining the life prospects for the
nation's Asian American citizens, the poem manages to keep alive the moment when it did so. The poem does not—or not yet—strike us as trite, even
though its central claim that the incarceration of Japanese citizens during
World War II was unjust is no longer controversial. As readers, we don't have
to work very hard to apprehend the dignity of Mirikatani's mother or grandmother as they respond to insult and injustice. But it is important to see that
the aesthetic achievement of these poems depends on depicting antiracism

rather than wealth inequities. That is not to say that these works are unworthy of study; it is, however, to say that we must be more circumspect and accurate about what this work can and can't tell us about our political situation.

NOTES

1. Kenneth W. Warren, *Black and White Strangers: Race and American Literary Realism* (Chicago: University of Chicago Press, 1993), 141.

2. Walter Benn Michaels, "Why Identity Politics Distracts Us from Economic Inequalities," *Chronicle Review* 53 (15 December 2006): B10; Adolph Reed Jr. and Kenneth W. Warren, *Renewing Black Intellectual History* (Boulder, Colo.: Paradigm, 2009), ix.

3. Wallace Stevens, "The Nobel Writer and the Sound of Words," in *Critical Theory Since Plato*, ed. Hazard Adams (New York: Harcourt, Brace, Jovanovich, 1971), 976.

4. Philip Fisher, *Hard Facts: Setting and Form in the American Novel* (New York: Oxford University Press, 1986), 8.

5. Janice Mirikatani, *Shedding Silence* (Berkeley, Calif.: Celestial Arts, 1987), 123.

6. Civil Liberties Act of 1988, "Restitution for World War II Internment of Japanese-Americans and Aleuts," 50 App. USCA s 1989, 50 App. USCA s 1989; *Personal Justice Denied: Report of the Commission on Wartime Relocation and Internment of Japanese American Civilians*, http://www.archives.gov/research/Japanese-americans/justice-denied/.

7. Mirikatani, *Shedding Silence*, 33.

23 |
TEACHING THEORY

DIANA FUSS

When I was a graduate student in the humanities at Brown in the heady theory decade of the 1980s, it seemed as if all the men were studying Marxism and all the women were studying psychoanalysis. There were a few border-crossers here and there in the graduate program, and quite often the Marxist theorists and the Lacanian theorists coalesced around deconstruction, but, for the most part, the men were in steady search of the real and the women were in hot pursuit of fantasy. While my male compatriots investigated material conditions, my female colleagues and I explored psychical emotions. The battle lines were drawn: hard and soft, economic and affective, public and private. Looking back, I find these highly gendered binaries surprising, especially in light of virtually everyone's shared interest in feminist theory, one of the great attractions and strengths of the Brown Ph.D. program, staffed at the time with some of the smartest gender scholars in the academy (Mary Ann Doane, Ann Fausto-Sterling, Ellen Rooney, Naomi Schor, Kaja Silverman, Elizabeth Weed . . .). And yet still we found ourselves splintering off into predictable byways, caught up in artificial theory debates largely of our own making: Foucault vs. Freud, Habermas vs. Irigaray, Marx vs. Derrida. Where our theoretical resistances found common ground was on the point of resistance itself: if you were not resisting something, we believed, then you were not theorizing. Theory *is* resistance.

Over twenty years later, the ghost of Paul de Man continues to haunt me still. For years his remarkable essay on "The Resistance to Theory" was my credo. De Man's great insight was to see that the resistance to theory is not something outside the act of theorizing but inside it. Resistance, he insisted, is intrinsic to the theoretical enterprise itself. Theory works as a practice that raises questions about itself, and resistance operates as nothing less than its built-in precondition. Can the resistance to theory ever be overcome? For de Man, the answer is no: "Nothing can overcome the resistance to theory since theory is itself this resistance."[1]

De Man's foundational essay is a tour-de-force piece of logic, a way to claim for theory the power of resistance while overcoming all our own. For a long time the paradox of this masterful definition of theory escaped me; only when I began to teach did I discover that the best way to lessen students' immediate opposition to theory was to show how their concerns were themselves resolutely theoretical. Ironically, de Man became useful as a strategy to mitigate student resistances rather than to cultivate them. De Man's "The Resistance to Theory" became the most effective weapon in my own theoretical arsenal for resisting the students' resistances.

There is no question that de Man was onto something. The best I have read, taught, and perhaps even written over the years is theory unafraid to resist itself, to challenge its own assumptions. Yet my thoughts on *how* to theorize have changed dramatically since I became a professor, largely because of my experience teaching theory to undergraduate and graduate students. I no longer think that resistance exhausts all the many possibilities and practices of theory. If I have a new theory of theory, it is far less resistance and much more persistence. My new credo, forged in the crucible of the classroom, sees invention where I once saw only subversion. It embraces theorization over theory, an intellectual labor that goes beyond uncovering and resisting dangerous old ideas in favor of venturing and testing responsible new ones.

Even today, the reigning approach to theory tends to privilege resistance and a host of related concepts, chief among them refusal, subversion, reversal, and displacement. For me these strategies of reading, writing, and debating remain useful, but they are just one set of practices I rely on in the classroom for teaching students how to theorize. At the end of the teaching day, the pursuit of resistance, when practiced in isolation, is too agonistic to produce lasting theoretical contributions, let alone productive classroom discussions. Speaking only "the language of self-resistance" (30), as de Man puts it, sets students in continual opposition to themselves and to each other, often blocking the opportunity to build on the strengths of their own best insights. While resistance makes good politics, it does not always make effective pedagogy. Good teaching involves fluency with a range of techniques, including elaboration, evaluation, clarification, amplification, explication, imagination, and collaboration. My own best experiences in the classroom have come when a class has collectively worked through resistance to reach the point of inventing something unusual, unexpected, or even uncanny. To be sure, resistance and invention comprise their own specious binary, for in truth each presupposes and relies on the other in order to do its work well. Yet resistance that stops short of invention, that settles for merely saying "No," is a theory devoid of action, a safe mode of theorizing that risks nothing because it resists everything. Every theory classroom needs eventually to make the critical and momentous shift from talking about theory to finally doing it; only then, in my experience, does theory really begin to happen.

Given the influential role Paul de Man has played over the past quarter century in shaping literary scholarship, it is easy to forget that his signature essay on "The Resistance to Theory," which first appeared in a 1982 volume of *Yale French Studies*, was originally intended for a volume on teaching.[2] Commissioned by the MLA for inclusion in a book called *Introduction to Scholarship in Modern Languages and Literatures*, de Man's assigned task was to provide, for an audience of literature and language teachers, both a definition of theory and a discussion of its implications for pedagogy. Since for de Man the "main theoretical interest of literary theory consists in the impossibility of its definition" (3), the assignment to produce a teachable definition of theory was doomed from the start. Summarily jettisoned from the volume, "The Resistance to Theory" quickly became its own compelling demonstration of the power of theory to challenge the academy's reigning orthodoxies on literature and language instruction.

None of this is to say that de Man was uninterested or uninvested in the practice of teaching. On the contrary, the entire book that emerges out of de Man's classic essay, also entitled *The Resistance to Theory*, offers a thoughtful and sustained meditation on the difficulty of teaching and the teaching of difficulty. Reading this energetic collection of essays more than two decades later, what now strikes me most forcefully is not what de Man says about theory but what he says about teaching, and indeed about the relation between theory and teaching. Whenever the question of pedagogy arises, which it does frequently, de Man waxes aphoristic. Consider these words of scholastic wisdom, culled from a single paragraph of the book's title essay:

- the only teaching worthy of the name is scholarly, not personal
- scholarship has, in principle, to be eminently teachable
- as a controlled reflection on the formation of method, theory rightly proves to be entirely compatible with teaching

- a method that cannot be made to suit the "truth" of its object can only teach delusion
- it is better to fail in teaching what should not be taught than to succeed in teaching what is not true

(4)

All five of these pronouncements are claims as contestable as they are quotable. (Is there really no place for the personal in teaching? Must all scholarship be teachable? Is theory always compatible with teaching? Do methods not suited to their object only teach delusion? And isn't teaching what is not true one of the things that should not be taught?) I am less concerned here with refuting de Man point by point than with highlighting the invitation that these aphorisms extend to do precisely that, to become the kind of resisting theorist de Man himself exemplifies. De Man's very predilection for argument by aphorism—with all this genre's air of unquestioned authority and claim to certain knowledge—cannot help but to bring out the resisting reader in me. De Man the aphorist is de Man the gadfly, goading his readers to further acts of theorization, challenging us to resist his own teachings on resistance.

But resistance is not an end or termination in itself, it is simply a place where the process of theorization starts. "The attempt to treat literature theoretically may as well resign itself to the fact that it has to start out from empirical considerations" (5). Over and over again in *The Resistance to Theory* de Man tells us that to be good theorists we must first be good empiricists, committed pragmatists. What de Man the theoretician values above all turns out to be the practical, which is to say, the pedagogical. For de Man, theory begins in practice—not just any kind of practice but a very particular kind of practice: the exercise of close reading.

In the most surprising section of a book that insists that the only teaching worthy of the name is scholarly and not personal, de Man suddenly shifts, in his essay on "The Return to Philology," from the worldly aphorism to the personal anecdote. Recalling the late Reuben Brower, author of the 1951 New Critical classic *Fields of Light: An Experiment in Critical Reading* and teacher of a popular general education course at Harvard called "The Interpretation of Literature" (Humanities 6), de Man pays tribute to a teacher who knew nothing about "high-powered French theory" but everything about the pragmatics of excellent pedagogy:

> Students, as they began to write on the writings of others, were not to say anything that was not derived from the text they were considering. They were

not to make any statements that they could not support by a specific use of language that actually occurred in the text. They were asked, in other words, to begin by reading texts closely as texts and not to move at once into the general context of human experience or history. Much more humbly or modestly, they were to start out from the bafflement that such singular turns of tone, phrase, and figure were bound to produce in readers attentive enough to notice them and honest enough not to hide their non-understanding behind the screen of received ideas that often passes, in literary instruction, for humanistic knowledge.

(23)

For a new teacher just learning the ropes, this simple rule of close reading—call it "Brower's Rule"—was electrifying. "I have never known a course by which students were so transformed," de Man writes in admiration; "henceforth, they would never be the same." Here, de Man suggests, was a course utterly devoid of theoretical pretensions, yet more successful in subverting and transforming critical discourse than any self-proclaimed theory class. The point is clear: the best theory is not always practiced by theorists. For de Man, the proof is in the pedagogy:

> Reuben Brower had a rare talent, not out of respect for the delicacy of language, for keeping things as tidy as a philosophical investigation ought to be yet, at the same time, entirely pragmatic. Mere reading, it turns out, prior to any theory, is able to transform critical discourse in a manner that would appear deeply subversive to those who think of the teaching of literature as a substitute for the teaching of theology, ethics, psychology, or intellectual history. Close reading accomplishes this often in spite of itself because it cannot fail to respond to structures of language which it is the more or less secret aim of literary teaching to keep hidden.

(24)

Because the practice of close reading cannot help but to respond to the figurative play of language, it also cannot help but to be theoretical. For de Man, the turn to theory was a turn away from theology and back to philology, and the turn against theory was a refusal of the power of rhetoric, at the very moment rhetoric was "being used and refined as never before" (25). Thus, to teach the pragmatics of close rhetorical reading through a strategy like "Brower's Rule" is to teach students to be theoretical, without "the conceptual and terminological apparatus" that, de Man admits, can sometimes interfere with the empirical demands of teaching.[3]

What de Man seeks vividly to demonstrate with this affectionate tribute to his former teaching mentor is not merely how the seemingly least theoretical of pedagogues can in fact be the most theoretical, but also how terminology is less crucial to the practice of theory than methodology. De Man's own thoughts on teaching methodology were quite specific, an outgrowth of his conviction that theory can only be accessed through a careful study of language and figuration: "literature, instead of being taught only as a historical and humanistic subject, should be taught as a rhetoric and a poetics prior to being taught as a hermeneutics and a history" (25–26). De Man went to his death thinking that the teaching of literature as rhetoric or poetics could never be successfully institutionalized, for such a radical change would require a fundamental shift in the practice of teaching away from standards of cultural excellence "always based on some form of religious faith" and towards a more subversive "principle of disbelief" (26). And yet this is exactly what has happened since *The Resistance to Theory* first appeared in book form in 1986. College teachers of literature, some in fact trained by de Man, have introduced courses, curricula, and even programs devoted to the teaching of rhetoric. While I myself am wary of the near pure distillation of language assumed by an exercise like "Brower's Rule" (which, like the New Criticism that inspired it, tends to isolate the literary text from the cultural, historical, and political contexts that produced it), it is certainly the case that the attention to figuration de Man so passionately espoused is now no less a common pedagogical practice than the historicism and hermeneutics it was meant to challenge. De Man's "principle of disbelief" has become its own kind of faith, though de Man himself professed to have lost faith in a profession he believed was fundamentally incapable of serious institutional reform.

So what is theory to me now, and what do I think I am doing when I teach theory? Theory is practicing self-consciousness about how I think. And teaching theory is showing students how to be self-conscious about their own thinking. There is a difference between self-resistance and self-consciousness, a distinction we may have lost sight of over the years. To assume that self-consciousness is always a form of self-resistance is also to assume that the self is an errant, guilty, or correctable self—the very kind of Puritan or theological subject that de Man rightly and repeatedly warns teachers to avoid falsely embodying and mimetically reproducing in their students. If de Man had any particular cautionary example in mind here it was surely Austin Warren, whose vision of the pedagogue as pastor powerfully shaped the New Critical understanding of "The Teacher as a Critic," the title of Warren's contribution to the original "My Credo" symposium in *The Kenyon Review*.[4]

By critical and pedagogical self-consciousness I mean an approach to thinking about thinking that takes the *how* as seriously as the *what*. Good theorizing, like good teaching, attends not just to content but to process. The most important element of responsible theorizing is also the most crucial element of successful teaching: attending not just to arguments but also to methods of argumentation, not just to posing answers but also to framing questions. If I have learned one thing in my years of teaching theory, it is that students learn best when they are answering their own questions.[5] In a theory classroom, the trick to getting students to theorize lies in creating exercises that allow them to generate their own problems of study, and ideally a set of terms and methods for tackling them. This means approaching theory more inductively than deductively, starting with the problems and examples that are meaningful to the students and bringing in more explicitly theoretical work as needed along the way.

Let me pose an example. My favorite teaching assignment to date, selected from a range of different theory courses I have taught, is an exercise popular in feminist classrooms, and with good reason. Easily adaptable to the teaching of race and class as well, the "gender diary" was the perfect starter exercise for a semester's worth of theorizing on gender and sexuality. In a class so cross-disciplinary that no two students seemed to share the same critical vocabulary, I decided to begin the seminar by asking students, for their first assignment, to designate a single twenty-four hour period in which they would keep a gender diary. Students were required to carry a notebook with them at all times, and to keep a careful record of every act that they believe engendered them. I suggested that, eventually, we might think together about how, when, where, and why they were performing gender or others were assigning gender to them. But for now we would embark on a more pragmatic fact-finding mission, simply observing and recording the play of gender in our daily lives.

This single exercise—more "personal" than "scholarly" de Man would no doubt argue—yielded more theoretical insights more rapidly than any other pedagogical activity that I can recall. When we reconvened to discuss the gender diaries (I did not read them but rather invited students to volunteer their favorite entries) the results were fantastic. In keeping their hourly logs, some students questioned if they could ever escape their gender while other students wondered if they would ever find theirs. Some felt that gender explained almost everything about them while others thought it explained almost nothing. Some found themselves asking what or where gender is exactly, while others found it all too recognizable and ubiquitous. The one thing everyone agreed on was that keeping a gender diary was far more exhausting than anticipated. Learning to become self-conscious about how gender operates moment to moment was fun but fatiguing, an insight that further led the class to ask whether it was even possible to be a gender 24/7. I could have simply assigned, say, an essay by Judith Butler to suggest that one cannot be a man or a woman all day long, but offering the class an incentive to formulate questions of relevance to them immediately transformed the students from spectators patiently watching other people theorize to participants actively theorizing on their own. We did eventually cover selected readings by Butler, at which point her questions about gender performativity met with more head nodding than head scratching. Exercises like these are so galvanizing for students, I think, because the hard-earned moments of insight belong to them. Such collaborative group thinking creates a forum for theory in action, an environment in which students' interactive and inventive theorizing constitutes its own best form of teaching.

Putting theory to work, inciting students to theorize, doing theory rather than just talking about it—this is my own credo for "teaching theory" in the twenty-first century. In the end, the title I have chosen for this essay is nothing if not tautological, referring not just to the teaching of theory but also to the teaching that is theory. If theory is to teach us, and not just resist us, one can do no better than to experiment with a pedagogy that practices what it preaches, offering students the opportunity to be every bit the theorist Paul de Man once witnessed, and himself soon became, in the classroom of a committed teacher.

NOTES

1. Paul de Man, *The Resistance to Theory* (Minneapolis: University of Minnesota Press, 1986), 19.

2. "The Resistance to Theory" became the lead essay in the journal's special issue, "The Pedagogical Imperative: Teaching as a Literary Genre," and was situated in the opening section on "The Lesson of Teaching." See *Yale French Studies* 63 (1982): 3–20.

3. Not everyone saw Reuben Brower as the inspiring and transformational teacher de Man remembers; another graduate teaching assistant for Humanities 6, William H. Pritchard, provides a less flattering description of Brower's pedagogical methods. Whereas de Man

focuses exclusively on Brower's rigorous and rewarding writing assignments, Pritchard also discusses his lackluster and disorganized lecturing style. Interestingly, de Man himself appears to have been the best teacher in Humanities 6, his four lectures on Yeats so original and powerful, Pritchard writes, that they were met at the end with spontaneous student applause (Pritchard, "Hum 6. and Reuben Brower," in *English Papers: A Teaching Life* [Saint Paul, Minn.: Graywolf Press, 1995]). Geoffrey Hartman further notes that de Man, in the tribute to his New Critical teacher, composes a "little family romance" in which he "forgets to mention, for example, that Reuben Brower still believed there was a 'key' that would emerge from all textual bafflement to unlock a particular literary work" ("Looking Back on Paul de Man," in *Reading de Man Reading*, ed. Lindsay Waters and Wlad Godzich [Minneapolis: University of Minnesota Press, 1989], 12). Famously resistant to psychoanalysis, de Man never questions his own idealizations of his former teacher in "Resistance to Theory," an essay Laurence A. Rickels later retitles "Resistance in Theory," precisely in order to lay bare the transferences between student teacher and master teacher that de Man himself entirely forecloses (Rickels, "Resistance in Theory," in *Material Events: Paul de Man and the Afterlife of Theory*, ed. Tom Cohen et al. [Minneapolis: University of Minnesota Press, 2001]). Finally, Elaine Showalter, citing Pritchard, identifies a clear discrepancy between Brower's exacting literary practice and his much looser teaching style in her *Teaching Literature* (Oxford: Blackwell, 2003).

4. Intellectually reared by "theologians and philosophers of religion," Warren saw the teacher's role to be not so much the priestly transmission of the past as the priestly prophecy of the future. His "devotion" to close reading in the classroom Warren understands variously as an expression of mystic vocation and a form of pastoral care ("The Teacher as Critic," *The Kenyon Review* 13, no. 2 [Spring 1951]: 230).

5. Currently the best pedagogy book I know, Ken Bain's *What the Best College Teachers Do* (Cambridge, Mass.: Harvard University Press, 2004), is based on a similar premise: "people learn best when they ask an important question that they care about answering, or adopt a goal that they want to reach" (31). Interestingly, Austin Warren also embraces the self-questioning mode in his early "catechism" of teaching when he writes that "the best criticism is the critic asking himself questions he finds hard to answer, and giving the most honest (even if tentative or uncertain or negative) answers he can" ("The Teacher as Critic," 228). It is worth noting, however, that in Warren's "The Teacher as Critic" the person posing the questions and answering them is always the teacher, never the student.

24 |
AFFECT IS THE NEW TRAUMA

LAUREN BERLANT

Here's a tale about a time an accident led to an incident that is still shaping up as an event. Once I was at a conference. The conference was on feelings—on how the dynamics of their circulation shape the normative and potential workings of institutions, aesthetics, politics, historical imaginaries, and ordinary practices of sociality.[1] People had a lot of feelings at the conference, too: boredom, nostalgia, engagement, admiration, anxiety, criticality (friendly), criticality (hostile), criticality (confused)—the usual. But it was a good thing; people came to listen hard, to think aloud, and to be curious. They stuck around, they acted like colleagues.

Another feeling they were having, though, was fear, but not the usual kind—of doing bad work or being useless. This fear was that other people, not at the conference, would think that we were being trendy by focusing on affect and emotion. What haunted the instigator of this anxious thread was the phrase "the affective turn." The instigator of this thread feared being seen as ambitiously having had the bad taste of being attracted to a glittering object or worse, a knock-off of a cutting edge. The fear was that we would all seem to have a shallow aspirational relation to knowledge, to be imitators and followers of the original pioneers who did all the real thinking.

My colleague's angst brought back to me a previous encounter with a bitchy colleague's dart-bearing phrase: "affect is the new trauma." This meant that one scholarly trend was replacing another. As I work on both things I felt immediately like a paper doll in a string of identical cutouts. But only for a moment. Apparently, I'd worn my ego armor that day. The logic of the critical pecking order is that, if we seem to be in one, we are both borrowing its authorizing glory and, at the same time, appearing diminished relative to the glory we have borrowed to inflate ourselves. In academia, reputation is gossip about who had the ideas. But this time, fearing to embody wannabe intellectual belatedness, my colleague wanted us to assert our originality and priority.

This circuit of anxiety about professional value irritated me, made me sad, and undid my composure a bit. I responded in a tone that mixed consolation and flippancy. I said something like, "Look, we're professionals here. Other people's desire to diminish your motives for pursuing your work, which relies on knowing nothing about you and paying no attention to what you're actually saying, can't seriously affect how you proceed intellectually or pedagogically, can it? No doubt you've been working on feelings since you were a fetus, but must we justify our work by making self-inflating arguments about longevity, ownership, and origins? The important thing is where we push the thought and what we make with it, isn't it?"

I had always thought the point was that we do our work collaboratively, in discussion and across publics; that we are always in the process of playing catch-up with what we've read, heard, and discovered ourselves saying; and that the context of professionalism provides important breathing space, at least for those of us who have jobs where we are licensed to gather it all up to test and take the ideas beyond what's predictable. We get to slow down around the objects/questions; we get to gather things up recursively and track their impact; meanwhile we find ways to hold at bay whatever kinds of anxiety or envy arise from taking the risk of having ideas in front of each other. Making work is always anxiogenic. And the conference, merging activists, artists, and critics in the hope that thinking affect and emotion in different registers, idioms, and media might open up new potentialities and scenes of convergence, demanded a lot of patient cross talk, for which there was voluminous time scheduled and yet never enough time. The scene was shaped by anxious desires to relate things and to create a discourse world through their circulation that could have effects elsewhere, and on ourselves. To achieve that at any time we need to hone the skills to diminish our anxiety enough to show up, talk, and listen: and above all to counter intellectual foreclosure at the hands of other people's tacit reductive and shaming derision of our intellectual appetites.

The conference then turned on me, in a way. The next four hours included a barrage of mainly passive-aggressive snarky side comments about the wrong-headedness of identifying with professionalism. People with tenure, on the way to it, or otherwise highly trained, claimed that they had an amateur relation to knowledge, a nonauthoritarian relation to expertise, or (because not everyone made the same argument) by virtue of their subaltern/biopolitical location, did not enjoy the entitlements of the profession, always pushing it radically from occulted folds within it. For a long while I remained quiet, because something good was happening, a discussion of the affective dimensions of having jobs and/or making worlds for the work and the teaching that we hope will matter. That most of this talk was in the genre of the aside said a lot about how disrupted by ambivalence engaged thinkers can become in reflecting on the very circuits of value creation that bring us to each other and to the variety of things we call "our work."

But toward the end of the second day, I thought it was worth responding. I disputed any claim by the tenured people that they are not entitled by their professional position; said that for highly trained people to call themselves amateurs was a wishful defense against facing the complex effects of ambition, institutional location, the desire for distinction, the history of self-cultivation and having been taught; and the normative force of pedagogy. I disputed the presumption that progressive political commitments just naturally valorize vocational practices as more authentic, anti-bureaucratic, anti-elitist, etc.; and claimed that the ways we benefit from the value distinctions between mental and manual labor constitute privileges we cannot neutralize by the other complexities of our historical trajectories. The academy is not the only location many of us occupy, and we all straddle a variety of zones of relative vulnerability and security. But this does not mean that we are not also advantaged by the situations that academic life allows its workers.

It made me anxious to say this, as so much obfuscation and incoherence shapes the ordinary disposition of promotion and informal career policing in academic life that it boggles my mind on a weekly basis; and because for those of us not securely embedded in academic life, the aspiration to be able to make worlds through work requires complex negotiations of loyalty, solidarity, distinction, aspirational insiderness, and sheer time. But the fact is that academic professionals are permitted slower productivity than most other workers. We are also, to a point, allowed to experiment and fail, to be wrong and revise, to get distracted, to not know what we're doing while we're doing it, to stop in the middle, and to follow out instincts and hunches, not just building on established foundations. We are allowed to demand patience for the obscure, the experimental, the political, and the pedantic. Not all of us at all times. Not without cost. Sometimes the risks do not succeed. Like all other labor, critical cultural production in and outside of the academy is becoming increasingly proletarianized and unstable, as well as exposed to new initiatives for "quality control" and transparent utility. And who knows what standards are being brought to evaluate our work and our thought? At the same time, it is important to appreciate, how a wide range of practices is denoted by the category "good work."

In any case, I said something like this: "Here's what I meant by professional. I did not mean normative according to the formal and imaginary meritocracy of any discipline, university, or particular intellectual cohort. I did not mean 'contributing to the "conversation"' of one's mainstream discipline, artworld, or activist world. By professional I mean pedagogical. It's our job to show up and think, to show up and think with others, to collaborate using what we know and what we don't know to push concepts beyond where they were when we entered the room. I mean all of us, whoever's in the room, nudging each other towards more and less clarity about the problems that engage us, and thereby changing the contours of the problems, and praxis, too. I mean slowing down enough to take in an idea and imagine the change that would come from it. Doing this, focusing on building chops for thought, discussion, debate, expressivity, critique, and becoming different, regardless of how we feel at the moment, regardless of the noise of ambition that creates our own and our colleagues' nervous conditions, is the practice of professional obligation to which I was alluding. To be 'a professional' had never been an aspiration of mine—quite the contrary. I'd begun to think about it because I had so many students presume that to work together had a private, intimate component separate from its institutional mediation, and that seemed wrong. Then, I saw so many of us presume that if *we* were managing and producing distinction we must be doing it in the right, anti-authoritarian, anti-bureaucratic, barely compromised way, and that seemed wrong. The narcissism of good intentions leads to serious self-misrecognition. As for amateurism, we are always working beyond our expertise and our training, *but this is our job.*"

Things got more difficult later. A panel on pedagogy, affect, and emotion turned into a long and serious debate about whether professorial anti-authoritarian avant-gardism contributed to or blocked the empowerment or disempowerment of students. The debate was open, honest, cracking, and sharp: lots of incompatible desires and foci for political analysis of institutional politics in and outside of classrooms were on the table. The word "useful" was uttered in acid tones, although not by everyone. But no students would talk. Many private e-mail exchanges happened later, but it seemed as though so much desire of the teacher was in the room, so much intensity of need not to be reproducing the deadening, corporate norms of expertise, utility, excellence, and sublimated creativity of the neoliberal university and the class distinctions and discriminations it foments, that it crowded many topics and certain interlocutors out.

No one wants to be a bad or compromised kind of force in the world, but the latter is just inevitable. The question is how to develop ways to interrupt their banality and to move them somewhere. Yet the stories that we so often tell about professionalism—it's what unimaginative people aspire to, it's what *the ambitious* aspire to as they game the system, it's a pedantic rank-based bureaucratic formalism defined against (our) genuine conceptual richness—bar serious talk about the ethics of collegiality and pedagogy under conditions of aspiration. This blockage undermines how we inhabit the very scenes in which we've invested our fantasies of flourishing at work, in collective worlds, with each other and our students, for those of us who teach. The oft unspoken enormity of the desire to sustain (ourselves in) these scenes is why it is so easy to be deflated, for example, when colleagues condescend to us for want of intellectual discrimination.

I think often about this conference episode. I don't usually make credo-style speeches, nor pitch my practice at a level of generality that's supposed to model a way of being for colleagues. I am well aware that I drag my own personality and history to the classroom, the conference, the committee, the editorial meeting, the working group, the panel, the roundtable, the solo talk, and the encounters around them, and while I try to generate practices that enable me to be reliable, focused, fun, and improvisatory, it's an ongoing project, as you can imagine. But developing an explicit pedagogical/collegial ethics (e.g., professionalism) to which I can aspire has helped me and my students fight the academic's tendency to personalize everything, including responsibility.

I know why the lure (the mirage, the alibi) of the amateur works for anti-authoritarian intellectuals and for people who try to maintain a foothold in modes of knowledge (activist, aesthetic, scholarly) that feel made up, processual, and more lateral than upwardly mobile. Amateurism is also a way of de-dramatizing the risk of having ideas in public, and points to a position that critiques self-authorizing claims of credentialed expertise and the tedium of reproducing disciplinary norms. It allows the creative type to mix things up.

But the claim also disavows many things. It suppresses the amount of training that can go into the ways that one interferes with normativity. It cloaks the relation of power and privilege to the less institutionally, socially, and economically secure people with whom progressives have solidarity—including students. Even my own desire not to be disabled by the tensions between politically engaged pedagogy and credentializing norms both manifests a liberal attachment to teaching as ideally a scene of unimpeded thought by universal subjects *and* solidarity with the contemporary work of autonomous universities where people join to gather up their singular knowledge and ignorance to create new social and conceptual imaginaries and practices.[2] I try not to become destroyed by the clash of fantasies. But living amidst the uneven rhythms and nonidentity of institutional, broadly social, and always affective norms, fantasies, and economies demands a professionalism that enables us to recognize what's impersonal, what's systemic, and what's mediated about both our anxieties and the openings we are trying to create.

Let us look at the historical present, manifestly organized by the rhetoric of crisis. We need to reinvent what it means to do engaged, solidaristic work for the current crisis, the spreading precarities, and the insecuritization of all labor contexts. What world are we teaching people for, reaching toward, trying to describe or make?[3] What is the relation between the fantasy of knowledge as a good in itself and pedagogy as a project of collective skill building, a mobile utility that can have concrete effects elsewhere? Do the norms of engaged pedagogy change in the face of a world where labor is protected by fewer and fewer safeguards, let alone guarantees? What's the relation among models of inequality, uncertainty, and survival? What world is required for pedagogical optimism? How does a pedagogy of the historical present provide ways for neither taking its appearance for granted nor as a mirage? Is it possible to make arguments for liberal education that are better than the Arnoldian ones of cultivated citizenship that we are hearing dusted off recently? What would it mean to claim the importance of *nonvocational* education to the well-being of the social at large? How does the cost of education affect our imagination of what it can do, what it is worth? The ethical and the professional meet in the nervous system in raw-making and destabilizing ways. These are the questions that should make those of us in the dreaming professions—analysts of power and alternative grids—*appropriately* fearful, anxious, and queasy.

I offered this self-referential anecdote for the "Critical Credos" issue of *the minnesota review* to honor its fantastic interviews. They have always focused on the force of the personal in professional practice, tracking the singular ways that thought is both personal and impersonal, motivated and also an opening to unpredicted consequences not only in scholarship and teaching but in being in the world. I tell my students that they always have to be pedagogical in the classroom, and inevitably some reply that pedagogical means "condescending." What I mean is the opposite: lifting. The process of being in the world pedagogically (as someone who wants thought to have a transformative impact) is impersonal in the best way, and my professional obligation, as things happen collectively that can never be made by one virtuoso, even in an explosion of sovereign invention.

NOTES

1. Anxiety, Urgency, Outrage, Hope: A Conference on Political Feeling, held at the University of Chicago, October 19–20, 2007.
2. For information about autonomous universities, see the blog *Constituent Imagination* at http://stevphen.mahost.org/CIResources.html. See a map of autonomous universities at http://www.edu-factory.org/mappa.html.
3. This paragraph emerges from a long conversation with Eli Thorkelson, a graduate student in anthropology at the University of Chicago who works on the overdetermined atmospheres of contemporary university life in the United States and France, and who blogs on this topic at *Decasia*.

THE DEFENSE OF LITERATURE

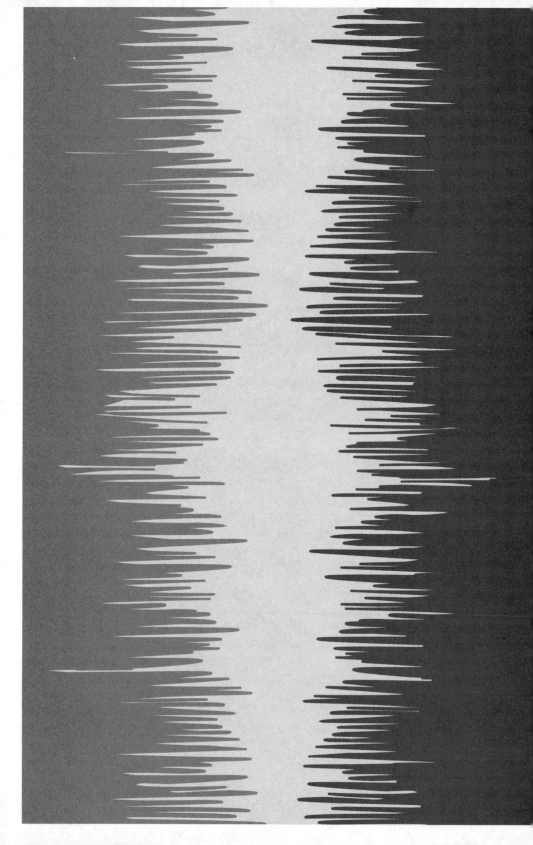

25 |
ACCESS TO THE UNIVERSAL
LANGUAGE, LITERATURE, AND THE HUMANITIES

TORIL MOI

I have been asked to write a credo, a declaration of what I believe in as a literary critic. The answer is: I believe in the value of language, of literature, and of the humanities. Yet I can't just write about language, literature, and the humanities as if these words were unproblematic. Throughout history, women have been denied access to the very fields I care passionately about. Even today, women's contributions to language, literature, and the humanities are often overlooked, undervalued and neglected. In many parts of the world, women are still denied equal access to learning and education.

Simone de Beauvoir defined sexism as the systematic attempt to deny women access to the universal. As long as man remains the norm and woman the other, the deviation from the norm, males will be taken to represent humanity, and human culture will remain unjust to women. In such a world "language," "literature," and the "humanities" will be represented by the words and experiences of men. As long as we continue to live in a sexist world, feminists have to continue to uncover the traces of women, revalue women's contributions to human culture, and insist that women's point of view be taken into account in every scholarly project.

LANGUAGE: THE IMPORTANCE OF TRANSLATION

Language is the repository of human culture. Language is expression and action, behavior and performance. Our words shape our world. As scholars and critics of literature, we specialize in the arts of language: we should respect the work of words. We should value good writing, strive to write well ourselves, and be passionate about training our students to write with pleasure, flair, and elegance.

Among the different arts of language, translation remains the most underestimated. Yet we live in a world in which people, ideas, and goods are constantly on the move. Transnationalism—the commitment to open communication across borders and cultures—has become a buzz word in academia. American universities set up campuses on the other side of the world, and students are encouraged to spend a summer, a semester, or a year abroad.

In a globalized world, translation is more important than ever. Translators shape a culture's perception of key works from other cultures. In spite of their commitment to transnationalism, American universities still do not value translation and translators sufficiently. Although many universities offer specialist training in translation studies, literary and philosophical translation is far too often considered a technical skill rather than an art and an intellectual challenge. Young faculty members in departments of languages and literature quickly learn that they can't get tenure for doing translations. Yet translation of literary, philosophical, and intellectual works is a highly demanding activity. The best translator is at once a linguist, a cultural historian, and a writer. Outstanding translators ought to find as much support in universities as creative writers.

Departments of languages and literature, including English departments, should train their students to understand and value the crucial work of translation. Publishers also need to value the work of translation. American publishers still publish fewer translations than publishers in other Western nations. Many publishers still don't realize that translation is a profession: they are still far too likely to think that anyone who can speak a foreign language well can also translate well. This is false, as the distressing example of the new translation of *The Second Sex* shows all too clearly.[1]

READING LITERATURE: BEYOND CRITIQUE

We have been far too uncritical in our embrace of critique. The hermeneutics of suspicion (Marx, Nietzsche, Freud) has dominated literary studies for the last fifty years. It taught us to read closely and well and remains useful as one tool for ideology critique of various kinds. But the hermeneutics of suspicion had a downside. It fostered a myth of critical superiority that turned teaching

and writing about literature into an exercise in faultfinding. The hermeneutics of suspicion made us suspicious of the simple, the unaffected, the artless,
the candid, the open, and the plain. It made us want to appear knowing and
sophisticated. It made it easier for us to criticize than to praise. In fact, the
very word "praise" is still likely to conjure up the idea of thoughtless gushing
rather than serious analysis. This is a *problem*. We need to move beyond the
language of critique and unmasking and relearn how properly to praise a work.

The task of the critic is to show others why a specific work merits our
sustained and undivided attention. Understanding must precede critique. To
understand a work is to get clear on its conditions of possibility, its historical,
social, and political situation and concerns, its aesthetic and existential projects and achievements. Clearly, there is no intrinsic conflict between critique
and understanding. After all, the most effective criticism emerges from critics
capable of understanding a text or an argument from within, capable of fully
seeing what it is the writer wants to accomplish and why he or she goes about
it in the way she does.

I am against the sense of superiority that the cult of critique breeds in
literary critics. I am not against critical thinking, understood as the capacity
to demolish a bad argument or find the flaws in a theory. Logical thought
and analytical skills are indispensible for anyone who wants to do significant
work. Of course, students and teachers must engage with the worldview and
the arguments of a text, whether philosophical or literary.

Writers and philosophers often engage with the same problems, sometimes independently of one another and sometimes as part of a complex
dialogue. Why, then, do literary critics so often fall for the temptation to
reduce the work to an illustration of preexisting theories or philosophies?
Or worse: to consider the work a *failed* illustration of a theory? (This book
almost achieves the insights of Derrida or Foucault.) To treat the work as if
it were intended to be an illustration of a theory or a philosophical doctrine
is to suggest that we value the literary work only insofar as it exemplifies or
illuminates that theory. But if it is the theory we want, there is no need to
read the work of literature. I remain convinced that works are illuminated
by being placed in relation to relevant theoretical and philosophical insights,
yet we need to learn to treat theory and literature as equal participants in the
discussion, learn to let the work challenge the terms of the theory we use to
illuminate it.

Literature and philosophy overlap in significant ways. Both raise the
normative questions of human existence: What ought we to believe about
the world and ourselves? And given our beliefs (what we think is the case),
what ought we to do? We can't get through a day without acting on our

own answers to these questions. (Do I think there will be a bus at five p.m.? Should I take it? Do I think he loves me? Should I marry him?) There isn't a literary work that doesn't convey its own response to the question of what to believe and what to do. As literary critics we need to show how profoundly thoughtful the best literary works are. By "best" I mean the works that the individual critic is willing to call the best. Her judgment will depend on the questions she has raised and the projects and purposes she has in mind.

By objecting to the hermeneutics of suspicion, with its excessive focus on critique, I am not trying to restrict the field of literary study. Literary study should be concerned with whatever literature is concerned with: that is to say, pretty much the whole of human experience in recorded time. There is space in literary study for the investigation of every aspect of human existence, from everyday life to revolutions and war. Feminism, postcolonialism, Marxism, and other political perspectives are not external to the work: most literary works already contain their own reflections on power and politics.

I don't mean to reduce literary works to thematics. I take for granted that literary critics should pay close and full attention on the work's struggle to find its form, to its relation to its own artistic traditions, and in general explore the way it gives shape to the conditions of possibility of aesthetic utterances. Yet literature is not just about literature, form, and the struggle with language. Literature is also expression and representation. We don't have to choose between formal self-consciousness and representation: the struggle with form coexists with the struggle to express and represent.

DEFENDING THE HUMANITIES

In today's technocratic and business-oriented world, the humanities are under threat. Bureaucrats all over the Western world wonder why they should continue to fund disciplines that appear so unworldly, so incapable of bringing in money. Faced with such arguments, we should remind ourselves of the value of research in the humanities. Such reminders may not sway the bureaucrats, but they can galvanize our resistance to a certain kind of technocratic reason.

The humanities are concerned with history, meaning, and values. The humanities study the historical records of human experience and the myriad ways human beings have found to express that experience. Humanists interpret signs and decipher the traces of lost cultures. In different ways, the study of art, literature, music, film, philosophy, history, ethnology, and religion helps us to understand what values individuals and cultures have been willing to struggle and die for, what values they have wanted to transmit to future generations, and what myths and ideologies human beings continue to live (and die) by. The humanities keep the history of a culture or society alive. The humanities give a society its memory and its identity. The humanities help us understand who we are. ("We" here does not refer to a given community: I mean "we" as in "any one of us," and "we" as in whatever community we claim allegiance to.) To imagine a society that no longer cares about such things is to imagine a society reduced to alienated technocrats.

I want to say something like this: The study of aesthetic expressions is a key area of the humanities because literature and the other arts provide an unparalleled archive of expressions of what it means to be alive, to be human, and to create, in a specific place and time. Yet there is something wrong with this formulation. "What it means to be human" is not quite right. I do mean to speak about human beings, members of the species *homo sapiens*. But in real life no human being is *just* "human," just as literature is never *just* about "human beings." To talk about "humans" is to run the risk of stripping away the particular characteristics we actually notice, pay attention to, and care about in interactions with others. We always exist in the world as some specific incarnation of the human: I am a man, a woman, an intersexed person; I am black, white, Chinese, Norwegian; I am a seamstress, an empress, a coal miner, a soldier, a peasant. I don't think of the people I know as examples of the species but as particular people to whom I have quite specific ties of obligations and responsibilities, people who present me with quite specific problems and opportunities and who inspire in me quite specific feelings. The word "human" is indispensable to anyone who cares about the humanities, yet it easily leads us astray, for, as Simone de Beauvoir points out, it carries a long tradition of exclusion. We still need feminists to remind us that one meaning of the "records of human existence" is the "records of women's existence."

NOTE

1. For details, see Toril Moi, "The Adulteress Wife," review of *The Second Sex*, trans. Constance Borde and Sheila Malovany-Chevallier, *London Review of Books* 32, no. 3 (2010): 3–6. My essay and the translators' and French publisher's letters to the editors are available on www .torilmoi.com.

WRESTLING WITH THE ANGEL

A MODEST CRITICAL CREDO

MORRIS DICKSTEIN

The role of critics varies greatly according to the roles they imagine for themselves, the course they pursue, and the audience they seek to address. Academic critics writing for their peers will take a different tack from public critics speaking to a general audience, large or small, or from writers themselves using criticism to carve out a space for their own work. Surprisingly, novelists and especially poets have proved to be among our best critics. Poet-critics form the main line of the English critical tradition while the critical foundations for the novel were laid by Henry James. Yet American writers are better known for their prickly aversion to critics rather than their appreciation, even when critics created the following for their work. My favorite example, one that set my blood boiling, was Saul Bellow's likening of the critic to a deaf man tuning a piano. (Had he merely said "tone deaf" I wouldn't have been so offended.) Then there are the old saws that continue to surface: "Those who can't, criticize." "No one ever grew up with the dream of becoming a critic." All this implies that critics are little more than clumsy mechanics or failed writers, stewing in their inadequacy and taking out this resentment on their betters, the really creative spirits. As one wag put it, a critic is someone who arrives late on the battlefield to kill off the survivors.

In fact, really good critics *are* writers, with their own style and literary personality, though their work feeds off other writing, as novelists and poets feed off the text of our common life. Both kinds of writers must somehow be faithful to their originals yet develop their own angle of vision. They have to tell the truth, a truth we'll recognize, but, like Emily Dickinson, "tell it slant."

They distill art into meaning, punish failure, and lionize success, but like all writers they work by way of selection, even distortion. We remember critics for their temperament as much as their critical judgment: the pugilistic vigor of Hazlitt, the digressive idiosyncrasies of Ruskin, the clerical acerbity of Eliot, the transparent windowpane of Orwell, the poetic conjunctions of Benjamin, the Hegelian dynamics of Adorno. We can forgive a great deal in a critic who works out of a striking sensibility or a startling point of view, as we are seduced by writers who give us a fresh take on the familiar world. Some critics survive on the strength of their prose alone; some, by introducing or promoting new artists and movements; others, by introducing seminal concepts (the objective correlative, the dissociation of sensibility), by sheer intelligence or depth of learning, or by helping reorient the history of an art form. As it happens, T. S. Eliot could qualify under any of these categories.

So let me lay down a few principles that are simply features of the kind of criticism I love to read and have tried to write.

• It was only in the mid-twentieth century, thanks to the New Criticism, that criticism itself began to play a major role in the academic study of literature, which previously was focused on textual scholarship and factual research. Because of the new emphasis on close reading, most academic criticism grew too long, too pedantic and detailed. The critic felt obliged to lay out every step of the reading, not simply the interpretive outcome, the take-away or upshot of careful reading. Such monographs too often became little more than stepping stones in the job market, rungs in the accreditation process. Earlier critics read just as closely but luxuriated in aphorism, intuition, and apodictic summation, writerly vices. They kicked away the analytic ladder that brought them to their goal. Most journalistic criticism, on the other hand, is too brief and superficial, too uninformed, almost weightlessly opinionated. Trapped by space limitations and deadlines, such pieces habitually default on context, ignoring much that undergirds the work and gives it meaning. With the exception of longer, more intricate reviews in little magazines and a few intellectual journals, they reduce criticism to consumer guidance. They strike attitudes and ventilate feelings, unsupported by argument or evidence. If criticism must make its case as illuminating commentary on works of art, then the best vehicle for criticism is not the extended monograph or the hastily written review but the literary essay, personal, reflective, attuned to an ongoing conversation. This is why critical journals (like the avant-garde magazines of the 1920s and 1930s) and critical schools (the New York Intellectuals, the New Critics) were so important to twentieth-century criticism: they kept a conversation going, they responded to new movements in the arts with strong revaluations and with critical methods that were responsive to difficult new writing.

• It follows that the criticism I enjoy is more affective than cerebral, more empirical than theoretical. The glory of the essay, since Montaigne, comes in the way it generalizes from the concrete, raising "perception to the point of principle and definition," as Eliot put it. Much of recent criticism works the other way around, setting up a template of theory or method and shoehorning arbitrary examples into it. It has little truck with aesthetics, all too readily dismissed as ideology. In rare cases this theoretical approach sheds light on some work in question or on a larger issue; too often it is counterintuitive, distorting literary works with its own ideological agenda or simply missing the mark. Do we experience a shock of recognition when we read such a commentary? Does it open up a new path of understanding for us or merely serve as a vehicle for our political or moral prejudices? Does the reading actually confront and convey the power of the literary work or its agonizing failure to muster that power? Love and hate are crucial for critics, along with deep-seated ambivalence. They indicate that the writer's work has really touched us. They feed the flame of good critical prose and supply the energy that empowers the critic to enlighten the reader. This is why sharply formulated, deeply felt literary judgment, not simply analytic interpretation, is vital to the critic's task. It tracks the subtle movement of a genuine critical sensibility. Make-or-break evaluation gives evidence that the stakes are high, the critic is engaged, the subject really matters. A critic needs an analytic mind but also something of a polemical style, for criticism is also a form of persuasion.

• The work of criticism is a juggling act, a discourse without clear borders. The critic must play the role of what I once called a double agent, balancing text and context, a sensitive grasp of form along with the social currents that help shape art. F. R. Leavis is usually seen as a formal critic, yet he insisted that "one cannot seriously be interested in literature and remain purely literary in interests." In principle, nothing is alien to the critic: the writer's biography, the history of ideas, the social history of the times, the tools of philology, the evolution of formal conventions, the parallels to the other arts, the insights gleaned from literary history but also from other disciplines. These blurred boundaries have been unconscionably abused in recent years as critics squander their authority by poaching on fields they know little about, pronouncing on subjects they know even less about. One result is that a stereotyped progressive mindset, the well-meaning agendas of political correctness, becomes their received wisdom; open-minded scholars are unable to take their work seriously. Historians recoil from the anecdotal evidence of New Historicism as social scientists resist ideological position taking in social criticism. Research gives way to fashionable cant, currently some form of postmodernism and antiessentialism, which caricatures the wisdom of the past, gives unquestioned sanction to all forms of relativism, and effectively assumes what needs to be proved.

• Despite the sins of critics in fields they haven't mastered, I call myself a generalist, a public critic, which is simply another name for an intellectual, someone whose first love is the exchange of ideas. As an undergraduate at Columbia I learned to pillage literature for ideas, to quarry it crudely for important themes, but somehow I also imbibed a strong historical sense, what Philip Rahv called the sixth sense of the critic. Eliot noted that this historical awareness "involves a perception, not only of the pastness of the past, but of its presence." This sense of the present became a watchword among the New York Intellectuals. Intrigued by the bold reach of their work, I grew attuned to the politics of literature, of literature as an actual intervention in the world. But it was only as a graduate student at Yale, then in the last stages of the New Criticism, and at later at Cambridge, still under the influence of Leavis, that I learned more about how literary works were put together, how they were made of language. This brought me back to my sophomore year of high school, when I first read *A Tale of Two Cities* and *The Scarlet Letter* and was amazed at the sheer craftsmanship of the whole work but also at the architecture of sentences and paragraphs. These books seemed ingeniously tooled, shaped to endure, yet their stories were also full of arrestingly concrete details, resonant symbols, and vivid re-creations of earlier times and places. They gave me intimations of both literary form and the pressure of history that I understood only years later.

• Despite the importance of craft, works of art are not so much objects as experiences. Critics are not like anatomists who murder to dissect but seismologists responsive to every rumble in the terrain of art and of their own inner lives. When Matthew Arnold called poetry a criticism of life, he meant that life itself, the stream of felt experience, is what gives art meaning and value. Before 1900 no one would have questioned this. But in the twentieth century we grew so concerned about the mediations of art—the conventions of realism, the techniques of modernism, the movements that defined different schools—that we sometimes lost sight of art's purpose and substance. Since art reshapes life into staged experiences, this further blurs the boundaries of criticism, creating an opening from aesthetic criticism to moral and social criticism. This was the trajectory of the great Victorian critics—Carlyle, Arnold, Ruskin—though it was also resisted by the successors they influenced, including Pater and Wilde, who disliked moralizing yet themselves wrote in this prophetic strain. For me the arts represent the inner configurations of a culture, its intimate depths of mind and feeling. The alienating effects of industrial society created the conditions for a social criticism grounded in aesthetics, for art pointed to a potential for human fulfillment that modern life had undermined. Twentieth-century critics like Orwell, Leavis, Wilson, and Trilling were heirs to this tradition, which has few successors today.

• Despite its ambitions as a critique of ideology, postmodern relativism lays down a path of acquiescence rather than social resistance. It rejects moral judgment as a form of hierarchy and elitism, though criticism has always demanded a trained sensibility, capable of doing the hard work of discrimination. Eliot described criticism, simply but memorably, as "the elucidation of works of art and the correction of taste." But "correction" rings oddly in contemporary ears, for it suggests that the few who know more or feel more deeply might offer instruction to the many and might improve society in the process. Yet taste and discrimination remain the ultimate tests of the critic, without which there can be no clarifying insight or understanding. Instead we have today the democratization of criticism represented by customer reviews of books and films on the Internet. Critical judgment increasingly resembles what we find on websites where hotels and restaurants are usefully rated by people impelled to write in or sound off. Their judgments are unedited, and we know nothing about where they come from. We must turn critics ourselves to weigh their worth. Criticism becomes a form of polling, in which we look for enlightenment from the man in the street.

In this context, it becomes wildly anachronistic to hold on to the Victorian notion of the critic as social or moral guide or to the modernist uses of the critic as mediator and expositor of difficult art or even to the more general view of the critic as an informed intellectual, someone who thinks hard about art and society, who has developed the faculty of focused attention, the rhetorical skills and the cast of mind, to craft those reflections into argument. This critical tradition is the heritage that matters; it speaks to the passions that drew me irresistibly to art and criticism in the first place. At bottom criticism is personal, agonistic, however measured its tone. It is Jacob wrestling with an angel, an existential encounter in which the full being of the critic confronts the full power of the work, which invites yet also resists critical translation.

27 |
EVERYDAY AESTHETICS

RITA FELSKI

Ibelieve art is worldly, not otherworldly: not ineffable, untranslatable, or
other. But I find myself increasingly troubled by the functionalism that
shadows social theories of art, as critics vault over the disparities between individual works and social structures in their eagerness to nail down
political meanings. The model of articulation, well known in cultural if not
in literary studies, redeems such trespasses by allowing us to do justice to the
contingency, mutability, and many-sidedness of cultural artifacts. And in the
thought style of phenomenology, most recently, I have found a newly productive irritant against the trend to over-contextualization, along with welcome
intimations of how to reframe questions of aesthetic experience. My current
convictions, in other words, draw on a seemingly improbable blend of cultural studies and phenomenology, modes of thought that gaze indifferently
past each other even though they are both, in their own way, committed to
everyday structures of experience.

The invitation to draft a credo offers a welcome spur to reflection and
self-reflection as well as a provocation to business as usual in literary and
cultural studies. As a first-person form, a blunt avowal of one's convictions
and commitments, it is a rarely glimpsed genre in academic writing, which
prescribes the subordination of personal belief to acknowledged authorities
and third-person sources. Literary theory prides itself on its antinomian and
antiauthoritarian spirit yet often accentuates such deference, as if multiplying citations of Foucault or Žižek will bestow a cast-iron legitimacy on the
writer's words. The credo, moreover, serves as an expression of faith rather

than a report on knowledge, reminding us of our obligatory enchainment in attachments, prejudices, and nonrational beliefs. We need to acknowledge, in Gadamerian fashion, that such attachments and prejudices are not obstacles to thought but preconditions for thought, and that even the most abstract and highly flown speculations build on our commitments rather than transcending them.

The method of articulation has driven much of my thinking about literature and culture, even though I stumbled across formal definitions of this method late in the day. A central tenet of articulation theory is the conviction that the social order cannot be conceived of as a seamless totality, that it is not a unitary whole ruled by a single overarching logic, and that it cannot be imagined as a quasi person capable of harboring desires or intentions. (Such personification is often enacted in claims that capitalism "wants" us to do something or that patriarchy "intends" women to behave in certain ways.) There is, in other words, no purposeful and omnipotent *Geist* driving the course of history in a given direction. Rather, we are thrown into a world that is fractured, multiform, and mutable, composed of myriad and multi-stranded relations of correspondence and noncorrespondence, of linkages that are made, unmade, and remade over time. To be sure, connections between social groups and patterns of action, belief, or cultural expression can acquire considerable permanence, cohesiveness, and power, giving the appearance of inevitability or second nature, but even such relatively stable and systemic regularities do not create or control the entirety of the social field. Political identities, in this sense, are not natural kinds but are forged out of the ceaseless play of correspondence and contradiction; they do not precede but are constituted by processes of articulation. The category of woman, for example, does not ground or explain the practice of feminism; rather, feminists seize hold of and redescribe the category of woman in the process of formulating and advancing their goals.

Such a framework dissents from more established ways of linking text to context in literary studies. It casts into doubt, for example, a critical procedure that claims to deduce political meanings and effects from the close scrutiny of texts, a method that I have elsewhere dubbed political formalism. Such readings hinge on an assumed identity or homology of literary and social structure, declaring the novel to be an inherently bourgeois genre or imputing to linear narrative the power to enforce heteronormativity or to sustain masculine privilege. Articulation theory, by contrast, insists that social functions cannot be deduced from aesthetic form and that past use does not guarantee the unfolding of future meaning. To be sure, texts bear the scars and residues of their histories and cannot magically shrug off their past associations, but by the same token, they also acquire new resonance and purpose in altered milieus. A genre such as the bildungsroman, for example, is invigorated, refreshed, and modified formally and thematically as it moves into contexts very different from those of nineteenth-century Europe. Literary and social interests do not line up in automatic or predictable alliances, and there are no short cuts to historically informed analysis of the density of context. Hence my reservations, back in the late eighties, about the possibility of defining a feminist aesthetic, defined as any necessary connection between women, politics, and particular styles or forms of writing. A related skepticism inspired me to reassess what was once a theoretical commonplace, that modernity was a quintessentially masculine phenomenon, and to wonder how modern women as well as men had unmade and remade the meanings of gender across a multiplicity of genres, frameworks, and social milieus.

This emphasis on contingency might seem to harmonize with poststructuralist theories of language that have dominated literary studies over the last few decades, yet I harbor extensive misgivings about the impact and effects of such theories. All too often, they shortchange the import and impact of artworks by turning them into meta-commentaries on the indeterminacy of language, the instability of identity, or the ungroundedness of belief. In addition, the vogue for performance metaphors, especially in gender studies and queer theory, has spawned an etiolated view of the self unable to do justice to the thickness of interiority and intersubjectivity, whether in literature or in life. Anti-essentialism is routed into a form of aestheticism that sees language as the sole shaper of human destinies and that wields this insight to trumpet the arbitrariness of beliefs and the artificiality of values. The literary text is hauled in to serve as star witness for the prosecution in this vigorously deflationary exercise.

Literary studies, in other words, remains stuck in a proto-modernist mindset that continues to prize self-reflexivity, dissonance, and estrangement as the most advanced forms of aesthetic consciousness. (Most of what passes as postmodern theory, at least in literature departments, does not seriously contest such a mindset, but kicks it up a notch or tinkers with peripheral details.) The negative, I've argued elsewhere, has become institutionally normative, alongside a paralyzing anxiety that reopening questions of how works of art enrich perception will trigger charges of naive mimeticism or retrograde humanism. Yet there is an easily discernable performative contradiction in theories enthralled with negation, subversion, and the glamour of marginality that sustain their case via entirely conventional and routinized forms of academic argument. Either the medium disqualifies the message, or we need to reassess the relative merits of novelty and familiarity, otherness and sameness, while also crafting more capacious and multidimensional explanations of aesthetic experience.

My fascination with the concept and the experience of everyday life stems from the stubborn resistance it offers to such critical theories of defamiliarization and demystification. On the one hand, the everyday is associated with habit, repetition, convention, the unthinking performance of routine activities—all those qualities frequently excoriated in modern art and criticism as indices of existential alienation or of conservatism and petit bourgeois complacency. On the other hand, an element of sheer necessity adheres to such elements of everyday living that the modern tradition of negative aesthetics seemed ill-equipped to capture or comprehend. My perplexity on this question first drew me to cultural studies, which trumpets its thoroughgoing commitment to the commonplace and the quotidian. Yet much of this work seemed intent on imbuing everyday life with the frisson of transgressive excitement rather than facing up to its mundane and humdrum qualities. It was the phenomenological idea of the life world that yielded the salient framework.

The life world identifies the heterogeneous assemblage of diffuse, distracted, semiconscious perceptions, beliefs, and reactions that make up much of our daily living. The act of seeing something as natural or taken-for-granted—hailed as a cardinal sin in contemporary theory—is here conceptualized not as an error to be rectified but as an inescapable facet of existence. Phenomenology, in this sense, attends to what is already in plain view; it looks at, rather than through, everyday modes of experience; it seeks to describe rather than prescribe, to attend to, rather than escape, the commonplace. What renders phenomenology a still timely framework is not Husserl's attempt at a transcendental reduction—one more expression of a recurring philosophical ambition to escape one's own shadow—but the gaze of wonder it directs at ordinary objects and mundane forms of feeling and thought. Its aim is to really see ordinary structures of experience—not in order to celebrate them or to trumpet their authenticity but to gain a surer grasp of the ineluctable nature of our first-person relation to the world.

In this sense, the concept of the life world is not just an attempt to capture the textures of everyday consciousness but a gauntlet thrown down to a tradition of modern intellectual thought enamored of displays of skepticism, doubt, and self-reflexivity. Phenomenology does not deny or devalue such skepticism but reveals its necessary limits by noting that any questioning of ideologies, claims, or belief systems depends on tacit meaning structures that allow critique to take place. As certain questions or problems move into the foreground of our awareness, others recede into, or remain firmly within, the background. Moments of rupture or flashes of disorientation explode into consciousness against a horizon of unchallenged and unnoticed assumptions. Critical theory, in this sense, cannot purge itself of ordinary patterns of thought; even the most iconoclastic gestures are rooted in taken-for-granted beliefs and tacit conventions.

While the idea of the life world is often equated with conservatism or quietism, to my mind it signals the exact opposite. There is something exceptionally invigorating in a mode of thought that suspends the usual distinctions between elite and vernacular knowledge, science and ideology, critique and naiveté, to elucidate their underlying affinities and connections. Such a framework, in my view, is neither anti-intellectual nor destined to foster complacency. It does not hinder us from scrutinizing the politics of everyday life—challenging, for example, tacit assumptions about the division of labor in the household. Nor does it preclude attention to the contingency and mutability of life worlds, as shaped, for example, by rapidly changing relations to media technologies. (I take for granted, after Merleau-Ponty and Ricoeur, a "neo-phenomenology" that assumes linguistic mediation and historical difference and sees subjectivity as ineluctably caught up with intersubjectivity.) But one of the gifts of phenomenology, in my view, is its power to puncture intellectual hubris and the Faustian dream that newer, more sophisticated, more self-reflexive theories will somehow absolve us of finitude, ordinariness, and error. (In this respect, as in others, it has patent affinities to pragmatism.) A repertoire of background beliefs, sedimented assumptions, and everyday practices turns out not to be the antagonist of knowledge but its fundamental precondition.

The promise of phenomenology for literary studies, then, is a more ecumenical and expansive account of aesthetic experience. While a thematics of disorientation and shock plays its part in such an account, other registers of response move into the spotlight and acquire new visibility and salience—responses that were always in plain view but occluded or overshadowed by the preoccupations of contemporary theory. Phenomenology, for example, allows us to do justice to the widespread conviction that works of art can enrich our understanding of the world without lapsing into the misapprehensions of reflection theory, given its orientation toward questions of meaning rather than truth. It is equally primed to investigate the quasi-magical state of absorption that can befall us while reading a novel or watching a film, a state famously described by Barthes as the epitome of plebian *plaisir* rather than radical self-shattering *jouissance*. Ideally suited to thick descriptions of the intensities of affective and corporeal response, phenomenology pays notice to subtle and multi-shaded discriminations of pleasure as well as meaning. It authorizes us, in short, to look afresh at the spectrum of aesthetic experience without rushing to judgment about which aspects of such experience qualify as truly aesthetic.

In underscoring the promise of phenomenology I am, to be sure, expressing a hope rather than reporting a fact. I have found only modest inspiration in a past history of phenomenological criticism associated with the Geneva school, Wolfgang Iser, and (early) Hillis Miller. Such criticism suffers, in retrospect, from a tendency to conjure unwarranted universals out of modest particulars. It takes its bearing from a limited practice of academic interpretation—broadly New Critical in orientation—which is subsequently equated with the experience of reading tout court. It imagines a reader whose response is cerebral rather than emotional, who pursues linguistic novelty while disdaining formulae, who hovers fastidiously over nuances of form and style but resolutely overlooks the sociopolitical resonances or real-world implications of works of art. Such an archetype of mandarin bookishness falls short of capturing the mindset of the Harvard English department circa 1960, let alone telling us anything substantive about the experience of reading across the social field.

Here, cultural studies provides a much-needed readjustment in its attention to occluded forms of reader or viewer response and the multifarious contexts and conditions of interpretation. Rescuing romance-novel readers and *Star Trek* fans from a history of condescension, it accentuates the difference of popular aesthetics while formulating a robust defense of its value. Interpretative frameworks, intertextual references, criteria of judgment, modes of engagement and affective response shift and change from one audience to another. Whether leaning on Bourdieu's statistical correlations between aesthetics and class or drawing inspiration from de Certeau's utopian vision of the unruliness of ordinary readers, cultural critics insist that academic and popular response cannot be compressed within a single analytical or descriptive rubric. Moreover, their resort to ethnography and social scientific method signals a decisive break with the supposedly more impressionistic and formalist procedures of literary criticism. Cultural studies often prides itself on embracing a radical contextualism that recasts the meaning of a text as the sum or inventory of its various articulations while studiously abstaining from normative interpretation or judgment. In surveys of reception theory within cultural studies, phenomenology often figures as an embryonic, putatively naive model of the reader-text relationship that has been superseded by more theoretically sophisticated and historically conscious frameworks.

I am not persuaded, however, that phenomenology is rendered obsolete by cultural studies nor, indeed, that practices of academic reading and ordinary reading should be seen as incommensurate. Ethnography, for example, once hailed as a magic bullet that would solve the problem of theorizing reader or viewer experience, has turned out to be less remarkable and revelatory than expected. To be sure, it serves as a useful reality check for wilder flights of academic fancy, anchoring armchair speculations about art's effects in nuggets of empirical information about audience perceptions and practices. But while ethnography ranges wide, it does not go very deep; the responses and self-descriptions of ethnographic subjects are rarely very revealing. The overarching context and framework of social scientific research, with its questionnaires and interviews, its demographic categories and functionalist explanations, is not especially conducive to capturing the experiential density of what is involved in reading a book or watching a film. We are confronted, in other words, with the classic hermeneutic distinction between explanation and understanding, between "seeing that" and "seeing as," between grasping an analytical proposition and "getting" something by having it described a certain way. Novelists, for the most part, have been far more successful than sociologists or cultural historians in crafting descriptions of aesthetic experiences that are not easily captured in words. The promise of phenomenology lies in a similar potential to convey, via metaphorical analogies, imaginative formulations, and processes of discernment, something of what it feels like to become absorbed in a film or lost in a book. Its orientation, in this sense, is neither subjective nor objective, but attuned to the copresence, communion, and interdependence of self and text.

In this context, overlapping modes of engagement and commonalities amongst readers are obscured by a model of social stratification that splices audiences into hermetically sealed compartments of high-, middle-, and low-brows. I've argued elsewhere that structures of recognition and self-recognition persist across many kinds of readership, even though the modalities of this recognition and the texts that inspire it are far from identical. Similarly, the sense of being utterly absorbed or consumed by a work of art is hardly restricted to a particular subculture or class, even if this state of enchantment has received only token acknowledgment in literary theory. Rancière's objection to rigidly class-based demarcations of aesthetic experience by sociologists and Left intellectuals is on target; a presumption of absolute cultural schisms and incommensurable regimes of interpretation turns out to be no less dogmatic than appeals to a universal model of reader subjectivity.

This question of the general versus the particular bears on my own recent shift toward broad questions of theory and interpretation, a decision driven, for the most part, by a desire to explore methodological issues in more depth than seems feasible within a feminist framework. But it also owes something to a deepening despondency at the limited audience for feminist work—a sense that, while I see my scholarship as in conversation with other traditions, other traditions show little interest in engaging in dialogue with me.

A ready-made explanation for this phenomenon lies at hand, and it is tempting to chalk up any indifference to feminist work to unsavory motives. In some cases, no doubt, such indifference is fueled by a conviction that women have little to contribute to intellectual thought. And yet it is not just the retrograde or the reactionary who do not keep up to date with feminist theory, but multitudes of other female and male scholars, many of whom would no doubt describe themselves as holding feminist beliefs. Given the intensifying pressure to publish and to achieve scholarly excellence in narrowly defined domains, few scholars have the luxury of keeping abreast of developments in a multiplicity of fields.

In this respect, the common targeting of universality as an oppressive, all-pervasive, proto-patriarchal norm falls notably short of the mark, at least in the context of scholarly work in the humanities. The realm of the universal, for the most part, remains the domain of the amateur generalist, the journalist, and the low-status teacher of introductory surveys and great-books courses. The structure of the profession, as evidenced in the hierarchy of the job market, grant applications, and professional honors and awards, remains heavily oriented toward specialization, whether in the eighteenth-century English novel or cutting-edge queer theory. We are rewarded for demonstrating our academic expertise in defined subjects and methods to small audiences. Feminism, in this context, functions as one more area of scholarly specialization, analogous to the history of the book or performance studies. While the latest publications in such fields are eagerly tracked by those who define themselves as members of the same interpretative community, only rarely do such texts travel across disciplinary and subdisciplinary boundaries to reach broader audiences.

There is, of course, an obvious exception to this drive toward specialization. In the last few decades the idea of theory has come to stand for an interest in debating theoretical, interpretive, and methodological issues that affect all forms of scholarship, not just some. To define one's work as theory is to make the rhetorical claim that it possesses general relevance. While such claims are often scolded for a putative arrogance based in white male privilege, such criticisms strike me as largely misplaced. To argue for the wider import of one's arguments is not to deny the specifics of one's location, merely to deny that such specifics are all-determining. The effect of such objections, moreover, has been to further entrench a system of academic subcultures and subfields in which scholars write for a handful of their colleagues, increasing the stranglehold of specialization. Such professional trends, in my view, need to be vigorously resisted. By engaging general issues in literature and interpretation, while giving them a feminist spin, I hope to reach readers unlikely to ever open a work of feminist criticism.

Such, at least, is my present conviction. But secular credos, unlike religious ones, are not divinely inspired but fallible and changeable, swayed by the force of the better argument or, less happily, by the winds of academic fashion. For the moment, at least, I hold fast to a conviction that attention to particulars can coexist with plausible generalizations, that contextualization need not exclude careful scrutiny of formal devices, and that political interpretations can only persuade if they also do justice to the felt density of aesthetic experience. And, above all, that we need to amplify our repertoire of interpretative styles and theoretical frameworks by venturing beyond the safe haven of skepticism, suspicion, and critique. Amen.

28

CRITICISM IS VITAL

DAVID R. SHUMWAY

W illiam Carlos Williams wrote, "It is difficult to get the news from poems yet men die miserably every day for lack of what is found there." My credo is a paraphrase: "It is difficult to get the facts from criticism yet people die miserably every day for lack of what is found there." By criticism, I don't mean merely the interpretation and evaluation of literature or other texts but a broader project and attitude of which literary criticism is only the most familiar instance. This project has largely defined the disciplines we know as the humanities, and genuine criticism is not to be confused with most reviewing done in popular periodicals. While during the first half of the twentieth century most criticism in the United States was produced by journalists and other nonacademics, it has largely disappeared from the media since then. This leaves the work of academic humanists as the major source of this vital activity.

I have always believed that criticism is vital because I believe that the world is comprehended most of the time not by means of science or simple experience but through the lens of representations received in the form of what we call art, culture, religion, and entertainment. However, I have not always been willing to state this conviction so forthrightly. My hesitancy about espousing the value of criticism lay in the critique of humanism associated with poststructuralism, especially with Althusser and Foucault. Foucault was a major influence on my thinking, and the dominant interpretation of his work held that humanism was simply the denial of the reality of power. For a period, like Fitzgerald's genius, I believed both this and its opposite and articulated each position when it seemed appropriate. Statements in support of criticism were appropriate when addressing administrators or nonacademics while statements critical of humanism were appropriate in most other professional contexts.

The critique of humanism in the United States became a critique of the humanities, a project in which I was centrally involved. We focused on the way that power, rather than the disinterested pursuit of truth, structured academic disciplines. A related critique highlighted the humanities' lack of power to bring about political change. While the critique of ideology is an activity of the humanities, in Marx's conception it ought to have an end wherein the class interests of the rulers are exposed and the oppressed learn to recognize their own interests. Alas, however, despite Herculean labors of decipherment on our part, the workers still did not seem to get it. Despairing of mere interpretation of texts, we tried to find more productive projects—for instance, the number of essays in this collection proclaiming belief in studying the academy suggest that if we can't change the world, we have a shot at changing our own domain.

I have no wish to denigrate this project. Ideology is a fact of life, and it remains in need of critique. Academic disciplines are, among other things, social institutions that exist to maintain their own and, to a lesser extent, broadly social hierarchies and relations of power. One of the ways in which such inequities are perpetuated is by the failure of academics to recognize that what we do is wage labor. Yet none of these projects, nor all of them taken together, is sufficient. It is not a mistake to focus the activity of criticism toward a practical end, but it is a mistake to regard only the end as valuable.

One of the reasons we got into that quandary is our skepticism about the value of the texts that we teach. It had long been a dogma of criticism that works of art are inherently valuable while criticism of them is only contingently so. Critics have long been prone to self-denigration, and the metaphor of the critic as parasite became a familiar one.[1] Thus the scandal of J. Hillis Miller's deconstructivist essay "The Critic as Host," where he asserted that literature was parasitic on criticism.[2] The self-loathing of critics, it is often implied, stems from their failure to become real writers, the assumption being that no one would actually set out to be such a lowly creature. But what if the value of literature were called into question? The answer, unless one is a Derridean like Miller, is that criticism will not become more valuable but less—a parasite must die with its host.

As it happened, the value of canonical literature and art lost its obviousness within the humanities. This is not to say that the value of the works humanists study has ever been a simple article of faith. Indeed, the humanities as disciplines arose as the conception of literature—meaning writing of all kinds—as a repository of truth or wisdom declined in the face of modern science. Philology, the ancestor of the rest of the humanities, is founded on the opposition between a critical attitude toward texts that questions their claims about their own status—whether as truth, art, organic wholes, etc.— but that also insists on their value in some other register. Early philologists focused on ancient texts, including both the Bible and works of Greek and Roman antiquity, explaining their origins and contexts with the goal of arriving at the truth the unreliable text could not by itself fully convey. Authority shifted from the text to the philologist, but the text remained the chief material with which the philologist worked. If the text became a mere artifact, useful only as a source of information about something else, the philologist's authority would become insignificant.

Philologists were not evaluators; aesthetic judgments were not their goal. Rather, they wanted to establish facts about texts, whether scripture, poetry, or historical documents. Philologists saw themselves as discovering facts just like other scientists, but they did not see these facts as entirely separable from the values conveyed by texts. If they did not regard it as their job to judge works aesthetically, they took it for granted that such judgment was necessary.

There have been some critics and theories of criticism—the New Humanism, for example—that have seen judgment not only as the essence of criticism but as a high calling, part of the eternal struggle to defend civilization. Diametrically opposed to this view is the one that emerged in the 1970s, where statements of taste were damned as "formalism" or "belletrism" and associated with the perpetuation of inequities of class, race, and gender. Yet both views seem to me to overlook the fact that judgments of taste are a ubiquitous part of everyday life. As Simon Frith argues, "The exercise of taste and aesthetic discrimination is as important in popular as in high culture," and functions similarly in both cultural sectors. Referring to Pierre Bourdieu's *Distinction*, where it is observed that the "accumulation of cultural knowledge and experience . . . enhances the richness and pleasure of the reading of cultural texts," Frith adds, "a similar use of accumulated knowledge and discriminatory skill is apparent in low cultural forms."[3]

Criticism can't avoid judgment because it is an integral part of the use of texts, of their apprehension and their pleasure. Cultural studies, which in the United States inherited the aversion to questions of taste from literary theory, has suffered from its unwillingness to engage in judgment and especially to offer any advice about what works are valuable.[4] Cultural studies has been very good at revealing the insidious effects of ideology in apparently progressive works and at detecting evidence of resistance or subversion in seemingly reactionary texts, but it has failed to make a case for the value of art, popular or otherwise. Since cultural studies has rejected old Marxist claims to science, it shouldn't replace them with a new set of inflexible rules. Rather, we should recognize that all art, just like all actually existing politics, is flawed, but that flawed art, just like flawed politics, may be valuable. More important, we need to affirm that pleasure is one of the things that distinguish art from propaganda, and we need to be willing to celebrate the pleasure we take in culture.

I have begun to practice this last element of my credo only rather recently, and with some difficulty. It has been hard for me to unlearn the habit of keeping my enthusiasms out of my analysis. In writing about rock stars as cultural icons, for example, my tendency was to rely on the judgments of rock critics in order to establish the facts of the stars' iconicity. But it became clear eventually that I needed to express my own appreciation because the critics had been reading songs or albums, while I was reading the stars as texts. And sometimes, I found myself having to argue that the critics had been wrong in their judgments of the stars' works. Similarly, in beginning to work on realist narratives, I've found it necessary to consider what is pleasurable about such works beyond the fact that they tell us something accurate about social life. The poor reputation realism has had since World War I has been the result of critics' failure to acknowledge this pleasure.

But if describing and celebrating the pleasures cultural works give us is a necessary part of criticism, it is only a part. Criticism is vital because the representations we make and consume are not transparent in their meanings or effects and are always in need of interpretation. While this assertion is widely accepted in some form or another within the humanities, it is apparently a hard sell to the rest of society. The rise of theory produced all kinds of complaints about its unfamiliar and specialized terminology, the complainers not recognizing that their own New Critically derived terms were at one time equally mystifying to older literary scholars and the public. Why not just write plain English, since literary criticism was obviously not rocket science? In this vein, such otherwise astute critics as Louis Menand have wondered why people need to spend so much time earning a doctoral degree when they are just going to be teaching and writing about literature.[5] I see no reason to apologize for the lengthy training needed to be able to read culture well.

Unlike rocket scientists, who need to know only one narrow set of problems in great detail, humanities scholars not only must establish detailed knowledge of a narrow specialty—say, the works of single author or American war films 1919 to 1939—but must also have broad cultural knowledge, including the relevant history, philosophy, sociology, and so on.

Unlike the popular conception of science, criticism never produces the final answer on any significant problem of evaluation or meaning. That's why it is difficult to get the facts from criticism, a condition that frustrates those who mistake facts for knowledge. Our students, conditioned by years of schooling in which one is rewarded for spitting back the correct answer, often have trouble with this. Historically they turned to Cliff's Notes, and more recently to anything they can get on the Web, in search of the "hidden meaning" they are convinced the professor is refusing to reveal.[6] Literary scholars have from time to time grown tired of the multiplicity of readings and have sought a science that would settle things once and for all. Theory, especially structuralism, was taken up in part as a response to this dilemma. But despite the frustrations of uncertainty, we all know the excitement of good discussion. Students appreciate it even if they may not be able to explain why. Adults in the book discussions I lead from time to time at local libraries are not there to learn the true meaning but to share their judgments and interpretations and to hear those of others. In these instances, participants understand at some level that the conversation is the point.

The conversation among professional critics often lacks the human connections of face-to-face meetings, but it nonetheless enriches the experience of the works with which it deals. And if no interpretation goes unchallenged, some do define the terms of debate for many years. Moreover, successful criticism is not done in disregard of facts. Humanities research cannot be purely objective, but it continues to be governed by the same quest for knowledge that drives research in other fields. Humanities scholarship thus serves the function of keeping cultural discourse honest. Without such scholarship, the meanings of history and texts can become ossified or be hijacked by those in power.

I realize I've made a number of distinct and perhaps seemingly contradictory claims about criticism. Criticism increases the pleasure we take in culture, helping us understand the value we as individuals and as a society find in it. Criticism helps us understand how familiar fictional or artistic representations of the world influence our beliefs. It helps us to think about our beliefs in comparison to others. Fictional representations allow for a freedom to speculate and adopt multiple perspectives. Similarly, the study of distant times and places enables the recognition that the here and now is not the only possible world. Such thinking is essential to civic discourse and enlightened leadership. Criticism and the humanities are more essential to genuine democracy than humanism ever was to the tyranny of Renaissance princes.

NOTES

1. A recent example by Graydon Carter in the *New York Times Book Review*: "Writing, remember, is the only art in which the creator is publicly judged by people who do precisely the same thing, but as a rule less well" ("The Summer in Italy," review of *The Pregnant Widow: Inside History*, by Martin Amis, *New York Times Book Review*, May 23, 2010, 1).

2. J. Hillis Miller, "The Critic as Host," *Critical Inquiry* 3, no. 3 (1977): 439–47.

3. Simon Frith, *Performing Rites: On the Value of Popular Music* (Cambridge, Mass.: Harvard University Press, 1996), 9.

4. See my "Cultural Studies and Questions of Pleasure and Value," in *Cultural Studies and Aesthetics*, ed. Michael Bérubé (Malden, Mass.: Blackwell, 2005), 103–16.

5. Louis Menand, *The Marketplace of Ideas: Reform and Resistance in the American University* (New York: Norton, 2010).

6. Gerald Graff, "Other Voices, Other Rooms: Organizing and Teaching the Humanities Conflict," *New Literary History* 21, no. 4 (1990): 822–23.

29

CRITICAL CREDO

MARK BAUERLEIN

My critical credo begins with a particular feature of humanistic disciplines. That feature is amply revealed by previous credos published in *the minnesota review*, specifically, by their variation. Review the entries and you see widely scattered interests and methods at work. One contributor aims to make students into intellectuals ready to enter tough forensic settings (Graff). Another one "remain[s] committed to looking for connections between the history of the left and the possibility of social change" (Cohen). One mentions his divorce after seventeen years of marriage while another describes a favorite class assignment in which students keep a gender diary, recording "every act that they believed engendered them" (Fuss). Another ends her discussion of service burdens on female professors with the sententious call for "an end to a kingdom based upon exploitation" (Massé).[1]

These are all more or less accepted practices and goals in the humanities today. If you sampled any hundred professors with the same question about credo, similar variations would emerge. Press them on what they think everybody should do and one would, of course, uncover common threads, most of them, I would guess, versions of exploding what philosophers used to term "the natural attitude," the mindset that takes things as given realities independent of human values and interests. But common grounds don't much excite the professorate. Everyone wants to be different. Our subject matter doesn't lend itself to hypotheses and truth telling the way scientific subjects do, and it encourages inquirers not to begin with the same question (say, "What is the structure of DNA?") but to pose unique questions of their own devising. Added to that, humanities professors receive awards and promotions and raises for individual effort so they wish to play up their distinctiveness.

The result is a bustling marketplace of purveyors vying for attention, a robust pluralism of ideas and interpretations. Or at least it purports to be so. Often it makes for lively conversations and a certain kind of progress within the fields, helping rising scholars and teachers carve out their own projects and say something original. But once we leave the arc of an individual career, the diversity of professional practices looks less advantageous. The problem is this: with so many professors envisioning different aims and methods of teaching and research, they can't come together as a united force in the full tournament of disciplines. Habitually addressing one another as interlocutors arguing over the nature and purpose of cultural study, they can't join as teammates to represent it vigorously to the university at large, much less to the public sphere.

Compare the habit to that of other fields. Chemistry professors, for instance, generally agree on the methods and content of chemistry at the high school and college levels; they don't interrogate assumptions and dignify "dissensus." Humanities folks do, and while it may demonstrate a virtuous self-reflection, in the arena of all the disciplines in the college it only disempowers humanistic study. The campus, we must remember, is a competitive environment. The natural sciences, social sciences, fine arts, and humanities vie for resources, funding, and enrollments, and they need all the weaponry they can muster. They scramble for turf in the general education requirements. They make annual cases to the dean for more tenure-track and graduate student lines. Self-criticism and individuality within the department are fine, but in a college-wide curriculum meeting they are suicidal. Get complacent, take your standing for granted, stress individual achievement, and highlight *my* credo, *my* thesis, *my* vision of the profession, and the department will be outmaneuvered.

At the high school level, rivalry works in the opposite direction. People and organizations such as American Alliance for Theatre and Education who mobilize instructors and safeguard individual disciplines don't want more— they want less. Not less material support, but less content for which they are responsible. Take the case of writing. Students complete writing assignments not only in English but in social studies, history, civics, and a half-dozen other subjects as well, and their grade depends in part on the grammar and style of the compositions. None of those other fields, however, want to assume the duty of *teaching* writing. When experts in them convene to draft standards that apply across the state and guide teachers' pedagogy, they focus on subject matter and modes of inquiry more or less unique to their discipline. Here is what we in discipline X have to do, they declare, and anything not included in the standards falls outside our purview. No need to burden teachers of government, music, and so on, with writing instruction, especially when they can say, "That's the job of English Language Arts." The same delegation happens with critical thinking, media literacy, and other so-called cross-disciplinary skills.

This is where disunity in the discipline and a plurality of critical credos proves damaging. When English teachers insist, "Wait a minute—we should all bear the brunt of writing," U.S. history teachers answer, "Well, we've got to cover the Constitution, the Civil War, the Progressive Era, and Civil Rights, not to mention historical research methods. What knowledge do you have to impart, huh? Besides, verbal skills are your job, not ours."

That query is fatal to English at the secondary level. When English teachers produce so many different answers to the knowledge question—which books to teach, which outlooks to emphasize, which literary histories, literary forms, and social/racial/cultural contexts to invoke—the discipline as a whole doesn't impress outsiders as creative and rigorous and exciting. It appears discombobulated and uncertain. Other teachers are more confident of their domain, and so they erect higher walls to keep out distracting and onerous cross-disciplinary skills. English teachers prize interdisciplinarity and devalue boundaries, in effect lowering the barriers and opening their field to educational duties well beyond the teaching of literature and composition. The State of Minnesota standards for Language Arts, for example, include customary items such as "read, analyze and evaluate traditional, classical and contemporary works of literary merit from American literature." But it also asks that students study "information contained in warranties, contracts, job descriptions, technical descriptions and other informational sources, selected from labels, warnings, manuals, directions, applications and forms."[2] It includes, too, "fallacies in logic," evaluation of "Internet sources," "the role of communication in everyday situations (e.g., advertising, informal social, business, formal social, etc.)," "the effects of media on society and culture," and "informed evaluations about television, radio, film productions, newspapers and magazines with regard to quality of production, accuracy of information, bias, purpose, message and audience."

These burdens cast English as a discipline all over the place. Students come away from those classes with a smattering of discrete "English" knowledge plus a set of skills transferrable to other fields. In effect, English Language Arts becomes a lesser discipline, with teachers elsewhere thinking, "We impart serious texts, important events, powerful ideas, and salient facts, while English teachers show students how to read them and how to write better paragraphs for us."

At the higher education level, the diversity of understanding among humanities professors has other, but still harmful effects. First of all, in the competition for turf and students, the humanities have slipped precipitously. The Modern Language Association recognized it in "Report to the Teagle Foundation on the Undergraduate Major in Language and Literature." The authors proclaimed, "Increasingly, programs of humanistic study that were once prestigious and highly regarded are receiving waning public support and are treated as marginal in their home institutions." One chart in the appendix documented a severe loss of "market share" of bachelor's degrees across the United States in the last four decades. Whereas in 1966 English picked up 7.47 and foreign languages picked up 2.94 of every 100 degrees awarded, in 2004 the rates stood, respectively, at 3.74 and 1.05.[3]

People have explained the decline of literatures and languages in a variety of ways. Some say that rampant political correctness, identity fixations, and adversarial postures of teachers in freshman and sophomore classrooms estrange a portion of students before they decide upon a major. Others emphasize the rise of vocational and careerist motives among college students, the explosion of the undergraduate business major (by far the most popular choice in America today) marking the obvious proof. Still others note the simple proliferation of new majors that inevitably disperses the undergraduate population.

Each of those explanations may be true, but we may still reasonably conclude that language and literature instructors have not persuaded entering students of the significance and value of their fields, at least not enough to counter the pressures that push students away. After all, some fine arts fields have prospered, and as for vocational motives interfering, people in business and the professions constantly harp on the value of reading and writing skills. But when people in the fields emphasize their own activity, they obscure the benefits of the whole major. For scholars, the conflict of interpretations may be an enabling condition, allowing them room to enter scholarly conversations with verve. For students, though, pluralism looks altogether different. Gerald Graff gives a nice rendition of their experience in his essay "It's Time to End 'Courseocentrism'":

> Once in college, a student can go from one teacher who passionately believes
> that interpretations of literary texts are correct or incorrect—or at least more
> correct or incorrect than other interpretations—to another teacher who smiles

or rolls his or her eyes at the naïveté of such a belief; or from one teacher who expects undergraduates to analyze literature by using a rigorous methodology and terminology to another who thinks it sufficient if they learn to appreciate books in whatever way is comfortable to them; or from one teacher who discourages students from summarizing, telling them, "I've already read the text—I want to know what you think," to another who says, "I don't care what you think, I want to see how carefully you've read the text."

From one course to the next, students pick up a "curricular mixed-message," Graff maintains, and instead of watching their courses accumulate into a vast reservoir of knowledge, they compartmentalize their syllabi into units that dissipate once the semester ends. The English major doesn't look like a formation, and students aiming for it don't sense a fortifying collective enterprise that endows them with an expertise, much less any holistic understanding.[4]

Moreover, the emphasis on individual perspectives demoralizes the teachers as well. Yes, it helps rising scholars publish quickly and push one critical point after another on five conference panels a year, but they soon find that their audience is dismayingly miniscule. More and more, the profession has subdivided into micro-niches, so much so that general and unifying communications are ever less heeded. It used to be that an important book in one subfield, for instance, *Natural Supernaturalism*, was read by pretty much everyone, even those far from, in that case, Wordsworth's poems. In the 1980s, theory became the common discourse, with everybody reading "What Is an Author?" and the rest. Soon enough, though, theory, too, splintered into ever more exotic species. By 2010, nobody could keep up, with the consequence that most monographs published by distinguished presses ring up less than 200 unit sales to individuals.

And so when it comes to scholarship and professional writing, my critical credo runs squarely against the differentiation impulse. For the humanities to endure, humanities professors must determine and reiterate common aims and core knowledge in the fields. We need less diversity and more commonality. That means identifying a body of works for which we are responsible, a canon of works that bear enough authority to underwrite the value of humanities scholarship and teaching. They form the materials of humanities practice, and the proper goal of research is to argue for the greatness, significance, meaning, and purpose of them. They constitute a tradition of expression open to addition and subtraction of this or that work, but only in a gradualist process. New theories and themes have their impact, to be sure, but the process should work more slowly than did the headlong disruptions of the last thirty-five years.

The very utterance of the word *canon*, of course, raises hackles, but the very term *critical* presumes it. Criticism entails value judgments, explicit appraisals of a work's worth. It describes, analyzes, and interprets, yes, and it also situates works in diverse social, historical, and ideological contexts. But criticism also renders verdicts, assigns merits and demerits. It aims to understand a work and to rank it. A critic freely rates a work a piece of high art or of pop ephemera. He tosses around labels such as "masterpiece" and "masscult" and "midcult." She presumes to pinpoint in the same text strengths here and weaknesses there. A professor might write about the 1997 film *LA Confidential* and draw parallels with film noir titles from the 1940s, highlighting the black-and-white cinematography, the corruption of public figures, and the seaminess beneath Hollywood glamour. A film critic would do the same but demonstrate how stupidly the film carries those traits forward.

For a supreme example, take T. S. Eliot's famous estimation of *Hamlet*: "most certainly an artistic failure." Eliot examined the protagonist intensely, loved Elizabethan language, and cited the play in verse and prose writings, but he still declared it wanting. He grounded that decision in a brilliant insight that Shakespeare pressed a complex psychological-emotional condition onto a dramatic mold (mainly, the revenge play) that could not contain it. In a word, Shakespeare couldn't develop the right objective representation of Hamlet's "problems." And for Eliot, it wasn't enough to uncover the confounded workings of Shakespeare's composition. Eliot had to draw the evaluative conclusion. That's what made him a critic.

Critical judgments needn't be so grandiose. A good critic can draw three sentences from a text and pick them apart to form a broad illustration. Here is journalist Andrew Ferguson in *The Weekly Standard* writing about *Game Change*, the inside story of the 2008 presidential campaign by reporters John Heileman and Mark Halperin. Ferguson begins with a quotation from page 279:

> "F— you! F—, F—, f—, f—, f—, f—, f—, f—, f—, f—!!!"
> McCain let out the stream of sharp epithets, both middle fingers raised and extended, barking in his wife's face. He was angry.

This was just the kind of behind-the-scenes moments that made the book a sensation when it appeared in January 2010 (Harry Reid on Obama's light skin and non-Negro dialect, and so on). Here, however, Ferguson has a critical point to make:

> As a book, of course, *Game Change* isn't any good. The haste with which it was thrown together shows itself on every page. The narrative zigs and zags,

subplots are left to dangle, anecdotes lead nowhere. The passage above, minus the dashes, opens a section of chapter 15 and then just sits there, completely unexplained. When did this happen? Where were McCain and his wife? Why was he so angry, what did she do in response, who else was there—all the old-fashioned reporter-type questions are unasked and unanswered; the authors merely drop the lines into the text for our enjoyment and then move on to a brief summary of the state of John McCain's marriage (assuming he still has one).

The writing itself is so careless that readers will sometimes wonder whether their legs are being pulled. Most writers would consider the descriptive phrase "sharp epithets" unnecessary after detonating ten—I counted—f-bombs, one right after the other, in perfect sequence. And I'm sure the authors could have done without that extra pair of exclamation points. Elsewhere they dredge up jargon unheard since the third grade. "The *Times*," the book tells us, "made Bill [Clinton] especially mental." They must mean *spazzed out*.[5]

This witty and compact deflation begins with a critical framework, "As a book," and a curt decision, "isn't any good." Ferguson applies an eye for style, cites bits of evidence, and derives a conclusion. After reading this clipped commentary, one can no longer regard *Game Change* as competent writing or honest reporting.

Rarely do humanities professors assume that kind of critical task, at least in so blunt a manner. Of course, they pick and choose works according to the reigning pieties and trends, but those gestures are so predetermined and generic that they don't count as independent judgment (which every critic must possess). Indeed, when it comes to the objects they interpret, humanities professors from undergraduate years onward are trained in circumspection. Hand them an Emily Dickinson poem and they'll delineate metaphors and ambiguities, then summarize ideas and themes with dispatch. But ask them, "What makes this poem great (or not)?" and they go reticent.

Why? Because evaluative judgments easily slide into bias or baselessness or insensitivity. People are afraid to voice them. Furthermore, to implement them well, one needs a strong measure of discernment, knowledge, and experience. We can reach back all the way to 1929 to find evaluative judgments discredited altogether in the classroom in *Practical Criticism*, I. A. Richards's far-reaching and enormously influential study of literary reading. Richards filled the first half of his book with specimens of poor evaluative judgments, displaying one student after another discussing poetry in hackneyed, plus-or-minus terms. He passed out to them bits of verse with title, author, and date redacted, and they proceeded to emote ("More irritating every time I look at it") and opine ("Not poetic in comparison with the Romantic age, it being *too serious and too of the soil and the streetcar for the average Romantic*"), substituting impressions and ratings for analysis.[6] But Richards didn't condemn them for their ineptitude. Instead, he interpreted their judgments as the outcome of misconceptions about verse, particularly their tendency to regard verse as merely moral and intellectual statements arranged in verse patterns. Good reading, one concluded, was to withhold judgment, to approach the verbal object as an expression to analyze, not to accept or reject.

Subsequent schools of thought reinforced the withholding on different grounds. In the general shake-up of literary studies in the 1970s and 1980s, value judgments acquired various psychopolitical overtones that sent professors scurrying for distance. Instead of asserting the work's worth, advanced practitioners questioned the very nature of such assertions. Recall the indeterminacies and aporias of deconstruction, *méconnaissance* in Lacanian psychoanalysis, and the subversion of masculinist, imperialist, racist, and heteronormative assumptions in later versions of theory. Each one shook the confidence of professors in one way or another. Everybody started interrogating and declaring their own subject positions, fretting about institutional legitimacy, racial and sexual identity, and pedagogical purposes, raising again and again the paralyzing question, "Who are we to pronounce such-and-such?"

We are still in that condition, and it needs to end. We must restore judgment to the regular duties of professors in their scholarship. And we need to incorporate critical judgment into our teaching—but not in the same way. Students aren't ready to make competent judgments of literature and language. They don't have the equipment, the knowledge and principles and seasoning. Therein lies our pedagogical mission: to instill in students the learning and savvy to make reasoned, informed judgments for the rest of their lives.

That's my credo, a modest and ordinary one. Teach students some literary and intellectual history, review the range of literary forms, introduce them to notions of tradition and innovation, high culture and mass culture and popular culture, compel them to take ideas and ideologies seriously, plant the "historical sense," cultivate an eye and ear for verbal surfaces—in a word, mix the ingredients of *humanitas* in the bowl of young people's minds. In the ordinary lives of adolescents today, our classrooms are often the only place where it will happen.

216 | THE DEFENSE OF LITERATURE

NOTES

1. "Critical Credos," Special Issue of *the minnesota review* n.s. 71–72 (Winter/Spring 2009).

2. "Minnesota Academic Standards, Language Arts K-12, May 19, 2003," http://education.state.mn.us/mdeprod/groups/Standards/documents/LawStatute/000269.pdf., 53.

3. Modern Language Association, "Report to the Teagle Foundation on the Undergraduate Major in Language and Literature," http://www.mla.org/pdf/2008_mla_whitepaper.pdf.

4. Gerald Graff, "It's Time to End 'Courseocentrism,'" *Inside Higher Ed*, 13 January 2009, http://www.insidehighered.com/views/2009/01/13/graff.

5. Andrew Ferguson, "How the Game Is Played," *The Weekly Standard*, 1 February 2010.

6. I. A. Richards, *Practical Criticism* (London: Routledge, 1929), 46, 28.

30 |
WHY I'M STILL WRITING WOMEN'S LITERARY HISTORY

DEVONEY LOOSER

Recently several colleagues asked me to defend my scholarly work. One of my areas of expertise is early modern women's writings, and these colleagues apparently found that specialization troubling. Indeed, what they wanted from me was less a defense of my scholarship than my participation in a funeral for women's literary history. They wanted a prediction about when the moment for studying women's writings apart from men's would be over—well and truly over. In fact, wasn't it already over, they asked? Hadn't gender studies in effect forced women's studies out of the lexicon? Wasn't a separatist approach to women's writings a fad, passé, reductive, erroneous? Shouldn't women writers always be studied alongside men? Wasn't studying female authors as a group like studying your subject in a vacuum?

Sometimes it is good to be challenged; I like a challenge. But it is no cake-walk to respond to someone who asks you the scholarly equivalent of "Are you still beating your wife?" You might respond, "Let me put a new spin on this and convince you why this field is relevant." Or you could take a reactionary tack, claiming, "Not everything that is worth doing is new." Refusing the terms of the question becomes part of the challenge.

Theirs was not a particularly original line of questioning, and women's literary history is not the only literary subfield addressing such concerns. Those in subfields that consider texts by or about marginalized groups could tell similar stories. And any scholars who have found their subjects inserted in the headline, "Is x dead?" know the phenomenon of which I speak. No doubt many have participated in exchanges like the one I have just described. (Where women's literature is concerned, there is even something amusing about our once-ghettoized area now being accused of turning exclusionary—a bizarre kind of progress in the reasons for its supposed irrelevance.) But the virulence with which my interlocutors grilled me was new to me, and the fact that one of them was a woman who had herself published books with the words *feminist* and *women* in their titles was also new.

How did studying women's writings and women writers come to be imagined as old news? It is true that the field is about as old as Shakespeare criticism, but few today seem to be complaining that studies of Shakespeare are old news; at least we do not dismiss *all* of them in one sweeping gesture. We might ask more broadly, "Why are supposedly old methods so often considered lousy methods in literary studies?" Or, "How does a literary methodology come to be perceived as old, and why does its age matter?" (Thomas Kuhn's *Structure of Scientific Revolutions* offers an interesting take, but it was published in 1962, so do with that what you will.)[1] Why weren't my colleagues asking me instead, "What's new in the study of women's writings?" Or, "What important work remains to be done in women's literary history?" Of course, they weren't asking those questions because they thought they already knew the answers: "Nothing" or "Nothing much."

I write here to advocate for both the old and the new in literary studies generally and in women's literary history specifically. This is, then, a credo that has its origins in a defense. (That in itself is nothing new for the genre of the feminist credo, histories of which are still being written.) I believe that writing women's literary history helps us better understand why we continue to have conversations like the one I had with my colleagues. It helps us to understand why the question "Are you still beating your husband?" (or spouse or partner) continues to sound so strange.

Women's literary history is part of a larger feminist project that attempts to make sense of how, when, and why we think words mean something different when they come from a man rather than a woman. Profound changes have occurred in the past several decades in literary and cultural studies scholarship—and, to a significant but lesser degree, in textbooks and classrooms—but we still don't know all that we should know about how we got to where we are today. In women's literary history, we still don't know a lot of basic facts—the life circumstances of women writers, what they wrote, what they published, and how their works were read and received. No doubt this is true about many male writers as well. But the fact is that we still don't know a lot about *highly successful* women writers, whether we define success as critical, popular, or commercial. This is simply not true, to the same degree, for men's writings.

It is important to acknowledge, then, that the writing of women's literary history is old. But it is not old in some kind of "back in the day" netherworld of the recent past. It builds on a foundation that dates back centuries, not decades. This is not to denigrate the important work that was done in the 1970s and 1980s. In *A Literature of Their Own* (1977), Elaine Showalter traces women's literary history back to the beginning of the Victorian era and examines its contours forward. Thanks to the opening of that door, we know now that women's literary history goes back much further than the 1840s. We also recognize that it is not a narrative of continuous progress. We have begun to describe how the writing of women's literary history in the past was by turns controversial and ho-hum.[2]

To be sure, scholarship on women's writings in the past remains vibrant because of the growth it has experienced since the late 1980s. Studies from that period fused the then-rapid developments in feminist literary theory with historicisms, old and new. Feminist literary historicism of women's writings has been punctuated by watershed moments, if not full-blown paradigm shifts. One of these was the publication of Margaret J. M. Ezell's *Writing Women's Literary History* (1993). Ezell enjoined us to look beyond what we might want, or hope, to see in our forays into the study of women writers prior to 1900. She enabled us to recognize patterns in our scholarship that were not faithful to the texts that we were (or, in some cases, that we should have been) studying. She demonstrated the pitfalls of slotting women writers as either feminist heroines or patriarchal victims. There was perhaps no one better situated than Ezell, whose graduate training was in both history and literature, to redirect second-wave feminist literary criticism, to bring it into conversation with emerging historicist and textual methods. Ezell moved us in a direction that Jean Marsden has called "Beyond Recovery."[3]

To go beyond recovery is not to eschew it but to recognize that the lenses through which we once recovered women's writings must shift. Aware of emergent identity issues of class/race/sexuality/nation/age, we must make sense of formerly unknown and unread (or little-known and little-read) female authors and their texts in multivalent ways. Aware that we ought not just to be looking for women writers whose politics match our own, we try to see more clearly the full range of women's writing and publishing in a given era. Instead of discovering in those writings hidden feminist messages, instead of ignoring or downplaying antifeminist statements, we aim to describe their complexities, contradictions, and contours. There is much work yet to be done to write women authors back into the literary historical record. Now is not the time to fold the study of women's writings back into some larger, indiscernible gender-mass.

Instead, we ought to be asking ourselves, "Why must gender studies be the trump card to women's studies or feminist studies?" For some, the desire to move to a gender studies framework may come from a well-meaning place—to be more inclusive. But it is a misperception to see today's women's literary history as a separatist endeavor, even if it sometimes still ought to strive to be a more inclusive one. Precious little feminist literary criticism on women's writings, whether of the past or present, has investigated women entirely apart from men. In most cases, it would be impossible to leave out the male publishers, reviewers, mentors, and family members in a woman writer's circle, not to mention the famous male and female contemporaries her work was often in conversation with.

Nevertheless, placing women writers at the center of our literary histories clearly makes some critics nervous. But if a single-sex concentration were no longer a viable literary-critical option, what would take its place? Would gender parity be the ideal, so that our studies would consider half male-authored and half female-authored texts? Or is it representativeness that we want to achieve—replicating whatever proportion of men to women authors existed in the literary past? (Of course, in some eras, we'd still have a lot of work to do to determine that formula.) Perhaps critical perfection is sixty men/forty women? Seventy/thirty? Eighty/twenty? What would proportional representation in literary and cultural studies scholarship look like, and what insights would it offer us? No doubt it would be an interesting experiment. We might even say that the past several decades of humanities scholarship have been giving proportional representation a whirl. Witness the meteoric rise of the obligatory chapter (often the last) on women and/or other marginalized group in the scholarly monograph. But if *that* period of literary criticism is now behind us, what has followed in its wake?

Maybe the notion is that, with the arrival of gender studies, we have somehow become the opposite of gender blind. We see gender everywhere in literary texts. Ergo, women writers need not be singled out for study because they, too, are everywhere. But here is the sticking point. They are not yet everywhere *in our accounts of the past*.[4] Despite their massive political and categorical differences from each other—which still need to be charted and described with greater care—women writers ought sometimes to be considered together, in order to ask new questions and potentially to reach new insights. Considering women writers in tandem allows us to recognize patterns that may be particular to that group. This is necessary not because individual authors thought of themselves as part of a tradition of women writers. (As we are learning, some did and some didn't.) Not all of them even wanted to be known as "women writers." But they ought to be considered together because, when their sex was identified or even just supposed, female authors were often embraced and dismissed by readers and critics in ways that demonstrate significant patterns. Many of these patterns appear to be based, at least in part, on assumptions made about their authorship and their sex.

The reception of women writers as a group seems to have changed dramatically, decade by decade, from one country or region to the next and from one genre to the next, as we are beginning to document. We are still putting together the data that would help us to create more effective descriptions of these relationships. These descriptions are important because they allow us to understand the cultural field into which all writers were entering and to which some of them at least were responding. It may sound tautological, but we need to study women writers together because, in the past, critics often assumed them to be part of a category and judged them categorically. Such judgments may have made a difference in how *all* authors packaged their work, what they were able to publish and what they weren't, and what was well received and what wasn't—in short, how texts were read and valued. These patterns of reception based on gender (and gender and race, gender and class, gender and age, gender and nation, gender and sexuality, etc.) may have made a difference in what the category of literature itself was, is, and is becoming. Writing about women's writing, then, is an unfinished disciplinary, sociological, and political project, as well as a literary and historical one.

To set such work aside now would be unfortunate. But as we know, if it happened, it wouldn't be the first time. We have begun to put together the story of how the category of "women's writing" has emerged at signal moments in the past, as if in an archeological dig, and thereafter been obscured, dirt heaped upon it as it went out of fashion. The turn of the eighteenth into the nineteenth century has been called by Clifford Siskin the era of a "great forgetting" of women writers—a concept that Betty A. Schellenberg and others are working to further.[5] We are in the process of documenting how eighteenth-century British women writers were for a time both newly professionalized and, in some genres, culturally dominant. A generation or two later, they had become difficult to trace. It seems mindboggling that by the mid-nineteenth century, Elizabeth Barrett Browning could not locate any literary "grandmothers" among British poets.[6] There were many forgettings and rememberings of individual women authors as well. One of the most dramatic was the 1970s feminist "discovery" of Mary Wollstonecraft (1759–1797), but other figures are no doubt yet to be located and described.

With the monumental explosion of information (and full-text search capabilities) in online databases, we have at our disposal new ways to be more capacious—and less selective or capricious—in writing women's literary history. Emerging information is allowing us to locate precisely when novels that can be identified as published by women came to outnumber those identified as by men and to determine when that trend reversed itself. For the first time, we can look broadly at women writers' reception and compare the vocabulary used across a wide range of sources, to notice new patterns and to test the accuracy of what we thought we knew. Our challenge is not to raid this mass of data to fashion cherry-picking answers—selecting the juiciest bits absent any discernable context. We must instead continue to attempt to read both widely and deeply in the face of this explosion of information. We must try to render branches, if not the whole tree, where women's literary history (and its place in literary history *tout court*) is concerned.

I would like to conclude by posing the friendly question that the skeptical colleagues I mentioned at the beginning of this essay neglected to ask: "What work ought to be done next in feminist literary scholarship on women's writings?" One thing I believe there is a profound need for taking more seriously is the role of aging, particularly old age. The reasons for adding the category of age to our work mirror those that have been made over the past decades about why our studies need to become more attentive to race, class, sexuality, and nation. We have ignored many writers of all backgrounds in their old age, and we're missing an important piece of the puzzle by doing so. What Susan Sontag long ago called the double standard of aging—that is, sexism plus ageism—has put women writers at greater risk than men for being forgotten in late life.[7] Despite the burgeoning of work on women writers, many of us continue to downplay our subjects' achievements and trials in later years. Adding writings by and about old women into our conversations is both an issue of literary historical nuance and social justice.

In my book *Women Writers and Old Age in Great Britain, 1750–1850* (2008), I argued that the cultural forgetting of the first generations of aged British women writers (and their selective remembrance as a group in the later nineteenth century) appears to stem from what we would now call ageism. This factor (often in concert with and inseparable from other ideologies, including sexism) played a role in the systematic neglect and ridicule of many women authors in their late lives. Readers and critics then were fixated (usually negatively) on women writers' old age. Many conceived of aged women writers, even those once considered great, as past their prime or even past being worth "listening" to on the page. Critics today carry this tradition forward, as British women writers' late works are on the whole less often read, republished, taught, or commented on. Nevertheless, there are some fascinating writings undertaken in old age and some compelling stories of female authorship in late life, a few of which I tried to tell in my book. But we need to know more—much more.

The ways in which literary history has been packaged have also affected our ability to see only the most visible writers across their entire life spans. In particular, the first generations of elderly professional women writers have become marooned in our literary histories. For example, when we as scholars of the eighteenth century or the romantic era stop attending to the works "our" period's authors published after 1789, 1800, 1832, or 1837—and when Victorian studies compatriots also consider those authors as "ours"—it is not difficult to see how partial views of long careers may take hold. Maria Edgeworth has often been classed as an eighteenth-century novelist, despite having published her last work of fiction in 1848. Jane Austen was admonished by Virginia Woolf to lay a wreath at Frances Burney's grave, though Burney died two decades after Austen did. We ought to be more aware of how we comprehend an author's entire professional career, published and unpublished writings alike, rather than focusing, as we so often have, on their productions in youth and middle age. We also have a great deal to learn about trends, particularly reception trends, by looking at aged women writers as a group.

In an interview that appeared in the pages of *the minnesota review* in 2006, Toril Moi expressed the opinion that "the idea of a field called *feminist literary theory* is probably over" and that we now have "various gender theories, theories of sexuality, queer theories, and you have postcolonial, transnational, and other theories—a series of fragmented, multiple set of fields with specific expertises."[8] Although I don't share Moi's sense of the end of feminist theory, I do agree that the fast and furious changes and heated debates that characterized the 1970s–1990s seem, for the moment, to have slowed considerably. From where I sit, however, this slowing down in theory production prompts little cause for alarm. Perhaps it is a sign that the theories that have enabled our work are still working. There is, after all, no concomitant slow-down in knowledge production. Few of us seem to be complaining that the books coming out in our fields don't have anything new to contribute.

What worries me, however, is the way in which this fragmentation that Moi rightly identifies has led to smaller and smaller collectives within humanities scholarship. There seem to be fewer works of theory or criticism that large numbers of us are reading in common. Even within women's literary history, though we have journals and conferences that bring our work together, we seem to be less often reading scholarship that falls outside of our own chronological, generic, or other more modestly imagined niche.[9] (A colleague refers to this phenomenon derisively as "My Stuffism," and that seems all too apt.) Our increasingly narrow scholarly focus within sub-subfields, within "our own stuff," has created new obstacles for all of us, in terms of audience, mutual understanding, and knowledge sharing. We might even say that these obstacles lead to the kinds of myopic conversation I had with my skeptical colleagues.[10] The challenge for those of us who write women's literary history, then, is to convince those of you who don't that our work matters to you and your work, too. This may be old news, but it is au courant as well.

NOTES

1. Thomas Kuhn, *The Structure of Scientific Revolutions* (Chicago: University of Chicago Press, 1962).

2. Elaine Showalter, *A Literature of Their Own: British Women Novelists from Brontë to Lessing* (Princeton, N.J.: Princeton University Press, 1977).

3. Margaret J. M. Ezell, *Writing Women's Literary History* (Baltimore, Md.: Johns Hopkins University Press, 1992); Jean Marsden, "Beyond Recovery: Feminism and the Future of Eighteenth-Century Studies," *Feminist Studies* 28, no. 3 (2002): 657–62.

4. I'll set aside the difficult question of the present here, for the sake of argument, but obviously, there is a great deal to say on that matter, too.

5. Betty A. Schellenberg, *The Professionalization of Women Writers in Eighteenth-Century Britain* (Cambridge: Cambridge University Press, 2005); Clifford Siskin, *The Work of Writing: Literature and Social Change in Britain, 1700–1830* (Baltimore, Md.: Johns Hopkins University Press, 1998).

6. Barrett Browning wrote, "England has had many learned women . . . and yet where were the poetesses?. . . . I look everywhere for Grandmothers and see none. It is not in the filial spirit I am deficient, I do assure you—witness my reverent love of the grandfathers" (Elizabeth Barrett Browning and Robert Browning, *The Brownings' Correspondence*, ed. Philip Kelley and Scott Lewis, 12 vols. [Winfield, Kan.: Wedgestone Press, 1984], 10:14). I discuss this quotation in terms of its implications for women writers, old age, and literary history in my *Women Writers and Old Age in Great Britain, 1750–1850* (Baltimore, Md.: Johns Hopkins

University Press, 2008), 3. On the poets that Barrett Browning might have located, see Paula Backscheider, *Eighteenth-Century Women Poets and Their Poetry: Inventing Agency, Inventing Genre* (Baltimore, Md.: Johns Hopkins University Press, 2005).

7. Susan Sontag, "The Double Standard of Aging," *Saturday Review of the Society* 55 (1972): 29–38.

8. Jeffrey J. Williams, "What Is an Intellectual Woman? An Interview with Toril Moi," *the minnesota review* n.s. 67 (Fall 2006): 65–82.

9. I include myself in this trend, and I applaud venues like *The Journal of Women's History*, which has instituted a "Book Forum" that seeks reviewers from outside of an author's subfield to start a conversation about her/his book's methods.

10. I readily acknowledge that I have probably misunderstood what's new, what's old, or what matters in these colleagues' work as well.

NEW TURNS

WITHOUT EVIDENCE

STEPHEN BURT

I am reading a first book by A., a poet who began as, and may remain, a performance poet—someone who writes for recitation, who evidently wants immediate reaction to oral performance from a live audience— along with a midcareer book by B., who is also a novelist, whose poems tell stories; as I admire the characters they reveal, the wayward insights and the comic self-description, I find myself thinking, *If these are good* poems, *then there is no difference between poetry and any other sort of writing.*

I am reading a book by C., a rather good if derivative poet, the sort of writer whom Pound placed among "good writers without salient qualities . . . men who wrote sonnets in Dante's time, men who wrote short lyrics in Shakespeare's time or for several decades thereafter," a writer who has taken over and as it were domesticated already existing ways to write. I find myself thinking, *these are good poems but I can predict what they do, because I know what kind of poems they are: the kind invented by D.*

I am reading a late-career book by D., and I like it. I find myself thinking, *I already know what kind of poems they are: they are the kind he invented twenty years ago and has simply continued to write.* Were I to come upon this book before I had come upon any of D.'s other books, though, I would have been bowled over, blown away.

I am reading the second or third poem I have ever encountered by E., who blows me away: she seems to have invented a new kind of poem, a new subgenre. When do my expectations settle enough to allow me to recognize *that kind of poem* when I encounter it again?

When does (when should) E. stop trying to write *that kind of poem*? After the second attempt? The second book? After E. sees other poets who have tried to write it? After she sees them succeed?

When students, when audiences, ask me what makes a poem good, I say that I call a poem good when I want to reread it several times with sustained attention to how it sounds. But that description also applies to works of linguistic artfulness that are not commonly called poems, for example, *Mrs. Dalloway*. I conclude that if I am to describe my own usage (rather than the larger, sometimes contradictory corpus of usage for "poetry" and "poem"), there is no ahistorical criterion that will separate all the works I call "good poems" from all the works I do not commonly call poems.

On the other hand, few of the works I do not call poems have the sort of compression, the invitation to be read not two but twenty times, that I find in the works I am likely to call good poems.

How many styles, how many developments, in contemporary poetry might be construed as reactions to the appearance, or allegation, that nobody reads it!

The hysterical boast, the style apparently meant to attract attention by any means; the strenuously topical headline-hammering culture critique, insistent (like so much journalism in prose) on speaking of matters in which we are already interested; the first book whose tone, whose "voice" gives for all the world (and for all its patina of theoretical justification) the impression of a destructive and willful child; the book of appalled satire indistinguishable from self-satire, supposedly immune from outside insult because the poet insults himself first; the book of in-jokes, designed to attract a great deal of attention from an in-group; the book of poems that double as reportage and would be of interest as reportage (the grim history of Guam, the travails of coal miners, the life of an airline stewardess) whether or not the poems were labeled as poems; the book whose compressed poems seem to seek the solidity and the humility we associate with solid objects, real things, natural or physical (as opposed to social) facts, which do not require our attention, our consciousness, in order to remain real.

And every one of these suspect modern strategies (which poets may not adopt *consciously*) gave rise to one or more books that I really enjoy.

Asked to contribute a "critical credo" (a well-established minigenre, I discover, dating back to the old *Kenyon Review*) I realize that I don't know what I believe. Or rather I know what I believe about particular works (poems, books of poetry), and only by generalizing, with some trepidation, from those beliefs can I make any guess about what I believe, or do, or know with respect to poetry, or to literature, in general.

Which is to say that either I walk around in an untheorized muddle, or else (as I prefer to say) literary reading and, hence, literary criticism are a habitual, accretive, impressionistic matter, that my habits of expectation and response (like those of earlier generations of readers, from whom mine differ in many particulars) have been built up over many small encounters, many cues and many chances to see how other people (teachers, friends, students, family members) read: these habits make up, for me (as they seem to have made up for earlier generations of readers) a more flexible and more interesting set of ways to respond, consciously and unconsciously, to a new text than do any ways that follow from explicit rules about how to read.

If this account seems "conservative," or Burkean—being a defense of intricate, partly unconscious, partly unselfconscious, pretheoretical traditions and habits—it also permits an account of how those habits change; and it should sound "conservative" only in the sense that environmentalists and ecologists are also "conservative," wanting to understand complicated and beautiful systems and also to keep them around.

I discover that I behave as if I believe:

• That there are people, individuals, who have ideas and experiences; these ideas and experiences are subjects of immediate and sustained interest in literary writing. Sometimes they have causal force; sometimes they are epiphenomena, comprehensible only when we see large social or even biological factors that make us whatever we are, that make us do whatever we do.

- That there are kinds of poetry, and in particular a kind or super-kind (a set of kinds) called lyric, in which poems represent individuals (so that "lyric" in general represents "the person" in general).
- That some of the most fascinating poetry of recent decades—especially but not only in the United States—attacks, or appears to attack, the two propositions above, claiming that there may be no individuals (that the individual, the person, is always the wrong unit of analysis) or that lyric fails to represent them: this poetry asserts, or seems to assert, that its characteristic forms and modes reflect our uneasy dependence on, even our emergence from, systems much larger and more interesting than we are. And yet we still say that somebody wrote these poems.
- That poems should have something personal and something impersonal about them at the same time. "All that is personal soon rots: it must be packed in ice or salt," wrote W. B. Yeats, implying (correctly) that poets have something personal which they, or we, want to preserve.

Poetry criticism should be easier to write well than criticism in most other arts because the poetry critic can always give the evidence: we can insert a bit of the art itself in the midst of discussions about it so that our readers can simply compare, as they go, a piece of the artwork to our description of it. (Music critics can do the same thing, albeit not in print: on the Internet or on the radio.)

But poetry criticism should also be impossible: if a poem is any good it should exceed and complicate any statement that you want to make about it—the trick is to say things that are true nevertheless. (If you do not feel that your task is impossible to execute completely then you are doing it wrong or else you are discussing a very minor poem.)

I am less often afraid of dying than I am afraid that I have already let somebody down; that I have neglected a real responsibility; that somebody I respect and trust will come to see me as a bad person, a slacker, a selfish type; and that this portrait of me will be *my fault*.

No wonder I choose to devote so much of my energy not to the making of original poetry (that most self-indulgent and supposedly autotelic of linguistic acts) but to the applied and even ancillary arts of literary criticism—describing, giving explanations to, proposing just deserts for, things that someone else has made; I give my time and attention to poems that represent another human being, that can never represent *only* me.

When I write poetry I reveal (as Kipling, teasingly, put it) "something of myself": when I write about poetry by G. I reveal something of myself, too, but only what the writings of G. permit me (by contrast or by echo) to reveal. I may then signal, or disguise, that revelation, as I try to write with constant reference to just what I have found in G.

When you are reading a poem *as a critic*, try to read it without thinking about who else might read it, who else would like it, who else may have already read it.

Do attend, however, to what sort of people, with what sort of knowledge and what sort of expectations, the poet expects her readers to be.

People who ask what distinctive role poetry plays for us, what distinctive moral, cultural, or intellectual gifts poetry alone can bring, are asking impossible questions. "Poetry," the word, at its most useful, denotes a set of techniques that writers can use and a set of frames that readers can adopt, frames and techniques that enabled Alexander Pope and Louise Gluck and Marianne Moore and Pablo Neruda to play their roles, to bring their gifts: these gifts, these roles, share less with one another than each writer shares with other writers who are not poets and with artists who are not primarily writers.

Poetry critics, as such, are people especially useful or eager or talented in their attention to those frames, those techniques.

When I see the damage that mistaken notions in other fields (in politics, in technology) have done, the harm that apparently innocent ideas (say, lead in gasoline, for a smoother ride) have caused, I take comfort in thinking that poetry is at least (as the *Hitchhiker's Guide to the Galaxy* said of our Earth) mostly harmless: to say with Auden that poetry "makes nothing happen" is to say that in our present state of civilization it is unlikely to hurt anyone.

J. came to understand contemporary poetry—her own poetry as she wrote it, the poetry of her own contemporaries—through an enthusiastic coterie of American West Coast avant-gardistes: poems had to speak to the systematic bad energies of late capitalism, to undermine the prison of conventional language, and "self-expression" was for bourgeois losers: under no circumstance should the contemporary poem project a consistent fictive "I."

J. has now written an enormous—and brightly readable—memoir, based on her journals and tracking her adolescence, more than 600 pages long; her new book of verse, moreover, addresses and mythologizes, with an unironized verve, her life partner and friends, almost in the manner of Shelley or Coleridge.

When you try hard and seriously to expel from your poetry the figuratively personal, the fictive "I," sooner or later it may return as the literal "I": as an attempt to present and preserve real people, with real names.

On the other hand, you can try to convey the personal, the fictive "I" by only apparently impersonal means: through description—I am the sort of person who would notice this and this and this and this and this and this, think them worthy of record (but who would probably overlook that). Elizabeth Bishop made this way of proceeding unmistakable and obviously useful; R. F. Langley seems to have taken it as far, in verse, as it can go.

Frost/Williams: Whose Era? Critics older than I am grew up asking, or arguing, whether Pound or Stevens ought to dominate whatever passel of tastes and techniques modernism has given us: hence Marjorie Perloff's title "Pound/Stevens: Whose Era?" But if we want to ask what the modern history of poetic technique can tell us about history in any larger sense the choice lies instead between Robert Frost and William Carlos Williams.

When we read Williams, even at his most pessimistic—say, "These" or "Impromptu: The Suckers" or "The Yachts"—the style alone tells us that societies do change, that they can become more (or less) just and more (or less) fun, that new styles can come into being to reflect those advances (or retreats). His style says, always, that we can solve old problems or discover new things, together if not collectively, through the shared medium of our changeable language. The same style, with its rough edges and its reversals, says that Williams himself does not necessarily know what we will discover next.

When we read Frost, the form and tone say the reverse: though we may be Americans in New Hampshire, we live, at best, in the universe of Virgil and of Horace; nothing can change, and nothing improve, from generation to generation. Whatever language we speak, whenever we speak it, the crops grow and die and we die, alone, and the poet at his most ambitious has to lead us, in code ("so can't get saved, as St. Mark says they mustn't") or in plaintext, to that one truth. We would know as much already, alas, were we (as he is) "versed in country things," and Frost writes, usually, as the man who already knows—so his finish, his flawlessness, even his sometimes jocular aura, confirm.

When I say that I would like to side with Williams, I do not mean that the weight of historical, nor of literary-historical, evidence has already convinced me to do so.

When we judge works of art we speak, quite rightly, about the value of surprise, of novelty. But there is a delight in finding difficult familiar patterns performed very well: perhaps the art of poetry has as much (or as little) in common with the sport of ice skating as with the work of scientific discovery. And—as with ice skating—the same difficult move may seem new, may hold our attention, may differ enough from the last performance of the same move, simply because we are seeing or hearing a different person perform it.

We hear, still, that one or another artistic move deserves praise and attention because it "makes us aware of our role in the construction of meaning" or some similar locution, but really we are already aware of that role: beginners are all too aware of it since they are often asked to find meanings, or effects, that they do not (yet) know how to construct. Sometimes construction is harder than disassembly; it is harder to bake somebody a cake than to give them a recipe, harder to make for them a working bicycle than to hand them a bag of bicycle parts.

We should not ask that all works of art be "subversive," any more than we should ask of gardeners, farmers, that they always plough up and turn over (sub-vert) new ground. (But there would be no crops, and no new flowers, if the people who grow them never turned over the ground.)

I don't want to read arguments about poetry when I can just read poems—but I cannot always read poems. I can read literary criticism and other sorts of expository and argumentative prose at the breakfast table, where I cannot read fiction or poems: they would be too absorbing, too distracting—I would neglect the people who eat breakfast with me.

Niedecker contra *Zukofsky*: I dislike in principle, though I might admire in the execution, any work of art that attempts to create a small band of devoted and specialized readers, readers who will devote their lives to its untangling. (For more on such attempts, see especially Bob Perelman's first book of criticism, *The Trouble with Genius*.) It seems to me arrogant, if not misguided, for an artist (if he has a choice) to ask us to devote so much of our time to himself (and it is usually *him*-self).

I am, however, happy to advocate work that in practice, for whatever reason—from the difficulty of its sentences, to the obscurity of local references, to the fact of being published by a small or badly distributed press—has only a hundred readers at present. Such work may seek attention (don't we all, sometimes?), but it does not aim to monopolize its readers, to take them away from other art, from other ways to see the world, which is, after all, bigger than even the most ambitious art that attempts to contain it.

I prefer to make claims about single authors, single works of art, by giving evidence and weaving arguments around it: in such cases, from a review-essay to an academic book, sufficient evidence *can* be given. But I prefer this generalized and fragmentary form when making claims about reading and writing and art in general, in part because I do not know, for such claims, what evidence would suffice.

32 |
ALL THERE IS TO USE

MARK GREIF

I

Ibelieve the right basis for criticism was once articulated by Kenneth Burke: "The main ideal of criticism, as I conceive it, is to use all there is to use."[1]

This precedes Burke as many great critics' method, and it will outlast those of us doing our short span of work now.

The reason Burke's ideal seems unprofessional is that histories of criticism divide us by our methods. They put critics into schools by their procedures rather than, say, by their subject matter, their styles, or their written personalities. There is something flattering about the seriousness with which they treat critics and also something irritating about the implacability of their categories—much in the way that you can't know your own character, but others are always eager and at ease to diagnose it for you.

I can't name or categorize my own practice. I do know what goes on in the workshop and what the procedures are. I possess certain problems that must be solved, for the sake of pleasure (while reading a book), on behalf of friendship (when talking about a book), and for the sharpening up of the self (because books describe the world and "self" names what guides us through it, with a keener or duller sense of direction).

My sequence of stratagems then retains a loose order, which I will dutifully undertake to identify with -isms. Facing a novel, for example, I look first for the moments of highest activity or voltage (instinctivism). Then identify implied authorial summary, direct address, and microcosmic encapsulation, to see what the narration argues openly (authorialism). Find typical passages of style and examine them, forgetting who wrote them and when, to see how they hang together internally (practical criticism). Hold in mind the central figures, images, geographical locations, proper names, physical actions, material objects, and familial or social structures of the book, outside the language in which they were depicted, to see what webs they form (psychologism, sociology, symbolism; here things learned from theory enter). Notice the worst parts (uncharitibilism). Discover where the spirit of the times of the book's writing infuses the written text and discloses itself (old and new historicism). Ask myself why I care (lunch break). Map out what parts have gone unnoticed to that point and why (completism). At this stage, I remove the protection of the intentional fallacy and end with sympathy and biography. I think a bit about the writer as a fallible human being, imagining I had created the object myself to see what I can learn of it as an object of human handicraft.

In other words, "using all there is to use" is not antimethod nor anti-ism (however facetious the ones above). But a singular method is an illusion made out of critics' plurality of methods fused with their private concerns and personalities. The era of grand theory in literature departments was essential for the humanities because it made a home for strains of Continental philosophy that had been exiled from Anglo-American philosophy departments. But it got a bad name when teachers not at home with philosophy thought it should be "applied" to literary works or that it furnished a reading "method"—with painful results, much as judging the duties of friendship or love on strict Kantian or utilitarian lines makes you a truly inept friend or lover.

II

What, then, is criticism? Criticism is thinking with an object, when the object is a work of art or an artifact. The object must be *fixed* in *form*, enough that one can study it, repeat the study, see round it, take some time with it. The same object must sit on others' tables—even if you sometimes have to point out to them that such an object is there. So criticism is also a kind of thinking together, in company.

The object of criticism may be made of words, of cement, of celluloid images. It may be the consequence of determinate instructions, made by humans, which it will require new humans to realize—as in a symphony or an act of legislature constituting a law. Or it may be a singular event, hemmed in by rules but shot through with spontaneity, like a trial judgment, a football match, or a battle.

Criticism is not the only activity of its kind that we should care about (we who are critics or have to do with literature). *Philosophy* I take to be thinking about the structure of many artifacts, or about nature, existence, and the general path through life. We do undertake it, many of us, and I wish we would give it some of the autonomy it deserves in our practice. Thinking that rests on the observation of what human beings do in common, their transactions, shared activity, and mutual practical understanding, is *social science*. I wish we did more of this, frankly: I wish, for example, it wasn't only "reader reception" that interviewed others (outside the classroom) to find out how they read. And then—always in a puzzling relation to this threefold division of the interpretive work we try to do—is making art, itself.

The connection of art criticism to art practice remains a source of grief. Criticism's way of turning over artworks in the mind is unusual for its wish to recover and communicate strong experiences in a medium distinct from that which inspired them. It always faces the challenge: Instead of doing criticism, why not either make art or sit silently in its presence? Why opine and scribble? The impulse is better understood if you acknowledge criticism's likeness to sketching or copying of masterpieces or making miniatures, and also to ornamentation, as we extend our pleasures by piling them up, laying tinsel on the Christmas tree. Done in common with others (real or imagined, contemporary or scattered over centuries), criticism might be like singing or making music together. In all these ways it is adjacent to art but is subordinate to artistic creation.

The balance changes, however, when criticism elects to show the ways in which a work or artifact speaks of a real world that is not yet good enough for us, inadequate to all that we could do or be. Such criticism becomes *critique*, which inspires criticism's bid, at times controversially, for a standing alongside the arts in the circle of original creation. And it becomes something other when it genuinely chooses to undertake philosophy or social science or art itself—and trouble will arise if you don't allow that critics can occasionally venture into these connecting fields.

Underlying all these practices is thinking, as a capability that is universally and evenly distributed. The democratic significance of criticism's real basis shouldn't be hidden. Thinking is something we all do, all the time, similar to speaking. But thinking and speaking are also capabilities that individuals come to perform with different manners of virtuosity and disparate outcomes of pleasure and entertainment for observers. So criticism, say, is finally just one track of thinking—practiced by some readers or observers or listeners for others who momentarily don't have the inclination or the freedom to dig into the mysteries of a particular object. Ideally, it is done for the imagined benefit of capable equals who just happen to have other things on their plates. All men and women are casual tellers of jokes. Society knows, however, the function of a comedian and is comfortable with it. The critic is a comparable figure. If criticism is associated with elitism, it's because of the supposition that when some people think publicly about art and talk about their thinking, they do so only because they believe others cannot think at all or botch it when they try. But that is a mistake born of other divisions and injustices that in general we ought not to tolerate and that have their roots elsewhere.

I suppose critics can always be convicted of one invidious judgment: We believe you have a choice, at base, whether to think more about the objects of the world or neglect them. Criticism contemns neglect.

III

The shape of criticism in practice is cut to the die of the times.

In 2011, the situation of criticism seems to be marked by contraction. The space in newspapers devoted to new books is shrinking. I heard the editor of the *New York Times Book Review* say two years ago that his section had been shortened from between thirty-two and thirty-six pages to between twenty-four and twenty-eight. The reviews of books that go in newspapers may not have been the primary location of the practice of criticism in a long time, it's true. In sheer bulk and hours, that title has belonged to the university. But newspapers and magazines have been the place of public notice for criticism of writing, and they seem the lap from which a public criticism originated.

The cause is not a loss of interest in literature. The withdrawal occurs across the board, in the loss of column inches, pay, and jobs—for critics of film and popular music, too. No one has become less interested in movies or pop music than before, not even the Great Imaginary Philistine who we all fear will lose interest in whatever we love. Nor is criticism less interesting in itself. The diminution comes from a reordering of commercial forces, in which the money that pays for the diffusion of cultural products has been helped by the Internet to lose interest in the print advertising that funded newspaper criticism sections. (Print criticism survives very well in the criticism-only weeklies that are not reliant on advertising, such as the *New York Review of Books*, *London Review of Books*, and *TLS*, which are less expensive to produce and are paid for by subscription dollars from steady readers interested only in books.)

Within the domain of criticism itself, the Internet has separated the consumer function—the thumbs-up or thumbs-down evaluative reviewer's obligation, which had also been a part of most public critics' job—from the "critical" function. Reviewing and evaluation is done now by volunteers who register opinions on Amazon.com, drawing distinctions among varieties of goods such as translations of ancient texts, DVDs of experimental cinema, opera recordings, fifty-foot garden hoses, and portable hard drives. The more recondite the area of consumer life, the better the answers and reviews tend to be. One learns obscure discriminations with precision and gains insights of great trustworthiness not because of the superiority of a hive mind but because individual reviewers' tastes and personalities come through with surprising vividness in these written paragraphs. You learn with whose tastes to identify and how to read between the lines. This kind of criticism takes care of itself online and is in perhaps better shape than ever before. The more ruminative critic is helpfully freed of its burdens.

Plus there are simply more objects to discuss. The material conditions of cultural production, archiving, and diffusion have led to a proliferation of things calling for a purely thoughtful criticism. Often people imagine that gatekeeping or selection is needed. Really, it is the hunger for a pleasure-giving, understanding-directed, conversational, and thoughtful art of analysis that most goes unsatisfied. Everyone knows that online this art, if not done badly, just isn't done enough. Its doing has few professionals now, and few structures by which to raise the stakes, or quality and abilities, of the existing volunteers. They, too, will need some kind of support to set their days free for invention and improvement.

I suspect universities will increasingly engross the former world of "public" criticism in the next few decades, possibly inaugurating their own reviews of various kinds to publish both professional and student criticism and beginning to offer more curricular initiatives in "public criticism" or "public intellect"—first at the graduate level with master's degrees, then as a part of undergraduate writing programs. The university has similarly engrossed other practices with a diminished commercial basis, such as American poetry and the American short story. Of course, this means that those who are newly trained to practice criticism in the university may not find money doing it later anyplace *but* the university.

It is hard to know how to feel about this. I don't think the taking-in of public criticism by the university would be a particularly good thing, but it would also only be an element in a larger movement. If it occurs, it will be part of the continued process whereby the university dilutes the humanities, here literature, by turning them into utilitarian tracks—as English departments are redirected from literature (and thinking) to writing (and quasi-professional preparation, or remediation of skills vanishing from secondary education). The university seems hard at work on many fronts, wherever it reconceives itself as a profit-making corporate institution, at indebting the American young and drinking up their early maturity—much as the health care system indebts us from the other end and drinks up savings and retirement. But the university, in its local operations, also saves and preserves so many things that make life worthwhile: it brings strange people together and, curiously, preserves certain visions of utopia, as well as the continuity of critique. So perhaps public critics, who also believe in literature (and utopia!), if drawn into the university, will help reorient writing programs to where university resources belong—by sending their students back to formal, humanistic literature classrooms.

IV

I think the new thing criticism ought to learn to do now is to grapple with the total aesthetic environment that has taken hold of ordinary life in our times, which criticism has not done all that well with—has, really, often been blind and deaf to—so far. From waking, when you put on one song then another to start the day in the right mood—while also listening to NPR (which is interviewing some writer or documentary filmmaker) and idly looking at the television or online weather—you can be environed by representations until you lie down again to sleep. Along the way you'll take in several fictions: *Law and Order* at the gym, a romantic comedy on DVD in the evening, and pages of Proust before bed. It's a matter for interpretation whether the "real" things you see (the news, reality television) also present themselves as fictions or art.

Criticism still deals primarily with single objects, and it separates aesthetic objects by their medium. Yet objects are not experienced singly today but in thousands, and often not sequentially but overlapping or simultaneously. There are people who put on music now to watch online pornography. No doubt someone, somewhere is trying to write a novel at the same time (during the dull parts). The archive becomes infinitely deep while new production foams the surface.

How can criticism possibly be alert to this? The temptation is to ask for an experimental practice, avant-garde in the manner of the modernist arts, collecting fragments of the aesthetic objects heard, read, and viewed, with the critic as a central, supersensitive reflector or perceiver. Yet one feels one has seen attempts at this collage—and nothing has been more miserable and narcissistic than these "experimental" attempts.

In fact, the subjectivism of such efforts to take in the diversity of objects through the single receiver have made clear just how much good "standard" criticism is impersonal and non-narcissistic, how firmly it turns away from the mere reflection of the self. It looks through the self to the object in its depths but also to the audience gathered round in similar position, imagined across great breadth.

I find myself looking to a few ventures of earlier critics for hope: short essays of Edmund Wilson, whom I do not ordinarily worship, and scattered moments of Pauline Kael. These instances all reconstruct the possibilities of the audience, imagined and assessed, in interaction with the work. Wilson's moments that I return to come in "The Greatest Show on Earth" (1925), where his eye travels the rings of the circus, and "Burlesque Shows" (1925–26), especially his account of the low-price workingman's Yiddish burlesque at the Olympic Theater. Also the strange "A Preface to Persius," in which Wilson reads an eighteenth-century preface to a translation of a Latin satirist in an Italian restaurant in 1927, where red wine is served despite Prohibition (and this fact becomes significant). In each essay, a mobile sensibility slides from the surfaces of some aesthetic object to a sweating, effortful performance staged in the real world—even when it is Wilson eating a gigantic dinner!— and to the audience that surrounds the performance and calls it into being. Wilson at the circus becomes an eye seeing the performance from every perspective in turn: audience, performer, introspective mind, naïve immediate admirer. The aerialist, Mlle. Leitzel, spins "costumed in silver, dazzled by white blades of light," yet once she leaves the arena, after death-defying feats, is seen as she "sinks into a chair, and her brow is rung with agony. She gasps; her great bright black eyes stare." Criticism takes in backstage, frontstage, the feeling from the cheap seats, the hidden emotions of the performer, and the shock to this critic, who never pretends he has seen it all.[2]

Kael is haughtier. (It takes spirit to be haughtier than Edmund Wilson.) But whenever you think she behaves as the isolated reviewer of a film, enthroned before the screen (as if she were watching it at home, if easy home screening had existed in 1969), you find that Kael is actually surrounded by people and constantly taking their temperature—haughty because she is attuned to them and mentally disagreeing with *them*: "people around me became rather hostile. . . . The atmosphere around me was as if the Church were being satirized before an audience of early Christians" ("Waiting for Orgy," on *Bob & Carol & Ted & Alice*). "*Bonnie and Clyde* keeps the audience in a kind of eager, nervous imbalance—holds our attention by throwing our disbelief back in our faces. . . . During the first part of the picture, a woman in my row was gleefully assuring her companions, 'It's a comedy. It's a comedy.' After a while, she didn't say anything."[3]

In the era of vast distribution but private screening and listening (and still-private reading), we critics will have to figure out what it means to reconstruct the feeling of the audience around us, to feel again the public pressure and exigency of so many invisible eyes upon so much visible *stuff*.

NOTES

1. Kenneth Burke, *The Philosophy of Literary Form* (1941; Berkeley: University California Press, 1973), 23.

2. Edmund Wilson, "Burlesque Shows" in *The Shores of Light: A Literary Chronicle of the Twenties and Thirties* (New York: Farrar Straus and Young, 1952), 274–81; Wilson, "The Greatest Show on Earth," in *The American Earthquake: A Documentary of the Twenties and Thirties* (Garden City, N.Y.: Anchor, 1958), 40–43; Wilson, "A Preface to Persius," in *The Shores of Light: A Literary Chronicle of the Twenties and Thirties* (New York: Farrar Straus and Young, 1952), 267–73.

3. Pauline Kael, "Waiting for Orgy," in *Deeper Into Movies* (Boston: Little Brown, 1973), 13–14; Kael, "*Bonnie and Clyde*," in *Kiss Kiss Bang Bang* (Boston: Little Brown, 1968).

33 |
OPEN

KATHLEEN FITZPATRICK

When I first started blogging, back in June 2002, I didn't have any sense at all that I was taking a stand or making a statement: nothing of the sort. I certainly wasn't setting out to change the nature of scholarship. On the contrary, I'd just finished rewriting the book that grew out of my dissertation—a four-year research and writing process based on a dissertation project that had itself taken two years. Six years already, and I figured, more than a little naively, that it would take at least another year or so for the book to be published. And here I was, itching to get some ideas in front of an audience. I'd started thinking that there surely had to be a better way, and maybe this "blog" thing was just the ticket.

The blog was an exercise in immediate gratification, in other words. I wasn't sowing the seeds of scholarly publishing's future; I was merely getting rid of excess writing energy, finding a place for the kinds of random ideas that took up part of my day-to-day attention, and satisfying the hunger for connection and communication that the solitary exercise of producing that first book left in its wake. I felt as though I needed all of that to happen in order to clear the mental space to be able to focus on my "real" work, the conference papers, journal articles, and monographs in which substantive scholarship gets done.

A couple of unexpected things happened, however, that changed my relationship to the blog in ways I would never have predicted. The most obviously significant was the fact that it took *four more years* for that book to reach print, not the hilariously optimistic one-plus I'd been imagining. Some of the delay was caused by the slowness in scholarly publishing that we all experience: the enormous lag time created by the peer-review process, the lengthy pauses between phases of the production cycle. But much of it was caused by the difficulty I had finding a publisher willing to take on a first book by an unknown author in the first place, much less in what was becoming an increasingly tenuous economic environment, still less given that this first book appeared to lie between multiple fields rather than squarely within one well-defined area of interest. The book was finally published, of course, but the four-year delay, coupled with my knowledge that even if it were successful the book would be unlikely to sell more than 400 copies, made me start wondering about the realness of the work that I'd done in it. How important could it possibly be, if so few people would ever see it, and only after so long?

The other thing that happened was that I started getting cited, in public venues, by increasingly respected members of my field. These early citations made an enormous impression on me—not least because the work that was being cited was never my book (which was still months, if not years, away from seeing the light of day), and it was only very rarely my journal articles. More often than not, these early citations pointed to blog posts or to reworked versions of posts that ran in more formal, if not formally peer-reviewed, publications. These were often pieces in which I thought out loud about the ways that scholarly communication was changing, and so perhaps these citations shouldn't have surprised me. Changes were, after all, afoot, and many of my colleagues were starting to ponder what those changes boded for the future as well.

But what did strike me about these citations and connections was that they were happening around work that I was doing in the open. Working in the open was for me not just a matter of publishing in open-access venues but of thinking out loud, in public, with a group of colleagues who were similarly thinking alongside me. Something odd would occur to me; I'd write a bit about it and post it on the blog; friends and colleagues would respond, sometimes pushing my thoughts further, sometimes changing their direction, sometimes disagreeing with me outright. In the days and weeks following, I was likely to return to the topic, to write about it again from a new angle, continuing the conversation and helping to develop the collective train of thought.

The vast majority of the formal work that I've published since 2002 bears some connection to my blog, whether literally developing out of a blog post or benefiting in more roundabout ways from the feedback that the blog facilitated. That feedback, and the community that produced it, was particularly important in the blog's early years as I was starting up my next projects, coming up for tenure, and otherwise getting my sea legs in the profession. My blog became a kind of permanent conference, allowing me to engage with key friends and colleagues from around the world on a more or less daily basis.

Many scholars worry about the consequences of working in the open, and a range of commentators have pointed out the dangers that apparently lie in being that visible on the Internet. Perhaps none of these commentators has raised more eyebrows than "Ivan Tribble," whose pseudonymous article "Bloggers Need Not Apply" ran in the *Chronicle of Higher Education* in 2005. In this brief screed, Tribble argued that as "a publishing medium with no vetting process, no review board, and no editor," blogs both put their authors at risk of being seen saying the wrong thing in public—the kind of "wrong thing" that an editorial process could ostensibly help to prevent—and make their authors seem silly, self-absorbed, indiscreet, and shrill. Tribble, of course, demonstrated all too clearly the degree to which blogging not only was looked down upon as an insufficiently serious form of writing but also served as evidence of a lack of seriousness inherent in the writer herself. Needless to say, despite strong rebuttals from a wide range of blogging scholars, Tribble's kind of thinking, imagined to be endemic in the academy, dissuaded many scholars from sharing their work in blog form.

Even where they understand that blogs can be used to do serious work, however, many scholars worry about the unintended consequences of exposing their in-process work to public judgment. They worry about the potential for political backlash, for painful critique, for the theft of their work. These are issues that I never gave much thought to, in the early days of my blog, for some reasons that were probably pretty blithe (though not, as it turns out, incorrect) and others that were more considered. The idea of worrying about my work being stolen, for instance, never occurred to me, precisely because every blog post I wrote was time-and-date stamped as I wrote it, undeniable evidence of the origin of my intellectual property rights. In fact, in that sense, putting my thoughts out there in the open seemed a safer way of laying claim to them than did hiding them from public view.

The concern about the unpleasant potentials of public critique is a real one, yet it's one we face down in other venues all the time: we present in-development work at conferences; we share drafts with writing groups; we routinely publish things with which others take issue. So while the blog required that I be prepared for the possibility of critique sooner in the writing process, and from a wider range of respondents, the difference was really one of degree rather than kind. It was a difference, however, that was productive: the moreness of more feedback was significant precisely because it came from a group of commenters who became a community. Our day-to-day interactions across multiple blogs built a strong sense of trust through the gradual development of a set of norms governing appropriate critical behavior. Each of us had to be willing to engage as honestly and openly as we would in conversation with close colleagues, and each of us had to be willing to accept and respond to criticism as it arose, without defensiveness or anger.

This is perhaps the most difficult part for many critically minded scholars contemplating working in the open: the fear of attack, whether intellectually or politically motivated. It's certainly true that the combination of speed and relative anonymity provided by the Internet has made possible some fairly shocking new forms of public incivility, as can be seen in the comments section of any local newspaper—or, indeed, in the comments on the *Chronicle of Higher Education*. Fortunately, the community norms espoused by many blogs (not to mention the blogger's ability to set commenting policy and to moderate out offenders) have made those sites generous and hospitable environments even as they promote vigorous discussion. Nevertheless, we worry, and not without reason, given the current political climate, about exposing ourselves not just to the responses of other academics who oppose our positions but to broader public backlash, interference, and even investigation.

Recent cases of such investigations—perhaps most notably that focused on the University of Wisconsin historian William Cronon, in which his e-mail was subpoenaed by the state's Republican Party after he published an op-ed critical of the governor's attempts to eliminate collective bargaining rights for public employees—suggest that there are two very different senses of "public" involved in the kinds of open work that I'm discussing. On the one hand, there are public issues, like those with which Cronon was engaged, issues such as immigration, reproductive rights, and the treatment of sexual minorities, issues that are rigorously, critically explored within the academy but are often subject to emotional rather than thoughtful reaction within the broader culture. Scholars working on such public issues are understandably concerned about the dangers involved in opening their work to widespread scrutiny. My own work, admittedly, hasn't been overtly focused on such public issues in ways that would have made me a desirable target. While the argument of my first book was grounded in an array of concerns about the gendering and racing of media forms and their representations, the project was on the surface about the relationship between television and the novel—uncontroversial enough for most readers. In fact, the only backlash the project inspired, a dismissive reading of the book's feminist grounding, came in a review in a scholarly journal. Similarly, the writing I have done on my blog, which has often revolved around a critique of assumptions held within the academy about new media forms, mostly generated concern among scholars.

In addition to the "public" involved in such public issues, however, we must also consider the "public" implied in engaging with critical academic issues in the open. The issues involved may not be hotly debated within the broader culture, but they may be of profound interest to some nonacademic intellectuals, and engaging with those audiences has the potential both to strengthen our work and to bring a deeper understanding of the significance of what we do as scholars to a broader group of interested readers. In fall 2009, I posted the full draft manuscript of my book in progress, *Planned Obsolescence: Publishing, Technology, and the Future of the Academy*, online at MediaCommons as part of an experiment in open peer review. In the weeks and months that followed, the manuscript received more than 300 comments from more than 40 different readers. Many of those readers were scholars, of course, but many of them came from fields other than mine, and several readers weren't academics at all. The librarians who commented on the draft were particularly helpful, as was one attorney who helped me think through the ramifications of several of the issues I raised with respect to intellectual property. Opening that manuscript to the world was a little scary, but the ability to engage with its reviewers—and the ability of those reviewers to engage with one another around the issues raised by the text—made the risk entirely worthwhile.

It's possible that I'd have felt differently if the oppositional nature of that text were located in its engagement with public issues rather than its advocacy for public engagement. But my root feeling has always been that hiding our work from the public is a terrible means of avoiding controversy, especially when our goal is working toward some kind of social change. In the same way that scholarship that draws out and engages with conservative reaction among scholars is far more productive than that which avoids it, politically oppositional work has to be brave enough to risk public backlash. And, in fact, work done in the open can draw some of its bravery from the community of scholars that can gather around it online, working together rather than alone in confronting such controversy and moving the culture in more positive directions. If the last decade has made anything clear, it's the degree to which U.S. culture needs its most careful thinkers to make an impact on its public discourse, and we simply cannot have that impact unless we're working in public.

Working in the open produced a tangible payoff for me: an increased visibility for the work that I was doing, a visibility that resulted in lecture invitations, article solicitations, and citations, as well as a community that helped strengthen my projects. But there are other more important if perhaps less immediately obvious reasons for espousing openness, which I breezed by earlier in my passing mention of open-access publishing, reasons that highlight a profound contradiction between the ethos of contemporary scholarship and the ethics by which it ought to be bound. Academics are trained, by and large, to privilege exclusivity: we rank journals by their rejection rates, and the more difficult a venue is to get into the more desirable it becomes. We understand a publisher's imprimatur as a sign of quality precisely because of its limited distribution. But that sense of the limited distribution of imprimatur too often bleeds over into our thinking about the distribution of scholarly publications themselves; texts that are made too freely available, we somehow seem to think, cannot possibly be any good. This disdain for openly distributed scholarship works in many ways against scholarship's very purpose: contributing to a developing body of collective knowledge. Openness is key to the entire enterprise; as my friend David Parry has said, "Knowledge which is not public is not knowledge."

Not only does scholarly writing that is published in closed venues limit its potential reach, but it restricts its reach to those with a certain kind of material privilege: institutional affiliation, and often affiliation with a narrow set of very privileged institutions at that. This restriction perversely undoes an enormous percentage of our labor. We spend our careers working with students, both at the graduate and the undergraduate level, teaching them about the value of a certain kind of critical inquiry, training them in the discovery and use of scholarly resources, instilling in them an interest in keeping up with what's happening in the field. But as soon as they graduate, their access to that material is abruptly cut off. Without a sponsoring library, they can no longer use the resources they've learned to value. We ought to want to keep our alumni involved in the kinds of intellectual conversations in which we engage as scholars—our former graduate students, most obviously, as too many of them will find themselves un- and underemployed in the years after they finish their degrees, but our former undergraduates as well. Perhaps it's only a tiny percentage of such alumni who would use those resources, but even those few could make a significant contribution to the general public's ongoing investment in the work that we do—and thus its willingness to fund higher education in the future.

I've come back to self-interest yet again, perhaps knowing that it's what motivates most of us in the choices we make. The self-interest we've practiced of late, however, has led us to mistake what we value today for what will sustain us tomorrow. As the results of the Ithaka S+R 2009 Faculty Survey showed, scholars' choice of journals in which to publish is far more influenced by the sense that a publication is well thought of among scholars in the field than it is by broader questions of access. For this altogether obvious reason it doesn't seem a problem to us that we place our work out of reach of the general public—but in so doing, we prevent that public from caring about our work or even from understanding why we do it.

Even more, we prevent a growing percentage of students and faculty around the world from engaging with that work as well, even when they have access to an institutional library. The predatory pricing structures of many journal publishers have increasingly placed some of the most important scholarship being produced today beyond the budgetary capacity of many less-affluent institutions in the United States, much less institutions in developing nations. Such inequities in higher education should not be allowed to stand, and particularly not where we have the capacity to create the change ourselves simply by publishing in open-access venues or depositing our work in open-access repositories. Ensuring that the knowledge that we produce is available to any interested reader should be considered an ethical imperative—even, perhaps, a moral one.

But don't let me be mistaken: working in the open is not all a matter of stern moral duty. The personal and professional benefits that I've found in the various aspects of my open work have been a key motivation, not least the community of scholars with whom I've found myself working over the last nine years. Their support at dark moments, their help running down the answer to a problem, their joy when there's been cause to celebrate—all of these have made this period of my career dizzyingly rewarding.

So while I didn't set out to transform scholarly publishing, this is where I've ended up: evangelizing working in the open. My hope is to spend the next phase of my career bringing more openness to the profession, in order to help more scholars find ways of working that are increasingly collegial, increasingly rewarding, and increasingly just.

34

TIMING

MARK MCGURL

I s it an actual memory or only a story I heard from friends and internalized as my own? In any case, it goes like this: It's the first seminar
meeting of the first semester of graduate school. The professor, a thrilling
devil, a guy with sparks flying off of him, slowly scans the room: "Let's get
one thing straight, you're all here because you think things are basically okay
with the world." The mix of outrage and merriment in response to this sally
is one I would see this man produce again and again in subsequent years,
even as the position from which he would do his skewering would somewhat
shift. This was long before anyone had heard the term "neoliberalism," the
economic ideology against which this professor's taste in art is now to be
understood as a point of genuine resistance. Times change.

The point back then had been to shock us out of our complacent assumptions about the political efficacy of academic literary criticism, the strange activity that we were now trying to make a career of. We wanted to be tenured
radicals, but the best we could really hope for was to be radically tenured. To
believe otherwise was to deny our fundamental embeddedness in the system
we would presume to critique. It was also to miss the fact of institutional
mediation, the way actions proper to one domain do not register elsewhere
without undergoing a process of dilution, distortion, or even ironic reversal. So it was with our largely symbolic "politics," but all was not lost. If we
were lucky, the institution of the university would mediate our relation to the
economic world while we engaged in the deeply satisfying work of serious
reading, writing, and (in reasonable amounts) teaching. In our delusions of

political efficacy, our ideas were strangely similar to those of the neocons who had lately been flattering literary scholars with their umbrageous attentions, holding them guilty of all sorts of subversion, not least of the Beautiful and True. In that seminar, at that time, we were told to leave those debates behind and get real.

My institution, if I'm not mistaken, was somewhat ahead of the curve in experiencing this deflation, this partial retrenchment of politicized literary studies in a chastened professionalism. It was the early 1990s, and the latest crop of initiates in that seminar room were all carrying different parts, differently combined, of the intellectual baggage of the 1980s, when Theory had reached the zenith of its popularity and scandalous prestige. Somewhat (I imagine) like the surprisingly popular phenomenon of Sartrean existentialism in the 1950s and 1960s, which entered my life in the form of used paperbacks, part of what it meant for Theory to be so sexy was that its attraction had been felt even among undergraduates of a certain kind, undergraduates like myself, which is to say, the pretentious sort of undergraduate who nonetheless eventually becomes a more or less real intellectual. We spent hours in the Theory section of the campus bookstore pawing the latest offerings from the University of Minnesota Press, whose sedate pastel covers could not have been more inviting, curiously. On our way to the bachelor of arts degree we had cathected Theory, which had conveniently taught us what "cathected" means. (It means having a "libidinal investment" in something.)

For all the diversity of intellectual activity—structuralist, poststructuralist, post-poststructuralist—conducted under that resonant term, one bedrock assumption in the advance of theory remained constant: it was important. Leading graduate students of my own through some of the landmarks of seventies and eighties criticism not long ago, I was struck by two things: First, the sheer strength and subtlety of some of the psychoanalytic, deconstructive, and Marxist readings of literature produced in that period, whose interest has, at least for me, if only as acts of writing, easily survived the transformation of the field since their time. That field is now dominated by dutifully untheoretical historicisms, with some newly framed theoretical interventions going on alongside, but any literary scholar in his right mind should be able to enjoy, say, Barbara Johnson on Lacan, Derrida, and "The Purloined Letter." I know my students did. The second thing that struck me about these essays was, simply, the aura of professional serenity emanating from them, however melodramatic their philosophical themes.

Nowhere in these texts is there any sense that "deconstruction" is something that might happen to the educational institutions where the deconstruction of literary texts was being conducted. In this they seemed the product, still, of the great era of expansion and enrichment of the U.S. system of higher education through the 1960s and into the 1970s. The liberal hegemony of that era made ample room for daring intellectual challenges to the status quo, of which Theory was apparently one. In the 1980s, in the centrist and right-wing press, these challenges were beginning to be resisted, often by way of grotesque parody and oversimplification. In the neoliberal hegemony of the present, they are simply being defunded.

When I arrived at graduate school in the early 1990s it was still too soon to see this clearly, at least from where I stood. But in retrospect the admonition to political modesty in that seminar room was an early warning that we would need to embrace an even more comprehensive modesty, a modesty of means. Someday people might look up and decide that the study of literature and, even more so, its theorization simply don't matter, whatever the political orientation might be. Apart from anything else, the New Class of technocrats and managers no longer felt it necessary to know something about (and perhaps even read) literature, as their culturally ambitious bourgeois forebears once did, and so our enrollments were bound to go down. Unlike the neocons, the New Class simply didn't care what we were up to. And while it was clear that we could not think of our scholarship as having an obvious "political" value and still be taken seriously, not at my school, no simple answer to the question of what kind of value our work *did* have seemed to be forthcoming. Most of the traditional ones, though they no doubt continued silently to motivate us, seemed even quainter than our gestures toward political relevance. To be sure, there were intimations, already, of a chronically bad job market, which was gradually effecting the objective devaluation of academic labor so unmistakable in our time. But at least for me, with my decent fellowship and very cheap, very cold apartment, the crisis in literary studies was first experienced as an existential one. What was literary studies for? How could it be justified?

My entire career as a literary scholar has been conducted in the encroaching shadow of professional doom. It is from this fact, I now see, that I derive my critical credo, which is in essence an existentialist one, though shorn of much of Sartre's confidence in individual freedom. I am a fatalist, that is, though one who believes we are fated to try and make life meaningful. You are thrown into the flow of historical time and make of your situation what you can. In the absence of transcendental guarantees, in the face of radical contingency, you commit yourself to something. You make something. That's the basic idea. I would only add that, if my friends and colleagues are any indication, you do so in a condition of unrelenting hurry ill suited to a properly scholarly mindset. A more recent version of existentialist commitment is to be found in Alain Badiou, in the ethos of fidelity to the revolutionary event whose outcome cannot be known in advance. Still another is to be found in and around the novels of David Foster Wallace, who made his commitment to institutions in the face of an abyssal infinity, an Infinite Jest. In my case—in this context—the commitment is more humbly to the value of the study of literature; to preserving space and time for the exhilarating sense of enlightenment I feel when I read good criticism and that I see occurring in the classroom all the time; and to extending this benefit to as many people as possible. Like Wallace's, it is conservationist in outlook, not revolutionary, but it also entails recognition of the absurdity of our endeavor, the dark comedy of error and irrelevance at its core. The only critical mode that would work for me, then, was a kind of affectionate satire.

It's already there in my first book, a revision of my dissertation, which had embraced the lessons in institutional mediation offered in particular by Pierre Bourdieu. Describing what I was doing as a "methodological philistinism," I applied these lessons to the emergence of U.S. literary modernism in the early twentieth century, which I read as a proto-professional discourse, an aestheticization of the burgeoning economic sphere of mental labor. I could not deny either that I was involved in that kind of labor or that my "sociological" approach to criticism was rather blatantly aestheticized, but it seemed important to try to see literary value, as it were, from the outside, from the position of the nonbeliever. If that "objective" position, taken too seriously, would entail the end of literary studies, we could at least "savor these intuitions of our pointlessness" and "take intellectual sustenance from our proximity to our own extinction (whether real or imagined) in a kind of autonecrophilic ecstasy of self-knowledge." Obviously I had been well schooled, by then, in the art of rhetorical flagrancy. However, the absurdist recognition of the approaching End Times of academic literary criticism it expresses still seems sound enough. The only problem with such statements is that they contribute to the future they prophesize. I know I was outraged when, a few years ago, the president of the University of California said in an interview that "the shine is off" higher education in the United States, thinking he was simply uttering a dark truth about our times. Lately I have been more inclined to make the case for literary studies than predict its demise.

With the application of our collective professional will, that end can be perhaps be staved off for a while, slowed down, or mitigated to some degree. You never know. We have some things going for us—inertia, for one, but also the greatness of great literature, whose worthiness of study will not be completely denied anytime soon. There is also the profound importance to human beings of storytelling, that pervasive practice in and by which we give meaning and direction to existence. And there is poetry, no less basic to human life. This is part of what fascinated me about the discipline of creative writing, the great success story of literary studies since the 1960s and an interesting parallel to the rise and subsidence of Theory. Devoted in many ways to the category of experience and to the creative subjectivity of the individual student, its motives were so plainly existential, so caught up in making the meaning of life. And this is partly why, even with my allegiance to scholarship, I wrote a book that refuses simply to trash creative writing as a massive spectacle of narcissistic anti-intellectualism. For all its faults, and in all its glory, the writing program was a sign of life for literature.

The literary works that emerge from writing programs can, of course, be accused of many things, not least of giving voice, or perhaps ideological cover, to the neoliberal economic order in which they appear. Do we really need to hear a bunch of sob stories when we should be staring at a graph? That graph shows the rich getting richer while everyone else goes into debt. Perhaps it should be more interesting to us than some nicely drawn fictional characters or the way we feel about our history or how incredibly good a line of poetry can sound. Even so, could it be that the neoliberal order is, not unlike literary studies, already careening toward its own end, its own creative destruction? Hasn't it been for quite some time? That was another thing that was not so clear in the 1990s but seems obvious now and needs to be integrated into our sense of the crisis in literary studies. There's no denying that increasing economic inequality is one of the central facts of our time, but so is waste. So is environmental catastrophe, militarism, sectarian violence, and macrofinancial instability. They yield their own grim, graphable statistics. The time of neoliberalism is also the time of disaster capitalism, as Naomi Klein calls it.

Seen from this perspective, the way literature participates in the stabilization of human identity by, as we say, *giving it a narrative*, appears something more than a distraction from economic inequalities. It appears essential and worthy of being studied by everyone. Against the withering torrent of time, technology, and markets, it represents so many efforts to remain recognizable to ourselves, to continue to be.

35

THE POLITICS OF SMALL PROBLEMS

FRANCES NEGRÓN-MUNTANER

It's good to feel even when you're so small and have nothing, you can do something.
—ILTEZAM MORRAR, Palestinian activist in Budrus

For as long as I can remember, I have been concerned about being seen as small and insignificant. Where I grew up, this anxiety came "in the water," so to speak, from that transformative moment when a child can make sense of the statement "Puerto Rico is a small island with no natural resources." The repetition of this axiom at home, at school, and on television was not so much meant to say that the island was "small"—a reasonable geographic observation—but that those of us who happened to live there could never survive without the wealth and protection of the giant up north. It also implied that the island's political location as "below" the United States was less the product of a specific history than a direct result of our unfortunate size, an accident of nature that no degree of human effort could ever alter.

This feeling of geopolitical disadvantage was compounded by a sense of bodily vulnerability. Since I was a small girl in an increasingly violent environment, my parents guarded me with their lives, monitoring my every move and never losing sight of me in public places. Not surprisingly, when new identities were imposed on me in my late teens—and I loosely embraced them—looking (out) for trouble became a critical survival skill. Like other young women, I learned how to read people's gaze to see if I was safe or in danger and to speak with my eyes when willing to take a risk on desire. When I moved to the United States, I came to know how racial shame burns in your flesh when others look at you in contempt and to discern when these dirty looks may be a preamble to bodily harm.

Four years ago, in an essay titled "Looking Good," I considered what kind of critical practice was produced out of such small circumstances. My initial response was that the recognition that *hay miradas que matan* made me both a filmmaker and a writer with a heightened concern about looking good. And I do not mean looking good in the sense of being considered beautiful (a desire shared with most of humanity). I mean it instead as a certain way to understand the coupling of glances that produce us as wanted or devalued bodies, unacceptable or permissible objects of violence.

Yet as it is generally hard to look good without putting some effort into it, this critical project was also about how working our looks—personally and collectively—may constitute a strategy to refashion whatever makes us feel unworthy and, in doing so, offer hope in our ability to become otherwise. In this regard, looking good is more than a thematic or a tactic; it is a method in the sense of looking closely or, in Spanish, *mirar bien* at the received knowledge that shapes how we understand our self and others. By looking both ways, I ultimately aimed to pose the question of what are the political and cultural effects of (not) looking good.

Perhaps the work that best embodies these ideas is my first single-authored book, *Boricua Pop: Puerto Ricans and the Latinization of American Culture* (2004). Here, I was interested in looking at the most conspicuous of Puerto Ricans—movie stars, artists, and writers—to see how their physical bodies and their bodies of work were being shown and showing off. Through collecting the detritus of high art and literature as well as mass culture, the book pieced together the performances of key figures to behold the role of shame in constituting Puerto Rican identity and how being seen contributed (or not) to its attenuation.[1]

A good illustration of the book's overall project is its most reproduced chapter, "Jennifer's Butt." Part of a section titled "Boricua Bodies," it spoke to entertainer Jennifer Lopez's massive cultural workout around her backside after starring in the biopic *Selena* (1997). Responding to what she viewed as American culture's hostile look at her behind, Lopez launched a one-woman crusade to affirm her body's beauty and right to be seen. At every opportunity, Lopez repeated a litany of complaints aimed at American anti-big-bottom attitudes, including that costume fitters and producers looked suspiciously at her butt and mentally rehearsed different ways to hide it. As Lopez well knew, the stakes over such a culturally small thing as her big behind were not small at all. At issue was not only her own career but how much public space Latina bodies could occupy, what they are worth to capital and state, and whether they remain outside of the norm of American identity.

After *Boricua Pop*, I realized that my interest in disrupting certain ways of looking and my attention to the smallest of details—be they of dress, gesture, or place—constituted a guiding politics, one that I have come to call the politics of small problems. This politics is evident in my writings that focus on what the critic Celeste Fraser Delgado called the "monumentally mundane" of popular culture, where I consider the small things that make up so much of people's affective lives and the marketplace, as well as in those that focus on the political economy of Puerto Rico and Guam, two small places to which I have dedicated much of my intellectual attention over the last two decades.

That the notion of a politics of small problems would partly arise from the study of Puerto Rico and Guam should not be surprising. These are highly strategic and symbolically important islands for U.S. global interests, yet they have been, and continue to be, politically belittled. Acquired as a result of the Spanish American War, Guam and Puerto Rico remain governed as unincorporated territories, meaning that they are still populated by U.S. citizens that have no voting rights in federal elections and are not fully protected by the U.S. Constitution. These are also islands that, while enduring the cost of being politically marginalized, have supplied much land and human resources to build power, institutions, and wealth to which they have little access. In sum, these are unusually valuable places from which to consider the enduring contradictions of modern democracy, the high costs of constant war, and the sizeable inequalities that sustain the global order.

A case in point is Guam: Affectionately called "the rock" and the "tip of the spear" by U.S. military commanders, Guam was literally ruled "like a ship" by an appointed naval officer after American vessels arrived on its shores in 1898. Thereafter, the island became a military outpost to support the refueling of coal-powered ships and to protect U.S. interests in the region. While most naval governors did not interfere much with the long-held rhythms of native Chamorro life before the bombing of Pearl Harbor, World War II proved to be doubly devastating. Not only did the Chamorros suffer a brutal Japanese occupation, but the United States also took advantage of people's fear of continued war to expropriate two-thirds of the island's landmass to build state-of-the-art military bases to ward off perceived Asian threats. The Chamorros had been a mainly rural community sustained by the land and close-knit extended families, and the "landtaking," as many called it, ended life as they knew it to make room for tanks, submarines, and brass.

When speaking about a politics of small problems, I am, then, referring to a set of political investments and critical assumptions: That despite the fact that major public and intellectual attention tends to gravitate toward "big" objects, places, practices, and peoples thought of as small are central to thinking about how the larger world works. Moreover, insofar as big forces often display themselves without shame in small places, it is possible from these locations to obtain a particularly pristine view of the logic that animates many of the globe's most powerful institutions.

The politics of small problems, however, is not only about what or how one can see from a place, important as this is. As Jamaica Kincaid, a writer who knows a thing or two about small places, suggests, a politics of small problems is also informed by a skepticism regarding modernity's core narratives.[2] A kind of disbelief, this skepticism emerges from having repeatedly brushed against the West's "dark side" as well as from witnessing how seemingly new national orders often produce similar forms of subjection. One of several potential responses to this disjuncture, the politics of small problems focuses on the most fundamental conditions of well-being and the varied instances of power inequities that make up our daily lives.

Which brings me to one of the most extraordinary examples of the politics of small problems that I have studied: the movement to evict the U.S. Navy from Vieques, an island municipality off the coast of Puerto Rico popularly known as *la isla nena* ("little girl island.") The story begins in 1941 when the navy purchased two-thirds of Vieques and squeezed the population between an ammunitions depot to the west and a naval bombing range to the east. Although many *viequenses* objected to the presence of the navy from the start, the island became the stage of large-scale protests only in 1999 after an errant bomb killed David Sanes, a local resident who was a security guard inside the base. A surge of activism bent on expelling the navy from Vieques sprang up across Puerto Rican communities on the island and elsewhere, confronting the legacy of six decades of expropriation, contamination, disease, inadequate transportation, and the impoverishment of the local population. Once the story reached the mass media, the movement went global as activists from Okinawa to the Middle East descended on Vieques.

On the ground, the legions of *paz para Vieques* activists, who could also be nationalists, ecologists, feminists, religious leaders, or transnational agents at large, were often guided by big ideas. But at the end of the day, the local groups seemed to know that to the extent that different political parties, corporate interests, and scientists had literally sold them off to grand signifiers like national security, the most productive politics was one that sought immediate solutions to a series of small problems affecting their bodies and everyday lives. At the top of their list was a stop to contaminating bombing practices, the construction of health facilities, and a shorter route between

Vieques and Fajardo, the nearest port. After four years of continuous protests, political negotiations, and favorable coverage, the *paz para Vieques* movement managed to do what many thought impossible: it forced the navy out of its self-described crown-jewel facilities during a time of war for the United States.

The politics of small problems, however, is not an American particularity. In the same year that the *viequenses* ousted the navy, for instance, people in Budrus, a village in the Palestine Occupied Territories with a population of 1,500, organized themselves around quite similar principles. As in Vieques, a small group started coordinating a series of nonviolent protests, this time against the building of an Israeli Separation Barrier on their land. While some of the leaders understood the struggle in the larger context of Palestinian nation building, what animated most residents was their rejection of the fence's proximity to a local school, its encroachment on village land, and, perhaps most importantly, the uprooting of olive trees that have provided sustenance for generations. After organizing more than fifty protests and attracting global support, the Budrus activists succeeded in forcing the Israeli military to move the fence closer to Israel's border. Equally significant, the activists not only addressed the immediate issues brought forth by the fence but also created conditions for a host of new political possibilities, including Hamas-Fatah cooperation, Arab-Israeli solidarity, and women's leadership.

Yet it would be a mistake to view the politics of small problems only in relation to the perceived scale of the issues addressed or the size of the geopolitical space from which they are fought. For this form of politics is fundamentally about a way of thinking and understanding political praxis in the post-1968 landscape. As relatively large structures like banks, legislatures, and political parties are increasingly considered violent, corrupt, or unaccountable to most people, small groups are also increasingly constituting themselves into what Archon Fung and others have termed "deliberative minipublics," with the objective of providing information, identifying solutions, and challenging mainstream institutions.[3] The fact that small groups can succeed against great odds further points to one of the key premises of the politics of small problems: that all macropolitics are fundamentally sustained by relationships and understandings that can be disrupted and reconfigured. Although one could argue that the world is actually getting bigger—more people, larger markets, and the emergence of huge superpowers such as China—it is no less true that the power of the small has grown in kind. In a tightly interconnected world made up of economic, political, and social networks with access to near instantaneous means of communication, any small thing can turn into a big problem.

A paradigmatic example is Tunisia's 2011 revolution. The trigger of what became a series of transformative struggles from Egypt to Syria was the feeling of powerlessness and frustration about a small problem: a young Tunisian man by the name of Mohamed Bouazizi, the sole provider for a family of eight, was trying to pay a fine for a confiscated fruit cart when an officer slapped, spat on, and insulted him. When he tried to complain to municipal officials and they summarily dismissed his concerns, Bouazizi set himself on fire, an action that came to exemplify the anger felt by millions of people regarding their nation's corrupt and authoritarian rulers. Fittingly, among those who responded were small groups of young people who successfully tapped into deep-seated dissatisfaction by providing information, engaging others through social media and expanding networks of discontent on- and offline. Although many measured the movement's success in its ability to oust the nation's president, undoubtedly a big deal, the aftermath remains a classic case of the politics of small problems: it gave way to a multiplicity of political actors who continue to press the many nodes of power that hamper radical democracy in Tunisia.

In this sense, the politics of small problems can also be thought of in relation to what some theorists, like Aníbal Quijano, call the coloniality of power, that is, the manner in which power relations characteristic of classic colonialism remain in place through an unequal international division of labor supported by racial, gender, and sexual hierarchies among and within nation-states.[4] Invoking smallness in this context is a way to critically call attention to the still-dominant idea that only when the "big" problems of nation building, state founding, or capitalist development are solved will the people be liberated. Moreover, an awareness of the "small problems" inherent in contemporary politico-economic arrangements offers a continuous means of critique and intervention.

At the same time, a politics of small problems does not exclude large-scale forms of organizing, such as massive demonstrations, nor ignore the difficulties in disrupting and transforming major institutions such as the U.S. military or the Israeli state. On the contrary, the politics of small problems entails both an understanding of the relationship between what Gilles Deleuze and Felix Guattari called "macro and micropolitics" as well as the importance of engaging with others in their singularity and difference.[5] But in taking into account small places, people considered small, and so-called small problems, it aims to expand our understanding of the world and the kinds of worlds we can imagine.

Accordingly, a politics of small problems assumes an ethical project invested in the idea that one has a responsibility toward others. Small countries and groups of people made small are more likely to be occupied, humiliated, bribed, environmentally compromised, and disadvantageously integrated into the global economy. In response, a politics of small problems speaks to the value of recognizing and acting on the other's concerns as if they were your own, before the scarcity of seed becomes a famine, before border friction becomes a world war, before bellicose talk on immigrants becomes hate crimes against anyone suspected of being one. The objective, however, is not only to "solve" problems, which can become a purely technocratic exercise, but rather, in the course of working through humiliation, injustice, and inequity, to enable meaningful political participation and the enacting of new possibilities.

A politics of small problems is then the kind of politics in which feeling small is completely optional—even for a Puerto Rican girl.

NOTES

1. Frances Negrón-Muntaner, *Boricua Pop: Puerto Ricans and the Latinization of American Culture* (New York: New York University Press, 2004); Negrón-Mutaner, *None of the Above: Puerto Ricans in the Global Era* (New York: Palgrave, 2007).

2. Jamaica Kincaid, *A Small Place* (New York: Farrar, Straus, and Giroux, 1988).

3. Archon Fung, "Recipes for Public Spheres: Eight Institutional Choices and Their Consequences," *Journal of Political Philosophy* 11, no. 3 (2003): 338–67.

4. Aníbal Quijano, "Coloniality of Power, Eurocentrism, and Latin America," *Nepantla: Views from South* 1, no. 3 (2000): 533–80.

5. Gilles Deleuze and Félix Guattari, *A Thousand Plateaus: Capitalism and Schizophrenia*, trans. Brian Massumi (Minneapolis: University of Minnesota Press, 1987).

36

THE POWER OF UNKNOWING

JUDITH JACK HALBERSTAM

C redos have always been a little off-putting to me: first there is the religious element, the Catholic chanting of a set of beliefs during mass; second, and probably deriving from the first, credos reek of piety and self-righteousness . . . not that I am *not* self-righteous much of the time, but why advertise it? Third, I have been turned off to credos by the saccharine "This I Believe" segment on NPR where some pious, self-righteous, and quite possibly religious person tells you what he or she believes and therefore what everyone else in the world must start doing as a consequence. These "I believe" segments rarely surprise: "I believe there is still a place for love in the world . . ."; "I believe in the sanctity of marriage . . ."; "I believe that we can find a way to eliminate phosphate emissions by the end of the year . . ."; and the worst, "I believe that everything happens for a reason." I always imagine myself on the show intoning: "I believe that random acts of violence really do make the world a better place" or "I believe that pet owning is akin to beastiality." But precisely because I have imagined myself talking back to the "I believe" people on the radio, I believe I can write a credo.

One of the first credos that actually appealed to me appeared in the unlikely form of Kevin Costner in *Bull Durham* (really unlikely! I know . . .) where, in a pitch to win over Susan Sarandon (a worthy goal), he lays down his credo for her, a list of life lessons he has learned from being "a catcher in the minor leagues"—a metaphor for some kind of smart but down-trodden masculinity. "I believe," says Crash Davis, "in the soul, the cock, the pussy, the small of a woman's back, the hanging curve ball, high fiber, good scotch, that the novels of Susan Sontag are self-indulgent, overrated crap. I believe Lee Harvey Oswald acted alone. I believe there ought to be a constitutional amendment outlawing Astroturf and the designated hitter. I believe in the sweet spot, soft-core pornography, opening your presents Christmas morning rather than Christmas Eve, and I believe in long, slow, deep, soft, wet kisses that last three days."

Okay, there is so much that is wrong with this credo: let's start with the obligatory hetero pairing of "cock" and "pussy," two words you do not want to hear Kevin Costner say, by the way, and then we can move down to the rejection of Susan Sontag's "novels" . . . hmm, she was not noted for her novels but for her incisive and clear-headed essays, and so why even bring up her novels? But the idea of outlawing Astroturf and the designated hitter and living for the hanging curve balls and the sweet spot, these seem like worthy goals. So, if I were to rewrite Crash Davis, what would I say? The short version would be something like this: "I believe in the queer and the freak, dying quickly and for a good cause, the long ball, the short book, strong coffee; I believe that high school students deserve better than *The Catcher in the Rye*; I believe that Bush lost. I believe that artists should let others speak about their work, that the push for gay marriage is a betrayal of earlier generations of queer activism, that *Finding Nemo* is one of the best films ever made. I believe in slow food, fast dialogue, hot baths, cold swimming pools. I believe that Ivy League schools tend not to be the places for intellectual innovation, and I do believe that anarchy, creative or otherwise, is possible, preferable, and perfectly doable. I believe that Lady Gaga is a genius, that Justin Bieber is a lesbian, and that Prince is Lady Gaga. I think we should abolish English departments, change disciplines every few years, go back to school, get rid of standardized tests, all speak three languages, and I believe in the living wage. I also believe that straight men don't try hard enough, gay guys try too hard, and butches should catch a break."

Well, maybe not, but that is what came to mind when I was asked to write a credo. So, having offered the quick and dirty version of my credo, let me draw out a few of my hastily offered rules to live by. In our line of work, professional scholars, there are lots of benefits and not a few downsides. The benefits include flexible hours, working without an onsite boss, summers without teaching, and job security. But the problems in academia are sometimes a consequence of those benefits, namely, complacency (produced by job security), laziness, absenteeism (flexible hours), elitism, nepotism, intellectual snobbery, and cronyism. I really do believe that many academics need to buck up and remember how to learn—many people teach the same classes over and over, repeat the work they did years ago in "new" scholarship and then jealously guard the gates of their discipline from intruders and newcomers who might shake things up to such a degree that their own work becomes irrelevant, anachronistic, or at least in need of an update. Let's remember what tenure is supposed to be for while we ponder some of the stagnancy of the university: tenure was supposed to protect scholars while they pursued possibly unpopular or at least counterintuitive ideas; it should provide a shield behind which socially useless along with socially useful work can be completed. Tenure, in its ideal form, allows scholars to take risks, try out daring theses, and innovate. But in a university where senior people often deny tenure to junior folks much more talented, skilled, and qualified than they are, we have to begin to question the validity of a system that protects the mediocre from the brilliant. And so I believe in shaking down the big disciplines once a generation, replacing dinosaur forms of knowledge production with improvised programs, and reinventing curricula, disciplinary knowledge, and knowledge clusters every decade at least. I believe that administrators are too often failed and bitter academics and that the university needs to dance carefully along the thin line between raising funds and becoming a corporation.

As far as my own intellectual path goes, like so many I was trained in English, but learning the discipline for me absolutely meant learning to betray it. And here I mean "betrayal" as a good thing, as an important part of learning. I mastered my discipline in order to dismantle it; we all did. The appearance within English of postcolonial critique in the 1980s and 1990s, queer theory in the 1990s, cultural critique from the late 1970s to the present has provided the tools for forms of knowledge that surpass English and that reveal it to be the discomforting product of its colonial past and its imperial pretensions. I learned in graduate school at the University of Minnesota in the 1980s how to expand my notion of culture to include the punk rock that had helped me to survive my dreary adolescence in the Midlands of England in the 1970s. I learned how to argue for popular culture, how to speak eloquently of subcultures, and how to argue against elitist formulations of knowing and being. And in my first job at UC San Diego, in a radical world literature department, I learned what it would mean to put English in its place as one set of literatures among many; I learned to see English as an imperial mission, and I learned to think about my own grammar school training as a kind of cultural brainwashing. My work, generally speaking, has ranged far afield of literary studies, and in my book *Female Masculinity*, I crafted what I called "scavenger methodologies" in order to create an archive for my project. My point was that every project produces its own methods rather than methods creating projects.

In recent years, I have been deeply interested in the politics of knowledge and in thinking through what some have called oppositional pedagogies. In pursuit of such pedagogies, I have come to realize that, as Eve K. Sedgwick once said, ignorance is as powerful a force as knowledge and that learning often takes place completely independently of teaching. In fact, I am not sure that I am teachable! As someone who never aced an exam, who has tried and tried without much success to become fluent in another language, and who can read a book without retaining much at all, I realize that I can only learn what I can teach myself and that much of what I learned in school left very little impression upon me at all. I thought about this while watching the extraordinary French documentary about a year in the life of a high school in the suburbs of Paris, *The Class* (*Entre Les Murs*, 2008, dir. Laurent Cantet). In the film, a white schoolteacher, Francois Bégaudeau (who wrote the memoir upon which the film is based) tries to reach out to his disinterested and profoundly alienated, mostly African, Asian, and Arab immigrant students. The cultural and racial and class differences between the teacher and his pupils make effective communication difficult, and his cultural references (*The Diary of Ann Frank*, Molière, French grammar) leave the students cold while theirs (soccer, Islam, hip-hop) induce only pained responses from their otherwise personable teacher. The film, like a Frederick Wiseman documentary, tries to just let the action unfold without any voice of God narration, and so we actually experience close-up the rage and frustrations of teacher and pupils alike. At the end of the film, an extraordinary moment occurs. Bégaudeau asks the class to think about what they have learned and each write down one thing to take away from the class, one concept, text, or idea that might have made a difference. The class disperses, and one girl shuffles up to the front. The teacher looks at her expectantly and draws out her comment: "I didn't learn anything," she tells him without malice or anger, "nothing . . . I can't think of anything I learned." The moment is a defeat for the teacher, a disappointment for the viewer who wants to believe in a narrative of educational uplift, but it is a triumph for alternative pedagogies because it reminds us that learning is a two-way street and you cannot teach without a dialogic relation to the learner.

"I didn't learn anything" could read like an endorsement of another French text, a book by Jacques Rancière on the politics of knowledge. This book was another revelation to me, a reminder that I, too, require a different model for knowledge transmission and reception. Ranciere's inspired speculations on "intellectual emancipation" in *The Ignorant Schoolmaster* (Stanford University Press, 1991) consist of a short series of essays in which he examines a form of knowledge sharing that detours around the mission of the university, with its masters and its pupils, its expository methods, and its standards of excellence, and that instead endorses a form of pedagogy that presumes and indeed demands equality rather than hierarchy. Drawing from the example of an eighteenth-century professor who taught in French to Belgian students who spoke only Flemish, Rancière claims that conventional, disciplinary pedagogy demands the presence of a master and proposes a mode of learning within which the students are enlightened by the superior knowledge, training, and intellect of the schoolmaster. But in the case of Joseph Jacotot, his experience with the students in Brussels taught him that his belief in the necessity of explication and exegesis was false and that it simply upheld a university system dependent upon hierarchy. When Jacotot realized that his students were learning to read and speak French and to understand the text *Télémaque* without his assistance, he began to see the narcissistic investment he had made in his own function. Jacotot was not a bad teacher who became a "good" teacher; rather, he was a "good" teacher who realized that people must be led to learn rather than taught to follow. Rancière comments ironically: "Like all conscientious professors, he knew that teaching was not in the slightest about cramming students with knowledge and having them repeat it like parrots, but he knew equally well that students had to avoid the chance detours where minds still incapable of distinguishing the essential from the accessory, the principle from the consequence, get lost" (3). While the "good" teacher leads his students through the pathways of rationality, the "ignorant schoolmaster" must actually allow them to get lost in order for them to experience confusion and then find their own way out or back or around.

In a less lofty vein, I believe in knowledge both practical and obsolete, knowledge that fosters collective forms of being and knowledge that breaks with conventional wisdom. To that end, I want to close my credo with my favorite film of the moment, a film from which I have learned much about masculinity, life, risk, wildness, love, loss, and survival. Based on a Roald Dahl novel, *Fantastic Mr. Fox* (2009, dir. Wes Anderson) tells the story of an aspiring fox who gives up his wild ways of chicken hunting to settle down with his foxy lady in a burrow. As the film begins, we find Mr. Fox striving for something more, looking for excitement in his life, wanting to move above ground and out of the sedate world of journalism and into the wild world of chasing chickens. From his new above-ground home in a tree, Mr. Fox can see the three farms of Boggis, Bunce, and Bean, and they present him with a challenge he cannot refuse. "Who am I?" he asks his friend Kylie, an eager but not gifted possum, and he continues: "Why a fox? Why not a horse, or a beetle, or a bald eagle? I'm saying this more as, like, existentialism, you know? Who am I? And how can a fox ever be happy without, you'll forgive the expression, a chicken in its teeth?" How indeed?

And of course, Mr. Fox (voiced by George Clooney) cannot be happy without that chicken in his teeth, and he reminds the viewer that the difference between a fox in the hole and a fox in the wild is just one hunting trip away. While this stop-motion animation marvel seems ultimately to reinforce the same old narrative of female domesticity and male wildness, in fact it tells a tall tale of masculine derring-do in order to offer up some very different forms of masculinity, collectivity, and family. But the best moment in *Fantastic Mr. Fox*, and the moment most memorable in terms of credos, comes in the form of a speech that Mr. Fox makes to his woodland friends who have survived the farmers' attempt to starve them all out of their burrows. The sturdy group of survivors dig their way out of a trap laid for them by Boggis, Bunce, and Bean and find themselves burrowing straight up into a closed supermarket stocked with all the supplies they need. Mr. Fox, buoyed by this lucky turn of events, turns to his clan and addresses them for the last time: "They say all foxes are slightly allergic to linoleum, but it's cool to the paw—try it. They say my tail needs to be dry cleaned twice a month, but now it's fully detachable—see? They say our tree may never grow back, but one day, something will. Yes, these crackles are made of synthetic goose and these giblets come from artificial squab and even these apples look fake—but at least they've got stars on them. I guess my point is, we'll eat tonight, and we'll eat together. And even in this not particularly flattering light, you are without a doubt the five and a half most wonderful wild animals I've ever met in my life. So let's raise our boxes—to our survival."

Maybe it is not quite a credo, something short of a toast, a little less than a speech, but Mr. Fox gives here one of the best and most moving addresses in the history of cinema. Like Mr. Fox, I believe in detachable tails, fake apples, eating together, adapting to the lighting, learning not to learn, risk, sissy sons, and I believe in the raw importance of survival for all those wild souls that the farmers, the teachers, the preachers, and the politicians would like to bury alive.

CONTRIBUTORS

MARK BAUERLEIN is the author of *The Dumbest Generation: How the Digital Age Stupefies Young Americans and Jeopardizes Our Culture; Or, Don't Trust Anyone Under Thirty* (2008), regularly contributes to the *Wall Street Journal*, *Weekly Standard*, and other popular journals, and writes a blog for the *Chronicle of Higher Education*. His academic books include *The Pragmatic Mind: Explorations in the Psychology of Belief* (1997) and *Literary Criticism: An Autopsy* (1997). He is professor of English at Emory University.

LAUREN BERLANT has written a cycle of books on American literature and culture, including *The Anatomy of National Fantasy: Hawthorne, Utopia, and Everyday Life* (1991); *The Queen of America Goes to Washington City: Essays on Sex and Citizenship* (1997); *The Female Complaint: The Unfinished Business of Sentimentality in American Culture* (2008); and *Cruel Optimism* (2011). She also is an editor of *Critical Inquiry* and George M. Pullman Professor of English at the University of Chicago.

MICHAEL BÉRUBÉ has regularly crossed the divide between academic and popular, publishing in *Harper's*, the *New Yorker*, the *New York Times Magazine*, and *The Nation* and blogging at michaelberube.com. His most recent books include *What's Liberal About the Liberal Arts? Classroom Politics and "Bias" in Higher Education* (2006); *Rhetorical Occasions: Essays on Humans and the Humanities* (2006); and *The Left at War* (2009). He is Paterno Family Professor in Literature and director of the Institute for the Arts and Humanities at Penn State University.

MARC BOUSQUET is the author of *How the University Works: Higher Education in the Low-Wage Nation* (2008) and blogs for the *Chronicle of Higher Education* (howtheuniversityworks

.com). In addition, he is coeditor of *The Politics of Information: The Electronic Mediation of Social Change* (2004) and *Tenured Bosses and Disposable Teachers: Writing Instruction in the Managed University* (2004) and founding editor of *Workplace: A Journal of Academic Labor*. He is associate professor of English at Santa Clara University.

STEPHEN BURT regularly contributes to the *London Review of Books*, *The Believer*, and other magazines. He published *Randall Jarrell and His Age* (2002); *The Forms of Youth: Twentieth-Century Poetry and Adolescence* (2007); *Close Calls with Nonsense: Reading New Poetry* (2009); and *The Art of the Sonnet* (with David Mikics; 2010), as well as two books of poetry, *Parallel Play* (2006) and *Popular Music* (1999). He is associate professor of English at Harvard.

VICTOR COHEN studies radical movements in the United States, compiling a 2009 issue of *Works and Days* on the New American Movement of the 1970s and early 1980s and an oral history of Ash Grove, a Los Angeles folk-music club that gave a home to radical political movements of the 1960s. He currently teaches literature at Oakwood School in Los Angeles.

JOHN CONLEY recently completed his dissertation on cynicism in twentieth-century American literature at the University of Minnesota, where he teaches as an adjunct and has been involved in the "Rethinking the University" project.

MORRIS DICKSTEIN'S books include *Gates of Eden: American Culture in the Sixties* (1977); *Double Agent: The Critic and Society* (1992); *Leopards in the Temple: The Transformation of American Fiction, 1945–1970* (2002); *A Mirror in the Roadway: Literature and the Real World* (2005); and *Dancing in the Dark: A Cultural History of the Great Depression* (2009), which received the 2010 Ambassador Book Award in American Studies. He is Distinguished Professor of English at the Graduate Center of the City University of New York.

DAVID B. DOWNING is the long-time editor of the critical journal *Works and Days*. He is the author of *The Knowledge Contract: Politics and Paradigms in the Academic Workplace* (2005) and coeditor of five other books, including *Academic Freedom in the Post-9/11 Era* (2010) and *Beyond English, Inc.: Curricular Reform in a Global Economy* (2002). He is professor of English at Indiana University of Pennsylvania.

RITA FELSKI'S books include *Beyond Feminist Aesthetics: Feminist Literature and Social Change* (1989); *The Gender of Modernity* (1995); *Doing Time: Feminist Theory and Postmodern Culture* (2000); *Literature After Feminism* (2003); and *Uses of Literature* (2008). She is editor of *New Literary History* and William R. Kenan, Jr. Professor of English at the University of Virginia.

KATHLEEN FITZPATRICK is the author of *The Anxiety of Obsolescence: The American Novel in the Age of Television* (2006) and *Planned Obsolescence: Publishing, Technology, and the Future of the Academy* (2011). She is also cofounder of the digital scholarly network MediaCommons (mediacommons.futureofthebook.org) and director of scholarly communication for the Modern Language Association.

BARBARA FOLEY'S books include *Telling the Truth: The Theory and Practice of Documentary Fiction* (1986); *Radical Representations: Politics and Form in U.S. Proletarian Fiction, 1929–1941* (1993); *Spectres of 1919: Class and Nation in the Making of the New Negro* (2003); and *Wrestling with the Left: The Making of Ralph Ellison's* Invisible Man (2010). She is professor of English and American studies at Rutgers University, Newark.

DIANA FUSS is author of *Essentially Speaking: Feminism, Nature, and Difference* (1989); *Identification Papers: Readings on Psychoanalysis, Sexuality, and Culture* (1995); *The Sense of an Interior: Four Writers and the Rooms That Shaped Them* (2004), winner of the 2005 MLA James Russell Lowell Prize. She also edited the collection *Inside/Out: Lesbian Theories, Gay Theories* (1991). She is the Louis W. Fairchild '24 Professor of English at Princeton University.

WILLIAM GERMANO was editor in chief at Columbia University Press and publishing director at Routledge through the 1980s and 1990s. He is now professor of English and dean of the Faculty of Humanities and Social Sciences at Cooper Union. His books include *Getting It Published: A Guide for Scholars and Anyone Else Serious About Serious Books* (2001; 2nd ed. 2008) and *From Dissertation to Book* (2005).

GERALD GRAFF has published six books, among them *Professing Literature: An Institutional History* (1987; anniv. ed. 2007); *Beyond the Culture Wars: How Teaching the Conflicts Can Revitalize American Education* (1992); *Clueless in Academe: How Schooling Obscures the Life of the Mind* (2003); and the textbook *"They Say/I Say": The Moves That Matter in Academic Writing* (with Cathy Birkenstein, 2006; 2nd ed. 2010). He is professor of English and education at the University of Illinois at Chicago.

MARK GREIF is a founder and editor of *n + 1* and contributor to *American Prospect, London Review of Books, Harper's,* the *New York Times Magazine,* and *Best American Essays.* He has recently published a book on midcentury American intellectual life, *The Age of the Crisis of Man* (2011). He is assistant professor of literary studies at the New School in New York.

JUDITH JACK HALBERSTAM has published *Skin Shows: Gothic Horror and the Technology of Monsters* (1995); *Female Masculinity* (1998); *The Drag King Book* (1999); *In a Queer Time and Place:*

Transgender Bodies, Subcultural Lives (2005); and *The Queer Art of Failure* (2011). She is professor of English, gender studies, and American studies and ethnicity at USC.

KATIE HOGAN is the author of *Women Take Care: Gender, Race, and the Culture of AIDS* (2001) and coeditor of *Gendered Epidemic: Representations of Women in the Age of AIDS* (1998) and *Over Ten Million Served: Gendered Service in Language and Literature Workplaces* (2010). She is professor of English and director of women's studies at Carlow University.

AMITAVA KUMAR writes for magazines in India as well as the United States and has published in the *Nation, Harper's,* and *Chronicle of Higher Education.* His books include *Passport Photos* (2000); *Bombay-London-New York* (2002); *Husband of a Fanatic: A Personal Journey Through India, Pakistan, Love, and Hate* (2005); *The Foreigner Carrying in the Crook of His Arm a Tiny Bomb* (2010); and the novel *Nobody Does the Right Thing* (2010). He is also editor of three books, including *World Bank Literature* (2002). He is professor of English at Vassar College.

PAUL LAUTER is founding editor of the groundbreaking *Heath Anthology of American Literature* (1990; now in its sixth edition). He is also the author of *Canons and Context* (1991) and *From Walden Pond to Jurassic Park: Activism, Culture, and American Studies* (2001) and coeditor of several volumes, such as *The Politics of Literature: Dissenting Essays on the Teaching of English* (1972). He is Allan K. and Gwendolyn Miles Smith Professor of Literature at Trinity College in Hartford, Conn.

VINCENT B. LEITCH is general editor of the *Norton Anthology of Theory and Criticism* (2nd ed. 2010) and author of *Deconstructive Criticism* (1982); *American Literary Criticism from the 1930s to the 1980s* (1988; updated, 2010); *Cultural Criticism, Literary Theory, Poststructuralism* (1992); *Postmodernism—Local Effects, Global Flows* (1996); *Theory Matters* (2003); and *Living with Theory* (2008). He is George Lynn Cross Research Professor at the University of Oklahoma.

DEVONEY LOOSER is the author of *British Women Writers and the Writing of History* (2000) and *Women Writers and Old Age in Great Britain, 1750–1850* (2008) and editor of *Jane Austen and Discourses of Feminism* (1995) and *Generations: Academic Feminists in Dialogue* (with E. Ann Kaplan; 1997). She is professor of English at the University of Missouri.

LISA LOWE's books include *Critical Terrains: French and British Orientalisms* (1991); *Immigrant Acts: On Asian American Cultural Politics* (1996); *Metaphors of Globalization* (forthcoming); and the co-edited collection *The Politics of Culture in the Shadow of Capital* (1997). She is professor of comparative literature at UC San Diego.

MICHELLE A. MASSÉ is the author of *In the Name of Love: Women, Masochism, and the Gothic* (1992); coeditor of *Over Ten Million Served: Gendered Service in Language and Literature Workplaces* (SUNY Press, 2010); and series editor of SUNY Press's Feminist Theory and Criticism. She directs women's and gender studies at Louisiana State University.

MARK MCGURL has published *The Novel Art: Elevations of American Fiction After Henry James* (2001) and *The Program Era: Postwar Fiction and the Rise of Creative Writing* (2010). He is professor of English at Stanford University.

TORIL MOI's books include *Sexual/Textual Politics: Feminist Literary Theory* (1985); *Simone de Beauvoir: The Making of an Intellectual Woman* (1994; 2nd ed. 2008); *What Is a Woman? And Other Essays* (1999); and *Henrik Ibsen and the Birth of Modernism: Art, Theater, Philosophy* (2006). She is James B. Duke Professor of Literature and Romance Studies at Duke University.

FRANCES NEGRÓN-MUNTANER is a filmmaker as well as a critic. Her books include *Boricua Pop: Puerto Ricans and the Latinization of American Culture* (2004) and *Sovereign Acts* (2011), and her films, *AIDS in the Barrio* (Gold Award, John Muir Film Festival, 1989), *Brincando el charco: Portrait of a Puerto Rican* (Whitney Biennial, 1995), and the upcoming television show, *War in Guam*. She is associate professor of English at Columbia University and directs its Center for the Study of Ethnicity and Race.

CARY NELSON is the author of nearly thirty books, including *Repression and Recovery: Modern American Poetry and the Politics of Cultural Memory* (1991); *Manifesto of a Tenured Radical* (1997); *Academic Keywords: A Devil's Dictionary for Higher Education* (with Stephen Watt; 1999); *Revolutionary Memory: Recovering the Poetry of the American Left* (2003); and *No University Is an Island: Saving Academic Freedom* (2010). He is Jubilee Professor at the University of Illinois and national president of the American Association of University Professors.

ANN PELLEGRINI's books include *Performance Anxieties: Staging Psychoanalysis, Staging Race* (1997); *Love the Sin: Sexual Regulation and the Limits of Religious Tolerance* (with Janet R. Jakobsen, 2003); and the coedited collections *Queer Theory and the Jewish Question* (2003) and *Secularisms* (2008). She is associate professor of performance studies and religious studies at New York University, where she directs the Center for the Study of Gender and Sexuality.

BRUCE ROBBINS has published *The Servant's Hand: English Fiction from Below* (1986); *Secular Vocations: Intellectuals, Professionalism, and Culture* (1993); *Feeling Global: Internationalism in Distress* (1999); *Upward Mobility and the Common Good* (2007); and *Cosmopolitan Attachments* (2011). He has also edited or coedited several volumes and edited the journal *Social Text* for a decade. He is Old Dominion Foundation Professor in the Humanities at Columbia University.

ANDREW ROSS'S most recent books include *No-Collar: The Humane Workplace and Its Hidden Costs* (2003); *Low Pay, High Profile: The Global Push for Fair Labor* (2004); *Fast Boat to China: Corporate Flight and the Consequences of Free Trade-Lessons from Shanghai* (2006); and *Nice Work if You Can Get It: Sustainable Employment in Precarious Times* (2009). He has also edited and coedited seven books, and he is professor of social and cultural analysis at NYU.

DAVID R. SHUMWAY is the author of *Michel Foucault* (1989); *Creating American Civilization: A Genealogy of American Literature as an Academic Discipline* (1994); and *Modern Love: Romance, Intimacy, and the Marriage Crisis* (2003). He has also coedited three books, most recently *Disciplining English* (2002). He is professor of English and director of the Humanities Center at Carnegie Mellon University.

HEATHER STEFFEN is writing a dissertation on higher education in the Progressive era. She has published in *Socialism and Democracy*, *Cultural Logic*, and elsewhere. She served as managing editor of *the minnesota review* for five years and is a Ph.D. candidate in the Literary and Cultural Studies Program at Carnegie Mellon University.

KENNETH WARREN is the author of *Black and White Strangers: Race and American Literary Realism* (1993); *So Black and Blue: Ralph Ellison and the Occasion of Criticism* (2003); and *What Was African-American Literature?* (2011), as well as coeditor, with Adolph Reed, of *Renewing Black Intellectual History: The Ideological and Material Foundations of African American Thought* (2010). He is Fairfax M. Cone Distinguished Service Professor at the University of Chicago.

JEFFREY J. WILLIAMS writes for the *Chronicle of Higher Education*, *Dissent*, and other magazines, as well as academic journals. His books include *Theory and the Novel: Narrative Reflexivity in the British Tradition* (1998) and three edited collections, most recently *Critics at Work: Interviews, 1993–2003* (2004). He also is a coeditor of *The Norton Anthology of Theory and Criticism* (2nd ed. 2010), and from 1992 to 2010 he was editor of the literary and critical journal *the minnesota review*. He is a professor of English at Carnegie Mellon University.

CRAIG WOMACK is the author of *Red on Red: Native American Literary Separatism* (1999); *American Indian Literary Nationalism* (coauthor; 2006); *Art as Performance, Story as Criticism: Reflections on Native Literary Aesthetics* (2009); and the novel *Drowning in Fire* (2001). He is professor of English at Emory University.